Tim

The Official Biography
of Avicii

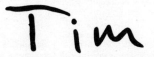

The Official Biography
of Avicii

Måns Mosesson

Translated by Bradley Harmon

SPHERE

SPHERE

First published in Great Britain in 2021 by Sphere
This paperback edition published in 2022 by Sphere

1 3 5 7 9 10 8 6 4 2

A CIP catalogue record for this book
is available from the British Library.

ISBN: 9780751579024

Typeset in Minion by M Rules
Printed and bound in Great Britain by Clays Ltd, Elcograf S.p.A.

Papers used by Sphere are from well-managed forests
and other responsible sources.

Sphere
An imprint of
Little, Brown Book Group
Carmelite House
50 Victoria Embankment
London EC4Y 0DZ

An Hachette UK Company
www.hachette.co.uk

www.littlebrown.co.uk

AT NIGHT THE RABBITS emerged from the bushes. Grey and shaggy, as if they had just fought a battle deep among the pine trees. It didn't take long before a falcon hovered silently in the sky, stretched its wings against the wind and waited for the opportunity to dive down towards its victims.

He saw so much from up here.

The scent of onions and rosemary rose through the air – the chef must have begun to prepare the evening's meal – and mingled with a whiff of the lemon trees standing down in the grove.

From the sprinkler came a quiet hiss, slowly showering the palm lilies by the pool.

It had been three weeks and Tim Bergling had started taking in his surroundings again. He was sitting on the roof of the rehab clinic, in a deckchair that the care staff had helped him to hoist up on to the red tiles. Through the haze out in the Mediterranean, he could make out the island in the distance, the one that people went to by ferry to snorkel and forget their hangover for a while before they downed the first pills of the night and started all over again.

But now autumn had arrived. The partying tourists had flown home. Privilege, Space and Pacha had closed for the season. Even the crickets had begun to go quiet.

The summer of 2015 had flashed by in a single dark daze; he realised that now. He had been sitting in the white villa on

1

the southern tip of Ibiza, stressed over the songs that were not mixed heavily enough and the fact that the record label wanted him to go to London to do interviews.

Stories was planned as the follow-up to the first album, which two years earlier had transformed Tim Bergling from a successful DJ in the clubs to a global pop phenomenon. The record had been delayed one year and Tim was having trouble focusing.

It had been a while since his body functioned like it was supposed to. And in the last year, after the surgery at the hospital, he had felt something new beginning to grow in his stomach. Tim had become obsessed with that lump. The more he thought about it, the clearer he felt it. Like a tumour that thrived inside him. And while that unknown thing had got bigger, he had played at summer festivals all around Europe and had sold out Ushuaïa, Ibiza's most prominent house music club, every Sunday.

When he woke up in the afternoon after the last gig of the season, he had been convinced that he would fly home to Los Angeles. Instead, they all sat together downstairs in the house. His father Klas was there, his manager Arash had flown in from Stockholm, as well as his older brother David. The tour manager, the bodyguard. And the bros, of course: the childhood friends who for the last year had followed him wherever he went.

They had expressed how worried they were. How tired they were of lying when they got the question every day of what it was like to work for Avicii. They had cried, been devastated.

Tim had eventually agreed to go to the rehab clinic, mostly to stop them nagging about how he had become unreliable and careless.

The first days, during the initial detox, he had mostly slept.

But then the treatment director Paul Tanner had advised him to start writing.

> My first memory is taking a bath with my mother or when she sings me a lullaby, or my father coming in and turning around the old cassette tapes with various children's stories on them from the A to the B side while I'm trying to sleep.

The words had come to him with sharp edges. He had lived in the soft deception of anaesthesia for so long that it was at first hard to write. But he understood the point: putting the experiences into words made them easier to talk about, helped him to see the life that had led him to this place in September 2015.

So when the sentences came, he naturally had trouble stopping them. Instead of sleeping, he sat at the computer and wrote himself through the nights. He told about his childhood, about his siblings, about how he discovered music and how his career gained speed. He wrote about the complicated relationship with his manager Arash and the time spent with his girlfriends Emily and Racquel.

The afternoons were devoted to long conversations with the treatment director. They discussed concepts like coping mechanisms and suppression. Tim analysed the new information systematically, as he always did.

He now realised how much he had pushed away. He had forced himself forward for so long that it had become the norm.

Suddenly he saw things in a totally new light. Even the difficult feelings that he really didn't want to have, that he had wrestled with ever since his childhood – nervousness, anxiety, fear – maybe even they had a purpose. He began thinking of them like a compass, an instrument that could help him point out a new direction.

The emotion itself can be positive or negative in energy,
but no emotion's purpose is negative.

For so long he had gone past his limits, lived in pain. The physical from his stomach, but also the psychological. He had not only hit a wall, he had crashed through it, several times over. He had been on the brink of death, that's how it really felt.

He wished that he had listened sooner.

THIS STORY BUILDS upon hundreds of interviews and count-less hours of conversation with those who knew and worked with Tim Bergling. Through his family I've received access to mobile phone notes, conversations, drawings, photos and reading tablets full of the books Tim ploughed through with ever-growing intensity. I've been able to see video recordings, professional as well as private, and have gained insight into how Tim structured his songs in the software program he composed with.

I have visited clubs in Ibiza and in Miami, his former homes in Stockholm and Los Angeles, had conversations during road trips through the desert in Las Vegas, at house festivals in Amsterdam, over tea and cakes in London and salmon and potatoes in Skillinge in the south of Sweden. To the greatest extent possible, I've tried to capture Tim's perspective on an often dense jumble of events and happenings. An invaluable source for this has been the over forty thousand emails that Tim received and sent over a ten-year period. There have also been personal notes, discussions on internet forums, as well as conversations over text, Messenger and WhatsApp to lean on.

When Tim himself typed he often did so on American key-boards where Swedish letters were missing – for the sake of readability, this has been corrected. In occasional cases spelling errors have been rectified and punctuation smoothed out, but with the original meaning maintained.

*

5

Tim Bergling celebrated his biggest successes as an artist during a time when mental health issues sharply increased among young people in large parts of the world. The reasons are many and complex, but that the figures have soared is measurable and indisputable. In Sweden mental health problems among young adults has risen by 70 per cent since 2006. The number of stress-related diagnoses only keep adding up: sleep deprivation, restlessness, depression, anxiety. The number of suicides in this age group is also rising in a concerning way – in many of the world's affluent nations, suicide is one of the most common causes of death of people under thirty years old. In Sweden the number of young people who end their lives has steadily increased since the turn of the millennium; in the US the numbers have soared in the last ten years. According to the World Health Organization, there are more people who take their own lives than who die of stomach cancer, cirrhosis of the liver, breast cancer and Alzheimer's. Suicide kills more people than war, assault, terrorism and domestic violence combined.

Behind a suicide lies almost always some form of mental disorder such as depression or anxiety. These are still topics surrounded by shame and silence. It can easily feel overwhelming to talk to someone who is feeling unwell. The worry of saying something clumsy, and thus perhaps even worsening the situation, can hinder the conversation. But research shows that those fears are unfounded: you do not need to have nice and perfect answers. The most important thing is to dare to ask, and be prepared to listen to the answer. It is through conversation, not silence, that we can save lives.

There are certain limitations when one writes about famous people who have taken their own lives. To avoid the risk that the depiction of such events triggers similar actions, one should avoid describing in detail both the physical location and the act itself. What is important in this story is not the specific details that surrounded Tim's final hours, but what led to them and what we can potentially learn from his passing.

If you feel that your situation seems unbearable or if you have active plans to take your own life, you should immediately call the emergency services.

If you've had thoughts of hurting yourself, or if you think someone close to you needs support, there is always help available. You can speak with someone you can confide in, or call one of these support lines:

UK:	Mind (mind.org.uk)
	The Samaritans (Samaritans.org)
US:	National Alliance on Mental Illness (Nami.org)
Australia:	Sane Australia (sane.org)
New Zealand:	Mental Health Foundation of New Zealand (mentalhealth.org.nz)
South Africa:	SA Federation for Mental Health (safmh.org)

I was born 1989 in Stockholm to two very loving parents, Klas and Anki. My father used to call himself a paper merchant (with a grin), a good testament to the humble values of the Swedish community. He actually owned several office department stores and was well off. My mother was a successful actor, as was my brother when I was growing up.

THE SMOKE ROSE UP towards the heavy chandeliers that hung from the ceiling of the hall. The hunters' arrows pierced the air and the magicians threw fireballs at the dragon's double heads, but this boss was a really tough bastard. His sharp teeth shone in the dark as he chased each one in the guild who dared approach him.

Together with druids, priests and magicians, the knight Important had fought for hours to get here, to the penultimate beast to be destroyed before the battle would be won. Their guild had been tactical and clever – sometimes all forty of them had joined into a united troop, sometimes they had split up to destroy enough dragon eggs without expiring.

Now Important was hidden behind one of the stone walls of the castle, which lay cut into a mountain in the Eastern Kingdoms. In his fiery yellow armour, he moved resiliently and swiftly. He was a paladin, a knight with magical properties, who came to the rescue when someone else in the guild was losing their vitality.

On the whole, Important was a character who justified his name. He had knives in both shoulder plates of his armour, flexible iron gloves and his belt was the most coveted. Between the helmet's visor and the dark cowl, his eyes shone an intense white. Sometimes the knight rode around the alliance's capital Stormwind, only to feel the envious glances of others when they saw the mighty horns of his horse's armour – a clear sign of what a devoted soldier he was.

The sixteen-year-old Tim Bergling was sitting in his bed with his back leaned up against the wall and steered Important exactly where he wanted. His fingers slammed against the keyboard in his lap as the knight ran to save yet another warlock in distress.

His friend Fredrik Boberg, who everyone called Fricko, was sitting beside him on the bed and looking on. It was evident that the guys had been playing for several hours – between glasses of stale Coca-Cola lay half-chewed sweets, crisp crumbs and spat-out packets of tobacco.

Fricko and the other friends had come to Tim's parents' apartment on the street of Linnégatan straight after school, dragged up their computers and monitors to the fifth floor and set them up in Tim's room. The clock had now reached long past midnight but the raid in World of Warcraft was still not over. One of the other friends had nearly fallen asleep on his keyboard.

In this little room Tim Bergling had grown up. Here he had drawn portraits of his parents and friends, written poems about the leaves of autumn and the girl in class he was most fond of. From his parents he had got a subscription to the magazine *Science Illustrated* and he ploughed through everything he came across about satellites and archaeological excavations and robots. Tim was especially fascinated by outer space. When he was a little boy, a telescope had been launched into orbit outside Earth's atmosphere. Hubble, as this dustbin-like machine was called, was equipped with cameras that, from their high position, could take sharp photos of everything from dying stars to luminous galaxies. Tim flipped through the close-ups of a giant gas cloud that seemed to be taken from a scary fairy-tale book – huge pillars of dust and gas lit up in ultraviolet light, reminiscent of monsters howling into the cosmos. It was probably in a similarly remote place that our

11

own solar system had been created once upon a time, impossibly long ago. With the fastest spacecraft man had ever invented, it would take over a hundred million years to get there, to the incomprehensibly eternal.

As Tim was sitting engrossed in his thoughts, his mother Anki busied herself in the kitchen, where she would cook meatballs and spaghetti for her son on the other side of the closed door to the right of the stove.

Her beloved little Tim-a-lim, who was so longed for when he was born in September in the last autumn of the 1980s.

When she reflected on it, Anki remembered how intensely she had wanted to have a child with Klas, even though they had both just experienced broken marriages and were already a little over forty.

By the time Tim arrived his other three siblings were well into their teens. Linda and David, his half-siblings from the father's previous relationship, had moved out first, Anki's son Anton left home not long after. There had only been three of them left in the household – Anki thought that that might have been one of the reasons why Tim was a little restrained and hesitant.

At the same time, he was stubborn, determined. In pre-school he had eaten neither pasta nor potato buns, neither fruit salad nor rhubarb cream. All the food that the other children snacked on, Tim rejected – he had stubbornly insisted on a diet consisting only of crispbread and butter. During the pre-school's annual Christmas show one of the teachers had to carry Tim into the hall because he did not dare to walk on the floor, and when they were on an excursion to a circus, Tim had wanted to stay outside.

'I don't know that clown,' he had stated and quite simply refused to go inside.

He needed to be at peace sometimes, to have his own space, he was clear about that. If he and Anki had been arguing about something, Tim would shut himself in his room. They would then communicate by pushing notes back and forth through the gap under the bedroom door.

'Okay! I admit it,' Tim wrote after one of those quarrels. 'I was wrong. And I apologise for that. But I think it was mean to call me a "couch potato". Do you understand that?'

'I agree with you, sorry,' Anki replied, pushing the note back into Tim's room.

And so they were friends again, and Tim came back out.

Maybe the careful and thoughtful family trait came from her side, Anki thought. She worked as an actress, had throughout her career been praised for the intensity of her acting – a few years before Tim was born, she had played one of the lead roles in the Oscar-nominated film *My Life as a Dog*. Now she commuted back and forth to a recording studio in Hallstahammar to portray a mother in the soap opera *Friends and Foes*. Like many others on the stage, Anki had been insecure about herself for much of her life. She felt too tall, too self-conscious and clumsy. When she laughed, she looked like a stuck Christmas pig, she thought, it was just the shiny apple in her mouth that was missing.

There was also a before and an after in Anki Lidén's life.

When she was a teenager, a stranger had dragged her into the woods and tried to strangle her. The incident had stayed with her for ever, making her sensitive and scared of the dark. She couldn't wear a scarf without feeling her airways tighten. Maybe this trauma had also affected her children, although indirectly?

In any case, Tim had a wait-and-see attitude that she recognised. At family dinners, when all six gathered, the other

13

three siblings could shout at each other without interruption and have a hell of a time. Tim would sit quietly out of the way and suddenly throw in a particularly drastic and apt comment. And then he would smile his wonderfully crooked smile and return to his room to carry on with his schoolwork.

Tim's father owned and operated Skottes, a business that sold office supplies to companies. At first glance, Klas Bergling could seem prim and proper, especially when he discussed purchase prices for pencils or perforators. If you scratched the surface, however, Klas also had an artistic vein, a creativity that wanted to be freed. He had grown up with the scent of white spirit, in the studio at the Royal Opera, where his father was head of decoration. At family gatherings, he could improvise small sketches in which he portrayed a zealous film director or a tipsy salesman. And on a free Saturday morning, it was not uncommon for Klas to turn up the volume on the stereo over by the bedroom. He rolled around in a bathrobe while the house god Ray Charles's powerful voice thumped against the stucco. The blind soul singer from the American South had an unsurpassed verve in his piano playing, could roar and whisper in front of the microphone so that he alone sounded like a whole orchestra. Otherwise, there was a lot of blues in the vinyl collection, often from Chicago, often guitarists like Buddy Guy or Freddie King, battered and bruised men who narrated stories of infidelity and jealousy, violence and misery.

Tim's older siblings had also listened to a lot of music, and had done their best to pass on their taste to their little brother. Linda had introduced the whole gang to the glam rockers in Kiss; David had listened to most things that went on MTV, from hip-hop to grunge; in high school Anton had started playing drums in a rock band.

In the summers, the family used to drive down to Skillinge

on Skåne's Österlen. In the old fishing village, they had bought a brick house that was worn and damp, but which had a view of the sea. As Klas played electric guitar without a shirt, Tim carved huts and learned to sail an Optimist dinghy down in the harbour. When he and a friend organised a flea market at a crossroads, Anki came over with burgers and soft drinks for her son.

The family were neighbours of the prominent trombonist Nils Landgren, who one day cleared out his studio and lined up assorted instruments for sale in the square. Tim bought a discarded synth, a Yamaha from the late 70s, which he put in the room next to the hall. Much of that summer was spent trying to understand the new instrument.

Tim plucked and pressed, never really finding the logic, but somehow it still felt right. He knew very little about what he was going to spend his life doing, but he knew he was creative. Anki's ex-husband, the popular singer Tommy Körberg, was somewhere in Tim's head – his artistic career was proof that it was possible to shape his own life.

Back in Stockholm, Tim got a six-string Fender in mahogany from his father. Compared to the synth, the guitar felt easier to handle. Tim trained on classics such as Eric Clapton's 'Tears In Heaven' and The Animals' 'House Of The Rising Sun'. With his lungs filled to the brim with air, he tried to sing the national anthem 'Du gamla du fria' ('Thou Ancient, Thou Free') and Nordman's 'Vandraren' ('The Wanderer').

The singing was swaying and skewed, but the guitar playing became more and more confident.

When his mother offered to arrange lessons for him, Tim thought it was an almost absurd thought.

He would, of course, teach himself.

I was a somewhat shy kid – not to the extent that it interfered with much, but there was a shyness in me for sure, most possibly inherited from my mother, who's always been very sensitive in general.

We used to watch movies every weekend and buy loads of candy and every now and again we'd party.

ONE BY ONE, the friends woke up in the living room. They must have fallen asleep in the early hours of the morning, when the dragons of World of Warcraft were killed and it was no longer possible to stay awake.

The teenage boys rubbed their gravelly eyes. Last night it was Johannes Lönnå and Fricko Boberg who had crowded on to the Bergling family's corner sofa, while Jakob Lilliemarck had spread out the green back cushions into a makeshift mattress on the floor. The friends stretched their stiff bodies and wandered out to the kitchen.

The door to Tim's room was closed as usual, which meant that their host was still asleep and did not want to be disturbed. Tim could get grumpy if they woke him up before lunch, they knew this. Instead, Fricko took out the toasted sandwiches and reached for the sausage in the fridge. Each friend mixed a glass of chocolate milk, said good morning to Klas and Anki and sat down in the living room again to watch a movie.

'Damn, I've found a way to get even more experience,' Tim exclaimed when he finally got out of bed and came out to the couch.

As usual, he had remained in front of the screen when the others went to bed, jumped on a griffin and flew to Kalimdor, the continent of the night elves and trolls, to look for black lotus flowers until six in the morning. The plants would make Important even more powerful and helpful in the guild's next raid.

'But you understand what this means,' he said and smiled. 'Fucking awesome!'

'We should go outside for a bit,' replied Fricko, who admittedly also cared about the computer game, but not to the same extent as his friend. Tim was unstoppably stubborn; once he had decided on something there were no other alternatives. But he also liked the sun.

The teenagers rushed down the stairs and turned right down Linnégatan.

Fricko had also grown up here, among the large stone houses in Östermalm. He lived by Gärdet, the large field that lay beyond the Radio House, and was an artistic person just like Tim. Fricko's father was a successful TV producer and he himself studied at the Adolf Fredrik music school. Fricko wanted to be an actor one day. He had got to know Tim a couple of years earlier, in the beginning of junior high, and they had found each other through their common interest in film. They now purposefully ploughed through classics such as *The Godfather* movies and everything by Quentin Tarantino and the Coen brothers. They could sit for hours and analyse the symbolism and plot of *Twin Peaks* or just relax with a musical like *Jesus Christ Superstar* or *Phantom of the Opera*. Tim liked Fricko's kindness and open mind. He was forgetful and absent-minded in a way that was impossible not to be charmed by. They were bros, brothers.

The neighbourhood around the square Karlaplan was the backdrop for the group of friends. In between Tim's home and Gärdesskolan, the junior high school he attended, was Fältöversten, a shopping centre where the corridors between sports shops and patisseries functioned as their leisure centre. In the grocery store Sabis, there were almost always sample tastings of aged cheese or slices of cold-cut ham that the boys could eat to their hearts' content. On the roof of the mall was a residential building – it was possible to get to the upper level via an escalator. Amongst the flowerbeds in the gardens up there, they ran around, smoked in secret, and made plans about who would buy from the kiosk near the Maxim Theatre next time. The old man there charged almost two hundred crowns for a six-pack of beer but never checked ID. Those who knew the code words even got to buy smuggled Russian vodka.

In the years just after the turn of the millennium, the boys' district had come into the spotlight in a new way. The rest of Sweden had certainly always related to Östermalm – for at least a hundred years, the district had been a symbol of prosperity and contentment. The houses from the turn of the last century that stood along the esplanade on Karlavägen radiated money and power. Here, business leaders, diplomats and friends of the royal family lived in interiors as magnificent as the façades, enjoying the sort of lives that gossip journalists loved to describe.

But in step with the growth of the internet, Östermalm also got its own kind of correspondents in the mid-2000s. Bloggers named Katrin and Alex and Sofi and Bella sat in the Hotel Anglais or Café Mocco and reported who hung out at which clubs, who was together and who had broken up. The clubs where all this drama took place were situated around Stureplan, the few blocks that lay between sleepy Karlavägen and the clamouring city.

During the day, Stureplan was the country's financial centre, where fund managers steamed forward with loud ties and leather briefcases under their arms. In the evening, the area became a noisy entertainment hub, where people shivered from the cold in the queues outside clubs and restaurants such as Sturecompagniet, Grodan, Berns and Spy Bar. The bloggers online kept a close eye on this nightlife. Here hierarchies were established, quarrels were started and peace mediated.

Tim's big brother Anton had become a part of this world. Like his mother Anki, he had played a leading role in a soap opera and now he was dating a celebrity photographer who took pictures of the gala premieres at Rigoletto or Grand. Sometimes Tim accompanied Anton to those events, but he thought of them as rather strange spectacles. Fashion bloggers, actors, politicians and reality-show celebrities who had received movie tickets in exchange for smiling professionally into the cameras.

Tim stood next to his big brother on the red carpet, looking a little sullen. As if on the periphery of everything, or perhaps rather hovering over it. It was as if the celebrity noise did not concern him.

He preferred to go to the video store at Östermalmstorg and buy sweets with his friends. Back in Tim's bedroom, they could watch the entire *Lord of the Rings* trilogy in one go, or action movies with Denzel Washington and Tom Cruise. On a family trip to Thailand, Tim had bought a whole bunch of pirated DVDs that they watched over and over. While they drank even more Coke and crushed crisps into the bed sheets they binge-watched the series *The Office* with Tim's favourite comedian Ricky Gervais. Tim loved the Brit's timing and clever humour. The friends watched the animated series *South Park* for the same reason: it was hysterically silly, but at the same time smart. Eric Cartman and the other major characters were utilised to heckle US President George W. Bush, hypocritical Hollywood celebrities, and basically anything else that was discussed at the time.

In the latest season, to the delight of the boys, there was an entire episode about World of Warcraft. Cartman had become obsessed with trying to destroy a particularly evil opponent and tried to persuade his friends to come and help him in battle.

Tim and the others sat laughing on the bed while Cartman hissed in his most mature voice that it was far more important to play computer games than to be out in the sun playing around.

Acne was introduced into my life for the first time, huge impact on self-esteem. Skipping classes on bad acne days. Kept me from going out during weekends, still did so but only when my skin was 'clear' enough.

Felt lack of interest from girls.

HIS FRIENDS OFTEN had to nag Tim to go out with them in the evenings.

'I'm just going to fix my hair,' he shouted from inside the bathroom in the hall.

'But you've already fixed it!'

'I promise, two minutes. Then we'll go!'

Tim examined his nose in the mirror. He had never liked it; he thought that the end protruded in a way that made it look like the snout of a pig. Now it had also become the epicentre of the craters that climbed over his cheeks and up to his forehead. He cursed the damn spots because they always found ways back.

Together with his parents, he had gone to a doctor in Aspudden, another in Östermalm. He had tried cortisone ointments, tested concealers and creams, but nothing seemed to help.

He himself thought it was lame to get so obsessed about the spots. It was a quality he disliked, that he sort of wound himself up and started thinking catastrophic thoughts. Throughout his upbringing, he had been worried about getting cancer. During game nights, it hadn't been unusual for one of his friends to have to feel around to confirm that he didn't have a malignant lump in his chest. But now? After all, he was in his final year of junior high, should be able to relax more. Still, those thoughts swirled in his head. When he imagined all the glances that would judge him as soon as he stepped outside the door, he was almost paralysed.

Like he said, lame.

'Come on, Tim!'

His friends were still waiting in the kitchen, annoyed that it was always like this. Tim seemed to have no sense of time, lived in his own little world. Did he even know what a watch was?

In the end, he gave in, he almost always did, going out with the guys in spite of it all. They followed the promenade towards the fiery yellow military buildings a couple of blocks away. At the edge of the park area, a rock formation shot up like a wall towards the street of Linnégatan and behind it lay a spacious depression. In the dry grass of this cauldron there were natural slopes and ledges to sit on and the teenagers became practically invisible to the adults who strolled by on the street. No one could have guessed that in the middle of the rock formation a party had started.

Someone had brought a portable speaker blasting out Swedish hip-hop artists like Snook or Fronda, or melodious Italian dance music by producers like Gigi D'Agostino or DJ Satomi. This style was called tween techno among the friends – they knew that it was considered a bit cheesy, but the snappy tunes were hard to resist.

If the boys were lucky, someone would have brought a bottle of coconut liqueur or a half of vodka, and if they were even more fortunate, some girls from the French school would come by, sitting and laughing in the grass between the crevices.

Tim had drunk alcohol for the first time a couple of years earlier, when he had managed to sneak a half-drunk bottle of gin from his parents' pantry. Now he was getting used to the tingle in his stomach and the heat that made his cheeks flare up more with each sip. He liked the person he became when the intoxication spread through his body. He settled into himself more naturally, became self-assured and quick in his

25

replies. Above all, alcohol helped him stop pondering so damn much. The nervousness was cut off and his head opened up. The girls and boys in the ravine who were more superficially acquainted with Tim would have had a hard time believing that only a moment before he had been fretting in front of the mirror – now the guy in the hoodie showed a completely different side.

Tim picked up a couple of sticks from the dry grass and held the cigarette between them so that his parents would not smell the smoke on his hands when he got home. Then he took a drag from the cig and exploded in an intense guffaw, unexpectedly loud.

A couple of blocks north-west of the secret rock crevice towered the majestic Östra Real. The high school in the middle of Östermalm was one with a storied history: here they had raised editors-in-chief, business leaders and even a Swedish prime minister.

Seventeen-year-old Filip Åkesson sat on the stone staircase that led up to the school's entrance and brushed some dirt from his Prada boat shoes. Åkesson knew how you should look – he was aware that Lacoste didn't cut it any more, for example. The poor guys that walked around with the crocodile on their chests probably thought it was snazzy, but in fact their polo shirts were more like something a parent had bought at the airport during their latest business trip. Filip, on the other hand, had combed back hair and a belt from Gucci. His trousers and shirt were just as tight as they should be.

The boys at school were ranked by where they lived and what their fathers did. Someone's dad was a finance man and they lived on a top floor on Strandvägen facing the harbour – they had it all. Another guy's father was the chief financial officer at an airline, another managed a hotel chain – also nice.

Filip Åkesson's dad was an architect, and they lived in Bromma on the western side of Stockholm. It could have been better. Nonetheless, Filip felt that he frequented the upper reaches at school. He was invited to all the house parties and had once taped up a kid in the school's stairwell and shot him with paintballs, something that had been well appreciated among his friends. Filip was loud-mouthed and definitely wanted something from life. Exactly what that was was still unclear, but it didn't matter so much. The important thing was that he showed he had some guts and energy.

From his parents he had got an iPod that could hold nearly four thousand songs. Like most of the guys in Östermalm, Filip had previously listened to Swedish hip-hop, but during the summer of 2006 he had discovered two Frenchmen who were making irresistibly bubbly dance music. Bob Sinclar's 'World, Hold On (Children of the Sky)' and David Guetta's 'The World is Mine' were on repeat on the MP3 player.

It had begun in Chicago some decades before Filip Åkesson was born, when Frankie Knuckles was spinning records at the club The Warehouse at the end of the 1970s. Knuckles was skilled at blending the disco songs of the time into a single unbroken flow, so that all sense of time and space disappeared on the dance floor. He used the very latest devices, like samplers and drum machines, to make his own versions of his favourite songs. He gradually peeled away the grand gestures and sweeping melodies of disco – the machines made the rhythms straighter, the drums harder, the bass more prominent. The vocals were reduced to suggestive moans and sounds, which were there mostly to reinforce the track's rhythm.

The style was baptised after the club in which it was created and would soon simply be called house music.

When Åkesson listened to those old tracks now they sounded ancient. It was possible to sense the editing of the magnetic tape and the mechanical scrapes and rattles of the drum machine. Almost three decades later it was instead software that ruled. The files in Åkesson's headphones were the first truly digital music, songs built of ones and zeros, with sounds so manipulated and warped that they no longer had any counterpoint in the physical world. It was music from the future. Filip downloaded the MP3 files from blogs with names like House Heaven, Project 1048, Face the Music and Living Electro, where whoever was first to put up a new remix of the Italian Benny Benassi became king.

Just like the others on the economics programme, Filip Åkesson had his locker on the second floor, under the mural where Thor, one of the Norse gods, swung his hammer to subdue the evil of the world. The footsteps echoed in the stairwell as Åkesson ran to yet another boring class on the first floor, where the social studies students had their lockers.

At the black wooden tables on the left was where Tim Bergling and his gang always sat. Filip Åkesson knew of Tim because rumour had it that his mother was an actor; it was said that she had even done a nude scene in one of her films. There were certainly other celebrity children at the school who were higher in rank – one was the son of the TV host Martin Timell, another of the singer Tomas Ledin. Compared to that, Tim's mum fared quite poorly; and in any case she did not seem to have imbued her son with any particular star quality. Quite the opposite. In Åkesson's eyes Tim and his friends were just nerds who sat and discussed Dota or World of Warcraft or something equally dorky.

It was enough to look at his appearance – Tim had spots, wore floral three-quarter trousers and a long-sleeved shirt with wooden buttons at the neck. The soles of his Adidas shoes had dried and turned yellow.

Tim Bergling didn't exactly give off the aura of Hollywood.

DURING THE SUMMER break before the second year in high school, Tim, Fricko and a few other friends went to Juan-les-Pins on the French Riviera.

One night they partied at Le Village, or maybe it was Whisky à Gogo – whatever it was, on the way home one of them had bought weed from some guy by the beach promenade. The gang went down to the water's edge, where Tim, under cover of darkness, took two or three drags of the joint.

At first nothing happened. And then still nothing. Then Tim's throat suddenly and completely dried up. He felt his heart beginning to race. A rumble intensified in his head, like a jet engine speeding up before take-off. Each heartbeat throbbed violently against his forehead, but when he checked his heart rate, it turned out that everything was in order, his pulse normal.

The knowledge that he might really just be fighting against his own thoughts did not help much. Maybe he would die now?

The feeling passed, Tim came home to Stockholm and forgot about the experience, until one day when he had sat in front of the computer for eleven hours straight. Tired and exhausted, he got up from his chair and his head started spinning again.

When he regained composure, he looked at the tobacco boxes in a high pile on a shelf above the head of his bed. Next to them hung a framed picture of himself; on the shelf above the desk stood the line of pirated DVDs. Wherever Tim looked, the objects suddenly felt distant, as if he couldn't reach them.

He thought it would be better if he slept for a while, but the next day it was the same. He was somehow encapsulated, no longer belonging to the real world. This was a different feeling from the fear of cancer. That discomfort he felt physically in his chest; this was something more elusive. Had he become mentally ill? Tim had heard that cannabis could trigger psychosis: a condition in which one found it difficult to interpret reality and in the worst case began to feel persecuted or hear voices, or got ideas about ruling the world.

After a few days of worry, Tim decided to tell his mother everything. He had smoked and now there was something wrong with his head. Maybe he had gone insane.

'It's as if I'm standing outside of everything,' Tim said to Anki. 'I've, like, lost contact with myself.'

His parents thought it was good that Tim had the confidence and courage to dare to tell them what had happened in France. This would all work out. Klas tried to reassure his son by telling him that he had had similar feelings when he was Tim's age: a kind of confusion and uncertainty. Terrifying nights when he felt as though reality was failing. He himself had handled it by writing down his thoughts. When he put his thoughts into words, the knots untied, life became steady again. Tim did not have to be afraid of that feeling of discomfort, it was just a matter of finding out what was haunting him.

They got in contact with professionals in child and adolescent psychiatry and accompanied Tim to the hospital in Sabbatsberg, where he was seen by a psychologist who specialised in talking to young people.

Tim left with mixed feelings. It was nice to talk about it, but the fact that he had needed to seek care strengthened his conviction that something was seriously wrong with him.

Anki was impressed with her son. She thought about how

she herself had been as a teenager – she had never revealed a single bit about her inner life to her parents.

'There is one good thing about this,' she told her husband. 'We never have to worry about Tim falling for drugs.'

On the surface, Tim was almost back to normal in the following weeks. In the corridor at Östra Real there were other things that caught his attention; he laughed as he sat at the table next to the lockers, talked about documentaries and games with his classmates.

The anxiety crept in in the evenings, when he was alone and going to sleep. He was afraid that his thoughts would start up again when he turned off the light. After three weeks, the discomfort was still not gone. On the contrary, it was almost worse. Now the thoughts no longer revolved around the actual bad trip in France, but around everything it had put in motion. Tim was worried about the fact that he was worried, and that he did not understand where the feeling came from. He lived a good life in every way, was lucky, even spoiled. A safe and secure upbringing in one of Sweden's richest areas, a childhood free of any major traumas.

It must mean that there was something wrong with him himself? That the toxic feelings were simply there in his interior, as steady as the stone houses in Östermalm? Maybe he was doomed to this, equipped with a brain that was damaged, already screwed up.

As he made an effort to analyse his situation, his thoughts bounced around in his head without ever gaining a foothold. Tim read online about the concept of derealisation, a condition in which one's environment felt unreal. It was reminiscent of the mother in *Requiem for a Dream*, a film he had been particularly taken by. A middle-aged woman dreamed of one day being able to take part in a game show on television. She started taking pills to lose weight and fit into her favourite dress. The madness escalated and after a while she nibbled on pills like sweets as her apartment closed in around her. Eventually, the entire living room was distorted and threatening, and when the paramedics came for her, she asked in a daze if they would drive her to the TV studio.

Derealisation. It sounded so frightening. Could this be something similar? Either way, Tim had lost the urge to go out and party. If he got drunk anything could happen, he thought.

In order to get advice from others who had experienced something similar, he started a thread on Flashback, Sweden's largest online discussion forum, where people from all over the country exchanged thoughts on everything from gardening to drug addiction to celebrity gossip.

Tim wrote:

> Feels like I can't really think clearly like I could three weeks ago, feels like everything is meaningless when the feeling is at its worst.

> I'm also worried about losing control of myself when I'm tipsy. Have never had these kinds of problems before but I'm worried that my anxiety will increase when I get drunk and that I'll feel like nothing matters and take my life or something :P.

As the weeks went on Tim worked out a strategy for managing his anxiety. He would simply turn off. Stop thinking so damn much. If he kept busy with other things, it would surely fade away.

IN THE AUTUMN OF 2006 Tim had other things to think about, anyway. There was a song that had dominated the radio the whole summer. Irritating, but still somehow irresistible. The bouncing synth bass, clattering drums, and lyrics that no adult in all of Stockholm seemed to understand. Those who didn't know anything about computers thought the song was about a boat. In fact, 'Boten Anna' ('Now You're Gone') was a digital love story about a moderator in a chat room; it was sung by a guy who called himself Basshunter. Only a few months earlier he had been a bullied computer nerd who posted his gimmicky song online as a joke for his mates. Within a few months the single had become the most downloaded song ever in Scandinavia.

It was a lame song in every way, Tim knew as much. It might have worked for the tweens in middle school, but hardly for someone who had begun second year in high school. But there was something about that melody. Once it got in your head it wouldn't disappear.

One evening at the beginning of the autumn term in 2006 Tim got an MSN message from Jakob, who had found a video on YouTube, a newly launched site where anyone could upload film clips.

Tim pressed play and saw a grey computer screen covered in chequered patterns. Furthest to the left ran a black-and-white keyboard, digital keys laid out just like on a real piano. The voice that spoke belonged to Basshunter himself, who was

34

showing how he created his hits. With the help of the mouse, he dragged mint-green bricks across the screen – within seven minutes he had the skeleton of the song.

It looked simple, and fun. Tim immediately downloaded a pirated version of FL Studio, the program that Basshunter used. This Belgian software had previously been called Fruity Loops and was one of the programs that had revolutionised the way music was created. Only ten years earlier, a musician would have had to rent a studio or spend tens of thousands of dollars on machines and instruments. Now you could do it all from your bedroom.

Tim tried to get a grasp of the software bricks; he'd plucked the guitar strings enough to understand the basics. If the green bricks were placed in the upper part of the grid, the notes got higher, further down were the lower octaves. What the program allowed Tim to do was to devise chords. He moved one block up, another down, then listened again. When he broadened the brick, the tone sounded longer.

To the left was a column of pre-recorded sounds: synthetic guitars, cymbals and violins. Some sounded like shy raindrops on a windowpane, some sizzled like bacon in a pan. The tones could scream like a gunfight between spaceships or be eerie like an unpleasant horror movie. An entire orchestra – no, hundreds of them – conveniently packaged in digital form.

Impatiently, Tim tried everything out, staying up all night, mixing and matching and moving. Failing and trying again.

Soon he understood that the same chords could have a completely different feel to them depending on what sound he chose from the column on the left. Something that pulsed calmly in one digital synth could become a sharp cry in another. He had discovered a synth that was called Z3ta+, where he could choose between sounds with names like Trance Delivery, Foreign Attack, Space Bell and Fusion Poly. Now he found a whiny tone that made the melody almost stressfully nasal.

It was perfect. He knew that Jakob and Fricko and the others would think it was cool if he made a song that was as irritating as possible. In the sound library Vengeance Essential Clubsounds Volume 2 there was a fervently whipping hi-hat which he sprinkled in quick succession. There was also a recorded voice that screamed: *The beat, the bass and the party – let's go!*

Now it started to resemble something. To really emphasise that this was a parody, he added yet another voice that, without interruption, said, *BASS! BASS! BASS! BASS! BASS!*

Maybe it wasn't good, but it was annoying and fun.

Filip Åkesson climbed in through the loading dock and followed the pulse that vibrated through the concrete walls. When he and his friend got further into the shabby warehouse in the industrial district in Nacka the whole space opened up and Åkesson looked around through the fog coming from the smoke machine.

It was something totally different from the boring classes at Östra Real.

The green laser beams hovering over the dance floor in swirling cobwebs, girls with blonde hair in tight dresses, guys from the suburbs in expensive jackets and shoes with shiny buckles. The hard banging electro that pounded against his eardrums.

For so long Filip had dreamed about getting to see this for real that he intuitively recognised the scene.

After its birth in Chicago, house music – and its more edgy cousin techno – had been picked up by curious Brits, who brought the sound from the US to Europe. And with the music came the parties. Filip Åkesson had heard about the mythological summer of 1988, when dance-craving Englishmen had organised illegal raves in the fields by the motorway surrounding London. He knew about Love Parade, which soon after had flooded the streets of Berlin with people celebrating equality and the new-found freedom of the early 90s.

Since then, the festivities had continued in derelict factories and solitary forest edges across the continent and turned dance music into a modern European folk music, a patchwork of different styles that occasionally cross-fertilised each other but just as often sounded essentially unique.

In 2007 the French built their house music on filtered disco samples that hovered over blurred bass lines. In England choppy bass rumbled over pirate radio in a sticky style called dubstep. The biggest and most powerful scene was in the Netherlands, where Tiësto filled arenas with his trance, built on grand string arrangements over blaring drums.

The scene in Sweden was not nearly as big, at least not numerically speaking. But there were tremors in the ground, signs that were noticed by those who, like Filip Åkesson, considered themselves as belonging to the vanguard. In Stockholm, a unique musical expression was growing, one that was as bombastic as it was euphoric, and could be heard not least on this night in the warehouse south of the city.

Filip Åkesson wove his way in among people who moved instinctively to the bass lines. Only a few weeks earlier he had tried Ecstasy for the first time and felt how the little pill made the music tingle and swell in each muscle. The melodies became wonderful, the snare drums were like an extra body part. Tonight as well they had started partying on the terrace at the house of a mate's dad, and the music now pulsed through Åkesson's body in pleasant convulsions. There was something magical in the way this music slowly grew.

Those who didn't understand may have seen the songs as

repetitive, but that was part of the point. The monotony made the music suggestive and prodding, teasing each and every sense. The night was a sea where it slowly blew up into a storm.

Up towards the small ledge that served as a stage came a guy in worn jeans, a T-shirt, and a backwards baseball cap with the LA Dodgers logo. He slowly pulled up the fader to play a new tune, threw off his cap, baring a tightly tied tuft of hair.

There he was. Steve Angello. Of all the house producers in Stockholm, this twenty-four-year-old was by far the coolest in Filip Åkesson's eyes. You just needed to look at him: how Angello's body language radiated that he couldn't care less what people thought. His back held straight and his chest protruding through any and all difficulties.

The Swedish press had of course yet to grasp what was happening – what a lively scene had been created in the capital over the last few years – but what did it matter when Angello's girlfriend had her own blog? Among pictures of high heels and skincare pointers, she talked about when her boyfriend spun in the booths at the clubs at Stureplan – the nightlife centre of Östermalm – at the venues that Filip Åkesson dreamed of one day getting into. She gossiped about the drinks at Grodan, F12 and Laroy, and posted pictures of Axwell and Sebastian Ingrosso, two other producers with whom Steve Angello was increasingly collaborating.

A bit playful and a little ironic – as if to emphasise how small yet prominent the Swedish scene was – they had started calling their trio Swedish House Mafia. In the summer they travelled to Ibiza, the party island in the Mediterranean that Filip already knew was the kingdom of heaven and played the clubs there. The pictures on the blog showed Sebastian Ingrosso with a sizeable drink in his hand at the legendary spot Pacha, where they performed with the star David Guetta. Steve Angello sat with a sunhat on the beach and read about himself in the music magazine *Mixmag.*

The dream life.

As the bass was bouncing between the walls, Åkesson started to box with his hands in the air to yet another one of the hard synth riffs.

This was his world, everything he was looking for.

Tim Bergling didn't go to any clubs, he was totally uninterested in them. Instead, he had sat in front of his computer for four months, engrossed, but still hadn't got any real depth into his songs.

When he described what genre he was working in, he hesitated. What even was this kind of music? 'Don't actually know,' he wrote in the forum Studio, a venue on the internet where beginners got on with seasoned professional producers. 'Tween-simple-Eurodance techno possibly,' he decided. At the end of January 2007 he posted a question about how he should approach FL Studio:

> I just wanted to ask if a FL veteran with a little extra time and energy would be able to help finalise a song I'm kinda happy with. I've basically been sitting for DAYS trying to fiddle with compressor and bass boost and vocoder etc. to make the voice and bass drum etc. sound good but haven't gotten anywhere :/. I don't understand the compressor and the song distorts like crazy at a 30% gain ...

Tim absorbed all the tips he got. He watched even more clips on YouTube, where other producers clarified the finesses and the settings.

The usual thing was obviously to start by looking for drums and a bass line that played nicely together. There was the bottom itself, the backbone of a song, that seemed to be the consensus. The recipe could certainly be spiced up with some sampling or a little moaning, but it was the drums and the bass that drove the production forward.

Tim's instincts led him to think differently.

He began with a melody.

If he didn't already hear it in his head, then it usually came to him when he played around with the chord bricks.

Once the right melody was in place then the next challenge began. Tim started looking for a fitting software synth and began to tweak, push and pull. The fun thing with FL Studio was that each and every sound could be twisted and distorted until it was unrecognisable. In the software program the instruments were freed from their classical roles – sweet strings could become blunt rhythmic instruments; a short and aggressive trumpet blast could be filtered so that it was perceived as a smooth bass tone.

Only once the chords sounded right sonically did Tim start building the rest of the song. Then he heard what kind of drums were needed, and what other effects he would use.

On YouTube the video to 'Feel The Vibe (Til The Morning Comes)', a song by Axwell of Swedish House Mafia, played on repeat. Tim studied the forward-leaning, soft production, the rolling bass that was as fat as cream. He noticed how the bass line interacted with the melody in an airy and elegant sway. Tim liked that the song was euphoric and soft without feeling cheesy. It was happy music that still had bite. He had a hard time understanding how Axwell had achieved such a saturated soundscape. If Tim's own beats were drawn in sharp pencil, Axwell's songs were painted with colourful pastel crayons.

Tim sat up all night, continuing to read and ask questions, just as he had done before on the gaming forums. When friends came to visit, it was clear that Tim was fixated on something new. When they wanted to watch a movie or start a new raid, their friend was sitting almost unreachable in front of his screen. It could be an hour of waiting, it could be two. It was as if Tim couldn't hear them.

He was captivated by his puzzle, had understood that a piece that felt insignificant on its own could be completely load-bearing when joined together with another. There was a logic in the process that was calming.

Tim forgot about his homework, forgot to eat, forgot about his spots.

In this room was nothing else.

When two and three and then four pieces of the puzzle finally fitted together, Tim began to bounce on his chair. A while ago there was nothing on the screen, just an empty grid, now a whole beat was pounding in his headphones. It even had some swing to it!

His chest tingled with joy and pride as he played the chords in the air with waving hands.

All of a sudden he could hear Anki getting up out of bed to go to the bathroom. He quickly turned off the ceiling light so that she would not see that he was still awake.

The rumour had started to spread among the teenagers in Östermalm about an artist who called himself Moonboy. The song 'En låda' ('A Box') had begun to be played from the wireless speakers in the corridors at Östra Real and Filip Åkesson heard it afresh in the kitchen at a house party during the last term in the second year, in the spring of 2007.

After a while a guy in Filip's German class said that Moonboy apparently went to their school. Åkesson thought this sounded ridiculous. The song was too professional to be made by someone their own age.

You mean the guy in E2C? The guy whose mum was an actress? The one who used to sit at the tables by the lockers and jabber about his computer games? The guy with yellow soles on his worn-out Adidas?

Was Tim Bergling Moonboy?

Filip Åkesson didn't want to miss the chance to get to know someone who made his own beats, no matter how stupidly the guy dressed. One Friday after school, Filip got a ride from his father to Linnégatan and took the lift up to the fifth floor.

'My parents aren't home, so we can be on the couch,' Tim said when he opened the door.

Even though they had gone to the same school for a year and a half, they had never really spoken to each other. Now they carried Tim's computer into the living room and hooked it up to the TV screen that sat on the wall in front of the green sofa.

Filip immediately began to play the songs of his Swedish idols. A remix by Sebastian Ingrosso, a rippling house piano from Axwell.

'It's sick, right?'

'Fucking sick!'

Filip suggested that they should try to do something that resembled his favourite song, 'Teasing Mr Charlie' by Steve Angello.

Tim quickly went to work. He clicked forward to a sound that was called Saw Dist Tube and began to lay out the components.

Bewitched, Åkesson watched the mint-green blocks dance across the grey grid as he heard a melody take shape. He had been listening to house music for several years, but had never seen it develop like this.

After only a few minutes Tim had created a pattern that was easy to loop. He copied and placed it under the first bricks – doubling a sequence was the best way he had figured out to make it sound heavier, he explained.

Then he slid in a bass drum and a little handclap.

'Then we have to *tease*,' said Filip Åkesson.

This is where Åkesson's experience came in. Even if he had been impressed by Tim's local hit 'En låda', at best it had lurched on. It never reached climax in the same way that the songs on Filip's iPod did.

Progressive house was a kind of music that was built on anticipation. That was the whole point with the word 'progressive' – that the songs would slowly develop and bloom like a flower in spring. The principle built on maximising the music's ebbs and flows. The listener was often tricked into a deceptive calm – just as the song was on the way to its crescendo, the drums could stop and be replaced by strings that gently swayed forward. Then the storm intensified in what sounded like a jet plane warming up. Once the song exploded, the effect became physical, a great drop made the chest explode.

It was like having sex, or at least what the boys imagined sex to feel like.

Filip Åkesson thought that he knew the recipe, second by second. First, it would be at least half a minute of just drums. This was so that the song could be imperceptibly mixed with another at the clubs. Then a short preview of the melody itself, maybe just a note or two, which made the listener want more.

Tim thought it was cool to meet someone who knew the rules so well, and followed Åkesson's instructions to a tee.

After exactly thirty seconds of drums, he allowed the melody to flicker, just for a moment. He extended it for another fifteen seconds and after a full minute of patient ascension, he finally let the whole melody detonate.

The screaming synth filled the living room while Åkesson cheered.

'Turn up the volume, man! You're a fucking genius, Tim!'

ARASH POURNOURI ATTACHED a piece of tape to the poster and hung it up at the bus stop.

His companion's mother had lent them her car so that, under the cover of darkness, they could drive around town and advertise the important message: in the summer of 2007 their club Dirty Disco would invade Café Opera, one of Sweden's most legendary nightspots, located in a beautiful premises with painted ceilings within walking distance of Stureplan.

It was in these neighbourhoods that the revolution had first begun.

At the club Sturecompagniet the DJ Eric Prydz had first met Sebastian Ingrosso, which had led to the birth of Swedish House Mafia. In the basement of the classic restaurant Grodan, people pumped their hands in the air to Swedish producers such as John Dahlström or Adam Beyer, and the club promoters Group Locomotives booked all the coolest names for the terrace on Fredsgatan 12.

Arash Pournouri – who was called Ash by those who knew him – was eager to take another step into the house music scene.

Arash had come to Sweden from Iran at the age of five with his single mum and two younger siblings. They had made a new home for themselves in Skarpnäck, a suburb south of Stockholm. Early on he had begun to dream of a future as a musician; as a boy he had won a local talent show with a song called 'Rosor av stål' ('Roses Of Steel'). His mother preached diligence and hard work and would have preferred to see her children become doctors, but Arash had always known that he would become a businessman. He had felt like an entrepreneur even before he'd known what the word meant.

Until now, however, his efforts had been in vain.

It had begun when, in his late teens, he approached Spray, one of the most successful IT firms in Stockholm, and presented his idea of a digital radio for mobile phones. Politicians had been promising faster mobile networks and Arash envisioned a streaming service where a mobile user could see in advance which songs would be played, like a radio with a greater ability to control the content. He later realised that he had been naïve and blue-eyed, he had even told the company's lawyers that he had not patented the idea. Six months later the company had sold a similar concept for big money, but without Arash's involvement. Humiliated, he had decided to study law; no one would ever dupe him again.

Alongside his studies Arash began to promote club nights, both in Stockholm and in Oslo. He would study three days a week and then ahead of the weekend take the bus over the border to Norway, where he played DJ at his own clubs.

Once during this intensive period, he lost his phone, which sparked his next business idea. Online Simcard Service would make back-up copies of the contents of a mobile phone so that important numbers and notes were always secured online. Since Arash himself could not write code, he took a loan of a quarter of a million Swedish crowns and invested his own savings to let a bunch of programmers develop the software. The project dragged on and became increasingly costly. When Arash gave the product demonstration, nothing worked. It was totally unusable actually, and all the investors dropped out.

But that was all history. Now he would get the people of Stockholm to understand the power of house music. He and his friend's agreement with Café Opera was actually quite crappy – the restaurateur took nearly all the ticket revenue – but they would get another foot in the industry. And they had booked some really cool names for the summer of 2007, including Laidback Luke from the Netherlands and the British duo Freemasons.

Now even more people would be invited into their fantastic world.

The flock would grow.

The newly found friends Tim Bergling and Filip Åkesson quickly developed a habit. They briefly met at school in the morning before they ignored the rest of the classes after lunch and took the short walk to Linnégatan.

There Tim lay flat on his bed, with the mousepad on the crumpled sheets.

Filip Åkesson would have no choice but to place himself behind Tim and stretch over his friend's shoulder in order to see the computer screen which remained on the desk. Pressed together on the bed, they continued to study songs by the German Tocadisco or Frenchmen such as Daft Punk and Joachim Garraud.

What they most often bickered about were the lower registers. Filip wanted a bass that was rumbling and aggressive. If the song was to work for the club, the thump would have to start from the bottom.

Tim was more interested in the composition itself. It would be enough to have a bass drum to give the song its bottom, he thought, and instead sought something more colourful and hummable. Open, welcoming melodies that were effective and immediate. Like children's songs, the kind you heard and which immediately stuck in your head.

After a couple of hours of work, all the oxygen had run out

and it felt like the only thing Tim and Filip were breathing was each other's farts. To avoid Klas or Anki noticing that they were skipping school, they would haul off for a while and grab a pizza in Östermalmstorg, then come back later in the evening, pretending to come home from school, lock themselves in Tim's room and continue to work.

Tim had got good at deceiving his parents. He would catch a cold or have a free period, often blaming the Spanish teacher for being ill. She was so old that it could almost have been true.

Although his parents let their youngest get away with a whole lot, they hardly bought all the stories he made up. In never-ending discussions, Klas and Anki tried to convince Tim of the importance of going to school but to no avail.

Their son was so incredibly stubborn.

In the same way that Tim had refused to eat anything other than crispbread in pre-school, he refused now to listen to his parents' admonishments about maths homework. His priorities were almost impossible to shake.

When graduation approached, the school administration sent a letter to Linnégatan. Tim had been absent so much that the tuition support was about to be revoked. Klas called the class teacher at Östra Real to find out what his son would have to do to improve his standing in this situation.

'Yes, well, he can start with coming to class.'

Towards the end of 2007 Tim and Filip felt that they maybe had some songs that were good enough to be heard outside their inner circle at Östra Real.

Tim was never really satisfied with the name Moonboy, it sounded too cheesy. Together with another friend, he had come across an article on Wikipedia about avīci, a kind of Buddhist hell reserved for the greatest sinners, such as those who had murdered their mother or an enlightened monk. Over and over again, these criminals were forced to be reborn in a place where they were tortured in an indescribably burning furnace, for an unimaginably long time.

Avici sounded much more hardcore than Moonboy.

Filip already knew what he would call himself, so under the name Avici and Philgood the boys emailed the song 'A New Hope' to some of the Swedish house music blogs. Now all they had to do was hope that someone liked it enough to post it.

At the same time, Tim discovered another place online where the discussions were even more savvy than on the Swedish website Studio. The Dutch producer Laidback Luke had a discussion forum on his site. Everybody that hung out there really knew what they were talking about. Tim had posted some of his songs – 'Mr Equalizer' and 'Who's The Wookie Now?!' among others – and immediately received knowledgeable responses.

'Just the crash on the first 4 kicks kinda gives a bad impression,' one person pointed out. 'Instead you could try some kind of white noise, this works great for me ;).'

'Only thing I'm missing is a bit of progression when the second take off comes,' wrote another. 'Try changing the bass/synth frequency or something after the second break. Anyways, a great tune. You could probably get a digital release with this one.'

Clearly, in the Netherlands it was possible to make a career out of producing house music. Every summer, the main football stadium in Amsterdam was filled with 30,000 partygoers, all dressed in white. At the festival, which was called Sensation, Tiësto was king. And he was so across the whole country, where he was called the Godfather. His atmospheric trance, built on grandiose synth patterns whopped by hot-tempered drums, had made him a superstar throughout Europe. Four years earlier, Tiësto had played in front of millions of TV viewers at the opening ceremony of the Athens Olympics; in his homeland there was even a special tulip named after him and the queen had honoured him with a royal medal.

Together with artists such as Afrojack and Chuckie, Laidback Luke belonged to the Dutch generation that came right after the Godfather – Luke was a superstar in the making.

One day when Tim opened the forum, he had received a private message that stared at him on the screen. Laidback Luke himself had sent his remarks to Tim.

Tim didn't dare open the message.

'Filip, can you read this for me?'

The concern turned out to be unfounded. The producer gave Tim straightforward but friendly criticism: he thought that the Swede should drop the attempts to make hard electro and instead focus on what he obviously had a knack for – melodies.

That became the catalyst for an intense dialogue, where the star listened carefully to each song Tim sent and gave personal advice on how the bass drum could be fuller or a synth loop crisper. Laidback Luke mentioned that he had his own record label, Mixmash Records, and if Tim continued to evolve at this pace, it was not impossible that he would one day release a song by Avici.

Now attention was coming from England as well. The DJ and radio host Pete Tong had played the hottest house music on his BBC radio show since the early 90s and in April 2008 he announced a competition for young producers.

Tim sent his song 'Manman', which to his great surprise was voted the winner by the listeners.

A few weeks later Tim and Filip went to Café Mocco in Östermalm, a place full of blogging girls and mums with baby strollers, to meet the club promotor Arash Pournouri.

The boys could see he was sophisticated and worldly just by the way he carried himself. Arash had a perfectly groomed beard and sparkling clean sneakers. He was grown up, twenty-six years old.

Arash had written a message on Facebook, saying that he'd heard a few of Tim's songs on the blogs and he would love to meet to see if they could work together somehow. Tim thought it was intimidating to go alone to meet a stranger out on the town, so Åkesson had come along as support.

Once they were seated Arash clarified that he heard something in Tim's songs. So many other house producers survived on unbridled intensity – Tim had another quality. A touch that at this point was still raw and directionless, but once refined could become something.

'House music is on its way up in Sweden,' Arash said. 'You can capitalise on that. I have the right contacts to push you.'

Arash promised that in one year he would make Tim bigger than nearly everyone in Sweden. After his unsuccessful business ventures he was filled with a lust for revenge. He would never again be played, never again rely on someone else. With his knowledge and experience he would be able to take Avici, and Philgood for that matter, to the top in no time.

'You'll have to be ready for this to be a full-time job,' Arash said to the teenagers. 'If you had a normal job you would put in eight, ten hours a day. But if you're going to succeed in this business, it'll have to be sixteen hours. At least.'

Tim and Filip just nodded, spellbound by what might be about to happen.

First meeting with Ash went well, started out as him just helping me out and eventually grew into our first management agreement. I remember him telling me he would make me the biggest DJ in the world, and that he knew exactly how to do so.

I was happy and thought it was cool as fuck to have a manager at 18 so I went along with it, having no work experience at all.

WHEN TIM WOKE UP the sun was scorching his face, the black tin roof almost boiling. When he lifted his head, he could look out over the conglomeration of rooftops of Stockholm's centre. Straight ahead rose Sankta Klara's church tower, to the right was the square Norra Bantorget; it was possible to catch a glimpse of the tourists gliding along the shopping street of Drottninggatan.

Right after graduation, just a few weeks after the meeting with Arash, Tim had moved away from home, to his older brother Anton's old pad on Kammakargatan in the middle of the city.

He had one year. During that time, his parents would pay for Tim's living expenses while he tested the waters to see if music could be financially viable. He had found a perfect strategy. At night he would stay up and work on songs and in the morning when it became impossible to stay awake, he would climb up on the roof and lie down on the small ledge. That way he got both sleep and sun. Although he fried himself red, he thought that the spots seemed to disappear with the burn.

Now he was lifting himself down through a hatch, continuing along the steps that sat against the wall, and landing in the building's attic storage. The one-room apartment was a few staircases down and was cluttered with unwashed plates, packets of tobacco, and burned CDs. The bed was supposed to be pushed up against the wall, but since Tim could never make a bed it basically filled the whole room, except for the area occupied by a refrigerator that he had filled up with Coca-Cola and frozen pizzas.

Tim squeezed himself through and sat down at the desk and continued working. He had got money from his parents to buy components and accessories for a computer he had assembled himself. It had fast processors, RAM and a hard drive that could handle huge amounts of data. The mousepad was called Razer Destructor and was covered by a metal coating that allowed Tim to make quick movements across the screen, which was not only good for playing World of Warcraft but also for building chords.

The best part was that Arash Pournouri had a plan. He had already explained how the music industry worked; he thought about boring stuff like distribution, positioning and marketing strategies.

The strategy was pretty hands-on. Through his experience as a DJ and club promoter, Arash had acquired email addresses and phone numbers for people in the business. He would quickly find a bunch of more established artists who were interested in letting a couple of young and promising Swedes do remixes of their songs. This way, Tim and Filip wouldn't have to start from scratch for each production and in addition they would be piggybacking on the bigger artists. If they managed to do one remix a month, their names would be established as producers who continuously delivered quality work.

Arash had already arranged the first assignment: the German DJ Francesco Diaz wanted an official remix of his song 'When I'm Thinking Of You'.

As Tim sat sandwiched in between the window and his unmade bed, his thoughts wandered freely, without pondering what was considered cool or quirky. He wanted to make his own versions of the Swedish 80s group Secret Service, or of Duran Duran or Eurodance artists like 2 Unlimited and Cut 'N' Move.

So far, Arash thought those were not good enough ideas. While Tim went entirely on gut feeling, his manager was more analytical. He praised himself for the ability to put himself in the shoes of the public. Arash listened to music at home, in the car, with headphones, constantly trying to analyse how different audiences would react to a song.

He emailed his comments on Tim's songs with bullet points, and they could end up being long lists of things that should be changed. A drop could be heavier, a sample should be cut off sooner, a snare could hit quicker.

Then they would go through the suggestions together. Getting rid of an element in a beat could be as effective as adding one. It was important to be frugal with the sounds, to refine them. The mass audience wouldn't remember the intricacies of a song, but the essence.

One thing was important: Arash wanted to have full control of the commercial side of things, while Tim would be free to focus on being creative. After his previously bombed projects, Pournouri would never lose control again. No one could work as excruciatingly hard as him, and every time he had handed responsibility to others everything had gone to shit. If Tim didn't trust that Arash would make him into a global phenomenon, then it was better that they didn't work together.

In return, Tim could focus on exactly what he wanted, namely to sit in front of the newly purchased twenty-four-inch screen and click melodies together. For Tim it sounded like a perfect set-up.

After graduation Filip Åkesson had taken a job behind the counter at a grocery store near the square of Karlaplan. He already felt as though he had fallen behind his friend: Tim was making great musical progress every week. But not everyone had parents who wanted to sponsor their son in such an uncertain endeavour as possibly becoming a house producer. Filip had to work, but after his shift he would hurry to Kammakargatan to see what Tim had accomplished during the day.

One evening, Åkesson arrived a couple of hours later than agreed because he had lost track of time on an errand. A guy at the Engelbrekt school had had a quarter ounce of Black Afghan for sale.

Tim was already angry when Filip walked in. It wasn't because his buddy was late, Tim clarified, but that he had spent their precious time buying hashish.

They had a chance to do something big now – Arash had made contact with the company Vicious Grooves in Australia, and Laidback Luke was still eager to release something, he was just waiting for the right track.

'Fuck you,' Filip yelled, 'don't be such a fucking pussy.'

Tim went up into falsetto, getting angry at his friend for the first time.

'If you're going to mess around with that then I don't want anything to do with you!'

One day Arash came to Kammakargatan with a few boxes of used equipment. They lined up two CD players on each side of a mixer from Numark.

At their first meeting Arash had explained that the real money was in performing live. It wasn't until they had some real global hits that would they make money on the tracks themselves. People had got used to downloading files for free and therefore the songs were more to be considered a way to launch their names than anything else. The real business opportunity was the gigs.

Arash showed how the cables should fit, went through the most important buttons and the basics of how a crossfade on the mixer worked. It wasn't so difficult, the technology they would soon get familiar with. The crucial thing was to learn to read the room, something that Arash had understood when he played his sets in Oslo. With a little practice they could learn to tell if the girls in the back were dancing for real or ironically or if the guys along the wall were ready for the harder stuff.

It was possible to divide a DJ set into three different phases, Arash explained. First it was a matter of warming up the crowd, so that they started vibing to the music and dared to move towards the dance floor. Then it was about getting them to turn up, playing more and more intense stuff. Finally, it was peak time, when everybody in the club would want to get fucked up for real. A good DJ at that point already had the dance floor in his hand and could control the audience's attention like a skilful film director. Once Tim and Filip got there, they could pretty much play anything, preferably the hardest shit they had.

Arash had already arranged the first gig. It was going to take place at Carlsson's, a school a stone's throw away from Tim's parents' home, where a dance was thrown for the students in the ninth year.

The afternoon before the school dance, Tim and Filip sat on the bed in Tim's cramped pad and burned their songs of Tocadisco and Eric Prydz and David Guetta on CDs. Tim drummed his foot against the floor, clapped his hands on his knees, stood up, walked around in circles.

'Can I play this?'

'Yeah, man, that's a vibe!'

'Are you sure that I can play it?'

Filip was nervous too, but Tim seemed totally freaked out. Each and every muscle in his body was tense, a cascade of words came out of his mouth.

The more they had got to know each other the more Filip Åkesson had seen that Tim was anxious about nearly everything. He had obsessive thoughts about pulling the door handle four times, he was forced to arrange the bottles of Coca-Cola in the refrigerator in a particular way. Without warning he could get a pain in his chest and make Filip feel if a cancerous tumour had grown or not. But this was still a whole new level of tension.

After a while Filip got tired of it. There wasn't really so damn much to think about, was there? You had to bite down and get through the hard stuff, be resourceful. No one else would solve your problems and those who believed so were Social Democrats and you weren't one of those in Östermalm.

'Can I end with this track?' Tim asked.

'Of course you can. Shit, just lighten up. Look for your balls and call me when you find them.'

The gig was to take place in a downstairs hall at the school. To Tim's great relief, it turned out that the students were much more interested in finding someone to make out with than listening to how his transitions between songs sounded.

During the summer of 2008 Tim and Filip got a more consistent gig. There was a café called Cozy in Södermalm that was open at night, perhaps a place that no one actively sought out, but it was located at a busy intersection where people ended up for a piece of pie after a full day of shopping.

Tim and Filip had to set up their equipment by the aisle near the kitchen, right next to the cash register. The café was actually a very good place to practise their DJ skills, as the only person who really moved to the music was the owner of the place, an acquaintance of Arash who always requested 'Body Language' by the German house duo Booka Shade. But suddenly, in the middle of a song, Tim happened to brush across the pause button, and the music stopped.

Ka-ka-ka-ka-ka-ka-ka-ka-ka-ka-ka the speakers stammered out, while Filip waited for Tim to press play again.

Nothing happened. Tim stood petrified, paralysed with shame. Filip had to lean over his friend and start the music again.

It had been an almost unnoticeable thing, ten seconds that the coffee-drinking customers hadn't even spotted. But for Tim it was a critical error, a moment of humiliation.

He no longer wanted to play at Cozy.

A few months later the pattern repeated.

Arash had another friend who worked with Young08, a festival that the Stockholm municipality arranged for the city's teenagers. The centre of the festivities was Kungsträdgården, a park in the middle of the city that for a few days filled up with tents where government employees tried to teach lustful teenagers how to wear a condom or how to act in the event of a fire.

Arash had arranged for Tim to be part of the closing show on Friday night – he would perform on the same stage as Miami rapper Flo Rida and the Jamaican duo Brick & Lace, in front of five thousand kids. It was like the greatest thing ever.

Tim reeled.

'Nobody cool goes there,' he said, 'that's for tweens.'

Filip Åkesson understood that it wasn't about the audience's age. It was about how many people there were. A packed Kungsträdgården was totally different than a café in Södermalm. Now Tim would no longer be an unnoticeable figure who anonymously played songs, now someone would loudly call him up on to the stage.

Tim refused. He had eight hundred arguments that all boiled down to one thing: he would not perform that Friday night.

Philgood had to take his place.

If Tim had a hard time getting used to the feeling of being a DJ, he worked all the more intensely in front of the computer. When a song was nearing completion the trio took a trip in Arash's car to get a sense of how the music was mixed, if the sounds were compressed and tight enough to work on the radio.

Tim and Filip had discovered that the Mornington Hotel on Nybrogatan had a gym that often stood empty. There, Tim was able to connect his phone to the system and turn up the volume in the speakers fixed on the walls. Among exercise balls and barbells, he and Filip evaluated the hefty bass line in Tim's latest song, 'Ryu'.

This piece of electro meant somewhat of a breakthrough. 'Ryu' along with 'Strutnut' were the first songs that Laidback Luke thought stood out enough for him to release them on his record label Mixmash.

And it wasn't just that. Luke also wanted to celebrate the release by inviting Tim, Filip and Arash to the US in March 2009 for a first gig on the other side of the Atlantic.

The party that Luke organised would take place in the basement of a luxury hotel in Miami. Besides Tim, a couple of Dutch artists were on the pink flyer: the veteran duo Chocolate Puma and Hardwell, a guy of Tim's age who had also hung out a lot on Luke's online forum.

If there was any place in the US where a house producer would like to be seen, it was in Miami in March.

The Winter Music Conference had started out as a traditional industry gathering at a conference hotel. Around the turn of the millennium a rave had been thrown in conjunction with the meeting, which had gradually grown into what was now called the Ultra Music Festival. The two events complemented each other: the Winter Music Conference offered seminars and panel debates for record company executives, booking agents and managers, and when the weekend came around the Ultra Music Festival attracted thousands of spring break-intoxicated students to party to death to explosive beats and laser shows. One year earlier, the Swede Eric Prydz had done his first festival show in the US at Ultra. At that time Lady Gaga had been in town, still a relatively unknown artist – now her song 'Poker Face' was well on its way to becoming 2009's best-selling single.

In general, dance music had long been overlooked in the US. While house music and techno had become mainstream genres in England, Germany and the Netherlands, they were still subcultures here. Of course, there had been sudden outbursts, moments when the scene had sparked – most recently in the late 90s when Brits like The Prodigy, The Chemical Brothers and Fatboy Slim had enjoyed successes on the charts. But at the same time, politicians had started to eye the culture and had cracked down hard on the raves held in warehouses and forests around the country. The seizures of Ecstasy had increased, and dance music was considered by many politicians a threat to young people. In 2002 the senator Joe Biden started to push through a bill called the RAVE Act – Reducing Americans' Vulnerability to Ecstasy. The proposal was criticised for being too extensive. Among other things, glow sticks were listed as reason enough for police to shut down a party. Even massage oils were seen as a sign of drugs.

Once the legislation came into force, it had been moderated, but Chicago, birthplace of house music, nevertheless became the country's first city to ban rave parties without a permit. Since then, a number of notorious night-time police raids had cooled the scene considerably.

The American radio stations had never really known what to do with music without traditional pop structure. Breaking through with a song that lacked verses, chorus and a bridge was considered virtually impossible in the United States.

There were certainly signs of change. The Frenchman David Guetta had just released a couple of songs that had started being played frequently on American radio. 'When Love Takes Over' was performed by Kelly Rowland, a former member of the American super trio Destiny's Child, and 'I Gotta Feeling' was a party monster by the Los Angeles-based group Black Eyed Peas, where Guetta had distilled the repetitive bounce that made him so popular in his home country. The Frenchman seemed to have found a magical formula – combining the energy of European house music with the greatest of American pop singers.

At the end of a long flight, Tim was leaning forward in his seat, hitting his knees. He looked out over the wings of the plane, seeing them rattle up and down in the strong wind. He knew that it would come to this. He hated flying, and every time he did, it was the landing that was the most unpleasant. Even for trained pilots, it must be a challenge to take a plane down, he thought, especially in this kind of turbulence. They had been circling the Miami airport for more than half an hour.

'Tim, now we'll probably die.'

Filip Åkesson, who had borrowed money from Tim's father to be able to make the trip, laughed at Tim Bergling, sitting in the seat next to him.

'We're going to crash, Tim!'

'Fuck you, man!'

Tim got a clean hit at Filip's shoulder, which dispelled the anxiety for a moment.

They had arranged a meeting at a sushi restaurant on South Beach. Tim's hand shook with nerves as he greeted Laidback Luke.

'I'm a little bit nervous about tomorrow, man. I haven't been DJing for too long, so I'm not very used to the set-ups.'

Lucas van Scheppingen, as Luke was actually called, knew exactly what Tim was going through. He himself had reached the age of thirty-one and had a long history of anxiety and self-doubt, although the cause was the opposite.

Lucas had no problem performing – on the contrary, he loved the stage. Up in his pulpit he could praise the power of music with intensity and technical bravery. But in front of the computer, it had for a long time been different. Lucas had been Tim's age when the legendary Carl Cox started playing one of his songs in the late 90s and he suddenly saw his name in the music magazines lined up in the record stores of Amsterdam. This was exactly what Lucas had strived for in his life. He had fought for so long – now he just needed to prove that he deserved to stay on top.

The mental block became overpowering. Lucas had built a small studio in the guest room at home in Aalsmeer, but no matter how much he worked on a sequel to 'The Stalker', he got nowhere. In an entire afternoon and evening he could fiddle with the sound of a bass drum which he then ended up throwing away. He turned up the volume until it felt like his ears were bleeding, yet he couldn't hear how it sounded. After a while, he stopped meeting up with his friends, stopped going out at all. When his friends asked, Lucas told them that he had been working in the studio all week. In fact, he had begun to spend the days in bed, where he veered between hubris and self-loathing.

There were so many who dreamed of this chance – why did he not just seize the opportunity? But then again, Carl Cox had played his song: that must mean that he had become someone!

One day as he stretched out on the couch to try to rest for a while, his body began to sting and tingle. At first almost imperceptibly, soon fiercely and intensely. Without warning, Lucas found it difficult to breathe. As he took in air, it was as if someone was pressing a hand over his throat. He tried to scream but was unable to draw in enough oxygen.

After a while Lucas realised that he was probably having his first panic attack. He had no plans to tell anyone. He was a man, strong and capable. Anxiety was for weaklings, for wusses, for pussies. He would bear his own burden, bite down, and work harder.

Twelve years later at the sushi restaurant Lucas just tried to look as calm as possible, to instil a little courage in his Swedish guest.

'Just try and relax and feel the vibe of the room,' he said to Tim Bergling. 'If you can just sense what the crowd wants you'll be fine.'

When the evening came, Tim played so early that the event was quite relaxed. Very few in the United States even knew who he was, no one came to just listen to him. They stood in the bar having a few drinks while Tim could calmly hone his beat mixing skills.

Soon the whole week in Miami had passed and Filip Åkesson thought it was time to relax. Tim and Arash had been nagging about how important it was that they focused: they were here to make contacts and learn, it was no damn vacation. But now they had done all that important stuff and Åkesson had two acquaintances from Stockholm who said that they had got hold of some blow. Filip had never tried cocaine and felt the tingle of anticipation grow in his stomach.

'Don't do it. It's totally not worth it.'

Tim was sitting next to him on the hotel bed. Calmly and sternly, he once again went on about his shitty trip in France. He did not give up until he had made his friend promise not to take anything during the evening.

'Don't do anything stupid, Filip, you'll only regret it.'

When they met again a few hours later, it was at a club down on the beach. Åkesson felt so alert that he wondered if it was even noticeable that he was high. He went into the club's bathroom to do another line. Three seconds later the door was kicked in.

The guards wrestled Filip down, forced his hands up behind his back and led him to a secluded room where they pushed him down on the floor.

'Where's your ID card?'

'It's in my back pocket,' Filip answered, with a knee on his back and adrenalin pumping to his temples.

Pretty fucking cool scene he had made here anyway. It was just as good to continue.

'There is some money in my pocket too,' he said, taking a chance.

The guard dug out the bills, counting them silently.

'One hundred and seventy dollars. I guess that'd be enough.'

Dazed, Åkesson stumbled out of the small room. What the hell had really happened? Did he just manage to bribe an American nightclub guard? What a fucking king he was.

The next day, the feeling had turned into anxiety.

On the flight home, Tim sat isolated, with his headphones on and his nose in the screen. When they had found each other in the club crowd again and Filip had boasted about what had happened with the guards, Tim had only been disappointed. They had been arguing all morning. Tim thought Filip had broken his promise. Besides, he missed out on his chances – think of everything Arash had done for them!

Demonstrably uninterested, Tim was now sitting in his seat and working on a beat.

There was only one way to handle the tense situation, Filip thought, and asked the flight attendant for another whiskey.

Arash commented on the situation by quoting a hip-hop track by Xzibit, where the rapper and his companions bragged about their excessive drinking habits.

Now Tim lit up. Suddenly he knew what the song he was working on would be called – 'Alcoholic'.

From: Tim Bergling
To: Klas Bergling
Date: 21 March 2009

Could you help me schedule an appointment with the doctor? Haven't had any more problems or anything but you know how I am and would be nice to just check one more time!

Feeling really good and I'm not particularly anxious at all but just wanted to like actually be totally certain!

Kiss kiss

Tim

> **From: Klas Bergling**
> **To: Tim Bergling**
> **Date: 21 March 2009**
>
> Hi Tim,
>
> You're not alone being a hypochondriac, I was a lot too, especially when I was young. Quite natural actually. So there is nothing to be ashamed of or think you're weird for. I'm scheduling a doctor's appointment on Monday.
>
> Kisses and hugs
>
> Mum and Dad

Klas Bergling stood in front of the ironing board in Tim's childhood room on Linnégatan and fiddled with a crumpled strip of paper he had found in one of his son's pockets.

Tim had turned out to be an administrative nightmare. For the most part, he forgot to ask for a receipt at all, and the ones he still collected, he immediately wrinkled and shoved into his pocket. With the iron on low heat, Klas straightened out proofs of purchase for burnable CDs, sound cards and train tickets.

Everything had gone so dizzyingly fast in the last year. One day Arash had just been sitting there at the kitchen table and Tim had signed a contract with At Night, Pournouri's start-up management company. Now Tim had someone who could negotiate and book and highlight him, and it was certainly lucky.

The old man Bergling was by this point sixty-four years old, had sold his office supplies company and set himself up for a quiet life as a pensioner without too much work, apart from the small side-business he had spent his time on in recent years. From his ex-brother-in-law's porcelain factory in Alexandria, Klas imported materials for building furniture, including metal tables with ceramic tops.

But his company, called Egyptian Warehouse, had quickly got a new core business and Klas had become some kind of unpaid accountant. He paid a salary of twenty-five thousand Swedish crowns a month to Avicii – since there was already another Avici on the music site Myspace, Tim had by now added a letter at the end of his artist name.

They had begun to develop a new kind of relationship, Tim and Klas, a small family business in the entertainment industry. In the spring of 2009, Tim sent a summary of the income:

1000 dollars for the first single
500 Euros for remix
800 dollars for remix
500 Euros for remix
about 3000 kronor for 2 gigs

Of course, Klas did not recognise a single one of the names his son worked with. Tim had remixed a song for some German named Roman Salzger, another for the Spaniard David Tort. He had made his own song called 'Sound Of Now', which apparently did well. 'Street Dancer' was another, a somewhat strange concoction of a breakdance song from the mid-80s, digital synths and elated flutes. Tim was represented on a compilation album called *Clubbers Guide to 2009*, where Avicii stood next to Sebastian Ingrosso and Laidback Luke, something Tim was clearly proud of.

After the first taste in Miami, more offers had begun to come from promoters outside of Sweden, for example in Zurich and Toulouse.

It was noticeable that Tim was working himself up as the trips approached. The stress seemed to take hold in his stomach – recently he had complained that he was in pain and wanted to be examined. However, the doctors had found nothing wrong.

The anxiety could also take other forms. When his parents were to drive Tim to the airport in May 2009, Anki found her son lying on the hall floor, smelling of alcohol and with his clothes half-shoved into a broken suitcase. At check-in, Tim discovered that he had left his computer in the car; Klas had to rush off and pick it up.

Part of it was probably about the fear of flying. But Klas also saw his son's stress as a sign of something more fundamental. Tim seemed to get nervous about simply leaving the safe neighbourhoods in Stockholm, anxious from being thrown out of his bubble in the messy apartment. He knew he would soon be seen under the bright stage lights and, not least, was worried that the audience would see his spots.

But on the other hand – once Tim got on stage and got into his groove, he was all right. And afterwards he was always proud, a little boastful in an adorable way.

For Klas, it was clear that Tim had found his calling in the music. Not only did Arash believe in this, so did Tim. Klas wanted to let his son grow, not deny him anything at all.

And Tim's goal was the top of the mountain, no lower altitude.

Towards the end of the summer of 2009, Tim Bergling sat alone in front of the computer in his flat on Kammakargatan. In the darkness behind him the blanket protruded from the unmade bed, out in the hall the bathroom door stood ajar. His shirt was wrinkled, he looked newly woken.

Only a few short sentences were to be read out, but by this time he had done over ten takes.

'Hey, this is Avicii. I will be playing at the Techno Parade in Paris, Saturday the nineteenth of September—'

He came to a halt, looked down from the camera lens, embarrassed. He reminded himself not to look too happy. He had tried to read from the script a few days earlier, but Arash thought those recordings were completely unusable.

Tim had made a peace sign with his fingers, something that was apparently never allowed to be repeated. Neither was puckering his lips or winking with one eye. It looked childish, Arash said, as if Tim were fourteen years old.

Things became increasingly serious month by month. 'Alcoholic', the song that Tim had made with Filip Åkesson as a model, had just been released by Joia, a Swedish record label run by Sebastian Ingrosso's uncle, and it started to spread online. The Australian company Vicious had released the songs 'Muja' and 'Record Breaker'. Tim had remixed 'We Are' for Dirty South and worked with the Frenchman Sebastien Drums. He had done one of his first interviews with a French magazine. 'Not even 20 years old, this young Swede is already stirring up excitement at all his gigs, with or without his partner Philgood,' wrote *Only For DJs*. 'The summer of 2009 will undoubtedly confirm the potential of this electrohouse talent.'

So now Tim was on his way to Paris, where he would play from a truck slowly driving along the avenues, surrounded by people dancing and making out.

For Arash, the situation was clear as day. It was time to start building a brand, and the emerging social media ecosystem was made for it. No longer would an entrepreneur have to wait for a reporter to come out with a photographer and give one's product half a page in the newspaper.

Online, you became your own publisher, and because the readers and viewers who started following you had made an active choice, it was possible to build a particularly strong loyalty.

The crucial thing about Facebook and Twitter was that it was not a mute one-way communication. Avicii would be built up to be a star, but still feel attainable. Behind the idol was a humble guy, one who gladly took the help of his fans – that was the impression that was to be communicated. On social media, there was a unique opportunity to interact with the audience, which was proved a success when Avicii's followers on Facebook competed to make the official video for 'Alcoholic'.

The fans showed both creativity and craftsmanship. A Swiss guy dressed up as a depressed fox and filmed as he drank his way through the streets of St Gallen, but the winner was a fan from Stockholm who documented a drunken night illuminated by streetlights. The winner was invited as a VIP guest to France, and in the comments section was exactly the discussion that Arash wanted.

Sick video!!!

awesome.

great editing.

What's happening with your prize? Are you getting a song named by you ... and did you meet Avicii?

Hey man, yes I went on a whole weekend with Avicii to France and 2 gigs! It was awesome man!

Tim felt that they were lucky that Arash knew how to work that brand, because he himself was not really made for it.

Musically, however, he continued to develop at a furious pace. At the end of January 2010, he sat in front of the chord blocks in FL Studio and sensed that he had something very special going on. It was an arrangement that took its time. Thick, sweeping chords that climbed up into the sky. He built and embroidered, had found digital marimbas, a West African xylophone-like instrument, which gave the music a pleasant and light Caribbean tone.

This song had the potential to be the sickest super banger, Tim felt it. He emailed Arash for help moving forward.

> So as it looks now, it's first marimbas during the break,
> very calm and kinda like an orgasm of sound, then what
> I want, or what I'm thinking in my head, is what it already
> does now, that it quickly changes to those fast stabbing
> strings etc and creates the sickest build up etc, so like that
> the song's gimmick should be a bit in that it changes so
> quickly in some way.

The tranquillity was torn by some really fat synth riffs – Tim thought they were reminiscent of the ones Axwell used in his remix of TV Rock's song 'In The Air'. It was the collision between the soft and the hard that made the song, the clash that made the music feel enchanting. The composition went under the working name 'Bro', as in brother. 'Fuck, I believe in this melody,' Tim wrote. 'You should see how people react to it already now when I play it and no one has like even heard it before!'

Overall a lot was starting to fall into place now, at the beginning of 2010. It was noticeable in how Tim let the bass lines interact with the melodies, in how he built layer upon layer without any element feeling out of place. The musical lack of direction that Arash Pournouri had talked about two years earlier, at the beginning of their collaboration, was gone. Now there was a clear musical identity. It was audible in Tim's remix of the Frenchman Bob Sinclar's 'New New New' or in 'Blessed', a collaboration with the Dutch sibling duo Shermanology.

The satisfaction that Tim felt while working in front of the screen was reflected in his elated melodies. The euphoria that washed through him as all the parts acted with each other was transferred to his playful drops, which in somersaults and turns jumped towards the sky.

Avicii had started to sound like Avicii.

It just so happened that the Godfather himself had at the same time bought an apartment in Stockholm. On Lästmakargatan, around the corner from Stureplan, the world's greatest DJ now spent his free time, when he was not out spinning around the world.

Tijs Verwest, as Tiësto was actually called, was a little unsure of where his life was going. Without really noticing it, he had become a nearly forty-year-old man, whose friends had started families while he himself still flew around for almost three hundred days a year. He had planned to marry his girlfriend, but when the wedding was postponed due to his constant travel, the relationship had gone awry.

Tiësto was also a little tired of Amsterdam and the Dutch dance music that had become so hard and highly strung in recent years. It was an aggressive and screaming style that could become tiresome after a while. On the other hand, he was attracted by the house music that was bubbling in Stockholm, which was more embracing and warmer in its tone.

It was a scene with roots.

In the beginning, of course, was ABBA, the quartet that had combined soft Swedish folk music with careful harmonies and tasteful chord progressions in world hits such as 'Dancing Queen' and 'Take A Chance On Me'. In the 70s many had seen the group as quirky, but history had proved their precise compositions right.

When dance music swept across Europe in the early 90s, the Swemix collective had made club tunes with a similar sense of poppiness – Stonebridge had achieved a world hit with his remix of Robin S's song 'Show Me Love' and Denniz Pop had produced Ace Of Base, whose hit 'The Sign' had topped the US chart for weeks.

Towards the turn of the millennium, Denniz Pop's adept Max Martin had for a few years defined the entire world's pop music. From Cheiron, their joint studio, Martin had composed hits for the Backstreet Boys, Britney Spears and NSYNC: methodically chiselled pop tunes with a heavy dose of American R&B and lyrics that followed the songs' harmony rather than English grammar. 'Quit Playing Games (With My Heart)', ' . . . Baby One More Time', 'I Want It That Way', 'It's Gonna Be Me' – so many hooks that had travelled the world from the small studio in Stockholm.

Now that the 2010s had just begun, the artist Robyn made stylish electropop and Swedish House Mafia emerged with their explosive style, but also their tracks were neatly produced behind all the bombast.

Clearly, they could make hits in Stockholm, a city that Tiësto experienced as amazingly clean and tidy. The inhabitants walked around smartly dressed in the latest fashion, always smelling good. The same precise efficiency was in the music, and it was a type of order that felt quite necessary for someone who had basically toured his private life to pieces.

Tiësto got help finding his way in Stockholm's nightlife from Sebastian Ingrosso of Swedish House Mafia, and in February 2010 he ran into Arash Pournouri at the club Berns. Arash gave him a USB stick with Avicii's latest songs. Of course, Tijs already knew about the young Swede, had listened to him with interest, but track five on this stick was something out of the ordinary.

Tiësto himself came from a tradition of making remixes. His breakthrough had come with versions of Delerium's song 'Silence' and Samuel Barber's 'Adagio For Strings'. He grew up cutting tapes, looping, putting one sample over another, always with an original to pick from. He could only imitate a chord when he heard it and he had only started to make his own songs when he became a star behind the turntables and needed to broaden his repertoire.

It was quite clear that Tim Bergling came from the opposite direction. Tiësto was a man of the booth – Avicii was a composer who had become a DJ.

Enchanted, Tiësto listened to the song with the vibrating marimba. Avicii apparently had a sense of space, a lightness and a tender nerve that set him apart. It was easy to feel a connection with the man behind the music, as if Tim Bergling's heart was in direct contact with his fingertips.

Tiësto was so impressed by 'Bromance', as the song on the USB stick eventually was called, that he invited Tim to the island that had become the centre of European club culture.

A few decades earlier, Ibiza had been an obscure island in the Mediterranean, a poor farming community that could only be reached by boat from the Spanish mainland. Here was where beatniks and bohemians, war-refusing Americans and gay Spaniards gathered, the latter finding a refuge from Franco's military regime among the olive trees. Protected from the outside world, a hedonistic club culture emerged, led not least by the Argentine DJ Alfredo, who held court at the club Amnesia.

By the end of the 80s, a group of British friends had come to the island to celebrate a birthday. With their nervous systems rejoicing in Ecstasy, the English had danced their way through the nights to Alfredo's magical selection of Italian disco, American house and Nigerian funk. When they came home to London, they started clubs in the same style, which made a new generation of Britons open their eyes to dance music and the parties on the small island.

Nowadays, the infrastructure was well oiled. Until six in the morning, special buses carried tourists to the clubs – in the summer of 2010, David Guetta played regularly at Pacha, Laidback Luke was every Thursday at Amnesia and, as usual, the Briton Carl Cox was the sickest with his legendary eight-hour gigs at Space.

Between three and six every Monday night, Tiësto performed at the island's largest club. Calling Privilege a club was in itself an understatement. The old bathhouse was as big as an ice hockey arena and had room for ten thousand people. Behind the worn-out diving platforms was scaffolding, and the narrow corridors up in the air had been decorated with a couple of sewage-smelling carpets and a sofa.

There sat Tim Bergling waiting to go up on stage.

It was incredible really.

Barely two years after he had sent his first songs to some Swedish blogs, Tim would be the opening act for fucking Tiësto, in Ibiza, several Mondays in a row.

Tim laughed and drank as topless girls got ready for their dance numbers out on stage. Next to him on the piss-smelling sofa sat another young Swede who, funnily enough, had also gone to Östra Real and had the same first name as Philgood.

Filip Holm was a year younger than Tim but already saw himself as a veteran on the club scene. He had grown up with a father who worked for the booking company EMA Telstar and had been running around arenas with laminated VIP tiles around his neck since he was a kid. In the short time since graduating from Östra Real, Filip Holm had made a name for himself in Stockholm's nightlife by running house clubs at Laroy as well as F12 and Café Opera. One night he had stumbled upon Tiësto outside one of the clubs, they had smoked a few cigs and discussed music and the rest was history. Now the twenty-year-old Swede was buddies with Tiësto, despite the big age difference.

'How weird that I never saw you at Östra,' Filip said to Tim when they finally got to know each other.

'But I was, like, kind of never in school, so it's not that strange,' Tim laughed in response.

The busloads of people poured into the old bathhouse. The music made the scaffolding shake and the sofa vibrate. Back here the bass sounded muffled and cracked, and even though Tim and Filip shouted at each other, it was almost impossible to hear what the other was saying. They downed Jägermeister instead. Tiësto loved the thick black German liqueur. Tim Bergling poured another glass.

It was serious now, show time, necessary to calm the nerves.

Up in the booth, Tim continued to have shots and bubbly. Some evenings he got really drunk, but the fact that he sometimes missed a transition didn't matter – the tourists had come to the island to party, very few cared about a perfect beat mix.

Afterwards, as the sun rose, they drove along roads flanked by huge hoardings covered with Tiësto's face. A gravel road wound up the mountainside at Sant Jordi, a gate was pushed to the side, revealing a salmon-pink stone villa surrounded by red rocks. This was Tiësto's house, and this was where the parties that really mattered were held.

Above the pool with tiled dolphins on the bottom was a terrace where they had installed DJ decks. As the morning ferries from Barcelona became visible on the horizon, Tim, Tiësto and the other guests took turns choosing songs. In front of the stone wall with the waterfall was a bar counter, girls were pole dancing and laser lights coloured the living-room walls in neon.

Surrounded by newfound friends, Tim was finally able to relax, and the more alcohol went in his body, the happier he became. Laughing, he passed around the green bottle with the red deer on it, inciting everyone around to drink right from the bottle. It was as if he wanted to share his experience; he tried to get everyone into that same soft state of mind.

Around lunchtime, he usually just leaned against something, still taking sips. Then he stumbled past ferns and fig trees and nodded off in one of the guest rooms under the pool.

One of these mornings, however, Tim had to travel on; it was around eight o'clock, the party in full swing. Tiësto's tour manager had made it his task to get the guests going to a gig in Stockholm.

'Tim, you have to go!'

'I don't want to.'

'You have to.'

When Tim laughingly ran away, he stepped straight on a drinking glass. A shard was pushed up into the sole of his foot, blood pumping out over the tiles by the pool.

After half a day in the hospital in Ibiza, Tim met Filip Holm at the airport. His injured foot was wrapped in gauze and a small piece of glass was still inside, a doctor in Stockholm would have to pull it out. Tim was hungover and happy, wonderfully resilient.

'What the hell happened?' asked Filip.

'Uh, I stepped on some glass.'

'We have to find a wheelchair or something.'

'No, jeez, grab one of those luggage carts and I'll get on that.'

That same summer, record company manager Per Sundin sat inside Pacha, a white stone building of several floors in Ibiza's port area. The club had become an institution of European party life – already in the airport's arrival hall, Sundin had passed a souvenir shop filled with the place's famous cherries printed on sweaters and ashtrays.

Dance music was a world that Per Sundin knew very little about in that summer of 2010, northerner and rock guy that he was. But now a friend was turning forty and wanted to celebrate by seeing Swedish House Mafia, a trio from Sweden that was said to offer spectacle and smoke.

Sundin was one of the major figures on the Scandinavian music scene, even though the last few years had not been particularly cheerful ones. Illegal downloading had punctured the record industry and Sundin had been forced to lay off more than two hundred people. When even the Prime Minister, during a televised debate, had shown understanding for the kids who downloaded illegally, Sundin's mother had called and begged her son to switch industries.

Instead, he had advanced to become head of the record label Universal and done his best to escape the crisis. Per Sundin had a career goal, as easy to formulate as it was difficult to achieve: to sign, from the office in Stockholm, a Swedish artist who eventually got a number one on the Billboard charts in the USA. That would be as far as a Swedish record exec could take it.

But tonight was hardly the night when this dream would come true. The birthday celebrators had been drinking wine since lunchtime and were now sitting on one of Pacha's terraces, waiting for a show that never seemed to start. The day was obviously turned upside down on this island – breakfast for dinner, lunch at midnight, the clubs full of people who swallowed pills and did lines right off the backs of their hands. Per Sundin had to fight to stay awake before pop queen Kylie Minogue finally took to the stage around half past two in the morning.

It was a great show with plumes and glitter. The record company manager wondered how three Swedes at some computer screens would top this.

When Swedish House Mafia finally thundered up into the booth, it was like a blow to the stomach. From the roof, a cloud of dry ice shot out as the audience pumped their hands in the air to 'One', a hard electro track that was the group's latest single.

Bloody hell, this was some heavy shit.

Per Sundin went down to the dance floor to study the

audience. Contrary to what he had expected, people were not here to dance. They were here to worship a band. This situation was familiar – it was just like a gig with Coldplay or Metallica, or Sundin's own favourite Bruce Springsteen. Artists who had all sold quite a few records, to put it mildly.

Sundin stumbled out into the dawn light with goosebumps on his arms and a revelation in his skull.

He would find a new Swedish artist who resembled Swedish House Mafia.

When Per Sundin came home and asked around the record company, he was tipped off about the song 'Bromance', by an artist who called himself Tim Berg.

Tim Berg also performed under the name Avicii, and Avicii sometimes called himself Tom Hangs, it seemed to depend a little on the mood of the songs. Sundin did not really understand the difference but when he reached out to Arash Pournouri he was immediately impressed by the manager's cocksure confidence. Arash seemed genuinely convinced that this quiet and spotty Swede would take over the world, and that any record company that was invited to take that journey with them should be grateful.

Now Sundin cycled the short distance from Universal's office to Styrmansgatan, a street that sloped down towards the bay, with the lush island of Djurgården glistening on the other side of the blue. This was where Arash Pournouri had set up an office for his management company, which he had named At Night. It was from here in Östermalm that Avicii was to be catapulted out towards the stars.

The address sure sounded lavish, but to get to At Night's location, Sundin had to walk through a long stone corridor, before a white-painted space opened in front of him.

He looked around the basement. The bright red carpet and

the equally red leather armchairs were probably meant to give the place the air of a luxurious lounge at warmer latitudes, but together with the light walls made the room look more like a cheap beauty salon.

'Take off your shoes!'

Arash's nasal voice echoed in the small room. He was sitting behind his desk in the far corner, in an armchair that dwarfed him. Sundin had to kick off his boots before he was shown around.

It was all a bit unusual that the country's most powerful record company executive would visit the artist and not the other way around. But that seemed to be part of Arash Pournouri's whole attitude: he wanted to point out that Universal could come to him if they were so interested.

Sundin was enticed by the cockiness.

'Do you wanna have a listen?' asked Arash.

Per Sundin sat down in one of the red leather armchairs, Arash turned up the volume and played him song after song.

The first single that Sundin wanted to release was a given. Avicii should do what Swedish House Mafia had done with 'One' – the trio had invited the star Pharrell Williams to sing over the beat and released the song again under the name 'One (Your Name)'. If 'Bromance' got some nice vocals added, it would even be able to reach outside house music circles.

The preparatory work for an updated version had actually already been done. The French duo Alviin & Da Frenchy had mixed Tim's beat with the singing on Samuele Sartini's track 'Love U Seek'. Tim had played the version with vocals during the summer and it had worked out well, so it was easy to build on the same idea. Singer Amanda Wilson was simply asked to record her vocals once more, so that they would sit nice and tight over Tim's production.

The new version was presented as if Avicii had remixed a song by Tim Berg and thus got the rather elaborate title 'Seek Bromance (Avicii Vocal Edit)'. Per Sundin signed an initial contract with Arash and Tim to have Universal release the song in Sweden, Norway and Finland.

'Seek Bromance' gained momentum very quickly, climbing up the charts in Norway, Denmark, Hungary, Poland, England and even the United States in the autumn of 2010. The tempo, which had already been high, was cranked up even more. In the Avicii Twitter feed, fans could follow as Tim burned CDs in hotel rooms, slept three hours in as many days and, after the accident with the glass, hopped around on his crutches in a frenzy of gigs back and forth across the continents.

It was exactly how it should be in this world. The old rock guys may have had a predictable routine where they made a record one year, toured the next, before they went into the studio again. Neatly organised tours and a somewhat loose schedule. For a DJ, the culture was completely different. House music was based on a constant stream of new singles, very few fans cared about albums, and if you got big enough, there was always a party somewhere in the world that needed some great music. Carl Cox had become an industry hero when he first performed at a party in Australia on New Year's Eve, then threw himself on a plane, flew across time zones and arrived at a new party in Hawaii, playing alongside the fireworks there as well.

Two New Year's Eve celebrations in one night: that's how a real DJ worked.

Tim had also started doing several shows a day – at the end of August 2010 he did a festival in the Netherlands at the beginning of the evening and a club in Germany that same night. In each place there was vodka and Red Bull, champagne and Red Bull, and Tim's eternal doubt about whether his songs were good enough.

'Did it work or not?' he asked Filip Holm.

They were on their way to the backstage area at the Dutch festival Lief.

Filip Holm had now started working for Arash and At Night, the old school friend from Östra Real travelling with Tim as tour manager. Holm was the link between artist, booker and promoter, and during the gigs he crouched under the booth to keep Tim company.

On stage in Utrecht, Tim had just played his rendition of Eurythmics' classic 'Sweet Dreams', and was unsure of the audience's reaction.

'Ooh, are you joking?' said Filip Holm. 'People died for it!'

'Meh, I didn't get that at all.'

'What are you going on about? They went bananas, man!'

Filip showed a video he had filmed from his spot under the DJ booth. Over by one of the speakers was the Italian producer Benny Benassi and he was surely digging it.

'Look, even he loved it! It was awesome, Tim!'

'Yes. Fuck, it looks pretty good when you film it like that.'

This was a recurring discussion. Tim was so incredibly self-critical, nothing mattered but that the audience liked what he was doing.

That's why he was always working.

Tim prepped for his gigs up until the last minute, often longer than that. To organise his sets he used Rekordbox, software that Pioneer had recently launched. There he arranged his songs in groups of three or four that he had already mixed together into a composite block. That way, he had ready-made transitions that were safe and sounded good. But he still wanted to mix it up, so that there was no risk of anyone hearing the same gig twice – each performance was filmed with hundreds of mobile cameras and ended up on YouTube, each setlist dissected by the fans.

He played by ear night after night, constantly putting new vocals over the instrumentals in so-called bootlegs, and had begun to be known for bold combinations. Some versions were a reflection of the music he grew up with on Linnégatan, such as the rendition of 'The Tracks Of My Tears', Smokey Robinson & The Miracles' soul ballad from 1965, or the slamming electro version of The Temptations' 'Papa Was A Rollin' Stone'. But Tim also made his own house bootlegs of the hip-hop group Beastie Boys and the classic rock band The Doors, played around with indie pop and mixed his fierce instrumental 'Abow' with Kings of Leon's howling pop vocals.

Photographer Marcus Lindgren let his camera film in the darkness of the hotel room, where Tim was leaning over the desk, preoccupied with a small drum sound that no one in the audience would notice anyway.

'When were you going to start playing then?' Marcus asked.

'Midnight,' Tim replied happily.

Lindgren filmed the clock's green digits.

It showed 00:26.

These images would be perfect on YouTube.

Marcus Lindgren was another of the additions to At Night, a twenty-four-year-old who with his agile Canon was able to film in high quality.

Arash Pournouri understood the value of posting clips to the fans on Facebook, and Marcus quickly learned the tricks. By framing the audience closely, he was able to give off a feeling that the club was packed even when there were some thin spots on the dance floor. Intense editing created the feeling of an ever-growing success. The optimal angle was in the middle of the dancefloor: there Marcus caught Tim's movements up on stage, and at the same time he could capture the feeling of a crowd that adored Avicii. With waving hands in the foreground, a focused DJ who looked out over his congregation.

As 2010 drew to a close, Tim had done over three hundred gigs during the year, a schedule that even Carl Cox could hardly match.

He kept the fear of flying in check by ploughing through books. On one trip, he was deeply immersed in *The Dirt*, Neil Strauss's biography of the heavy metal band Mötley Crüe. The quartet had survived fatal car crashes, overdoses and internal strife, but after ten years they fired their manager, one of the few people who could handle all the idiotic quarrels. There had been fights over money, meetings with greedy lawyers and their seventh album had ended up as a confused concoction that none of them could stand.

Tim looked up from the book.

'I'll never fucking change my manager!'

It went without saying that Arash Pournouri delivered. Leading up to Christmas 2010, 'Seek Bromance' had sixteen million views on YouTube and was on heavy rotation on the BBC. Tim had performed at the festival Sensation and had remixed a Daft Punk song. The Frenchman Bob Sinclar had bowed to him in respect, Chuckie called him this year's breakthrough in *DJ Mag*. He had bought a used Rolex, in sapphire crystal and gold with eight diamonds on the dial, and there was still over twenty thousand euros in the company account.

The most important thing for Tim himself, however, was that he had finally started to get a treatment for his spots that actually worked.

The medicine was called Tetralysal and consisted of red-yellow capsules that contained an antibiotic that inhibited the growth of bacteria in the pores of the skin. Of course, there were some potential side effects: the medicine could upset the body's bacterial flora and should not be taken on an empty stomach, the patient could get headaches or feel nauseous. In rare cases, the treatment could lead to inflammation of the pancreas. But after just a few weeks, Tim had started to see results.

The intruders had retreated, the assault to his face had ceased.

It was starting to go really well, indeed.

AT THE FAR END of At Night's basement space on Styrmansgatan was a long, narrow room with a singing booth, the white-painted stone wall covered with a rug to dampen the sound somewhat. There was a desk with a computer and speakers, on the floor a keyboard on a stand.

One day in February 2011, a slender figure with curly and unruly hair stepped into Tim's small studio. Salem Al Fakir was eight years older than Tim but had a bubbling energy that made him seem younger.

Tim had known about him since his breakthrough five years earlier. Delighted journalists had repeatedly told Al Fakir's story: growing up in a home with almost as many pianos as siblings, he started nagging about playing the violin as a three-year-old, writing his own pieces in preschool. At the age of twelve, he began studying with a music professor in Russia, soon touring as a concert violinist and prodigy before he got tired at sixteen and instead began composing distinctive pop.

By this time, the twenty-nine-year-old had managed to release three albums, win four Swedish Grammys and well establish himself in the industry – when the Crown Princess got married six months earlier, Salem Al Fakir had performed a specially composed song for the royal bride and groom during the festivities.

Salem did not really know what to expect in the basement studio; what he had heard of Avicii so far sounded to him like blippy computer game music. But their co-publisher had insisted that they do something epic together.

'I think this sound is cool,' Tim said, and screwed a digital synth on the screen as the studio was filled with a deep howl.

'What do you think about this? Do you like it?'

On the keyboard that stood by the wall, Salem began to improvise based on a simple major chord. The rhythmic stomp slowly grew.

When Salem let his ring finger wander away to an unexpected tone, Tim reacted immediately.

'There! What did you do there?'

Salem played the same keys again.

'Yes, exactly! That! Damn what a hook!'

And so they met, an instrumentalist drilled in classical music theory and a self-taught guy who did everything out of emotion.

Salem was impressed by Tim's lightning-fast ability to capture a tone that glimmered. Even a simple accompaniment needed variety and life, and Tim seemed to have a perfect ear for the small shifts that gave a song its spark. In addition, it was interesting to be around someone who moved so freely around the traditional structures.

Tim was now sitting at the computer and working out a drop that didn't gave a damn about the framework that the 4/4 time signature would usually create. He stretched the sequence out, pulling it far beyond the first beat, in a way that went against all conventional ways of composing house music. It was noticeable that Tim wasn't educated – it was also clear that he had total control over what he was doing.

Tim, on the other hand, envied Salem's ability to master the instruments. He himself used the keyboard only as an idea machine, to get a feel for the sound and melody. Then he drew up the corresponding chords; with the computer mouse he could control the nuances with greater precision. Salem's fingers seemed to be able to handle every single instrument on earth, it didn't matter if it was strings or keys or boulders that were placed in front of him.

This was the direction Tim wanted to go in. With the help of a musician like Salem, he would be able to make songs that in the future wouldn't be out of place next to Ray Charles or Nina Simone or any of his dad's favourites on the vinyl record shelf in Skillinge.

Tim could not hold back when he wrote to Arash: 'THIS IS SO DAMN SIIIIIIIICK!'

What a fucking anthem they had made. And it went so quickly. How long did it take, like three hours? When they parted, they basically had a finished song; Salem had promised to go home and finish the lyrics.

It would be called 'Silhouettes'.

'We have to get him to fall in love with house too, so we can do 1000 things together!'

Outside of the studio, in the office space in the basement, the work went on day and night.

The others sat around Arash's black armchair, in cheap folding chairs from IKEA.

By this time, the main squad of At Night had formed.

Carl Vernersson had gone to the same school as Tim in both junior high and high school, Tim had always thought he was well behaved and proper. Together with Panos Ayassotelis, a club promoter from Gothenburg, Vernersson booked gig after gig while the filmmaker Marcus Lindgren took the main responsibility for how Avicii was portrayed in the video clips on Facebook and YouTube.

Filip Holm now also belonged to the office crew – he had slowed down on the touring and instead started working as an assistant to Arash.

Filip Holm watched his boss's drive with fascination. Arash Pournouri had the entire repertoire of a salesman, could be presumptuous and persuasive when he needed to, cold and calculating when it was convenient. The opponent was an enemy to be defeated, the competition ruthless.

Holm adopted the same techniques. They would do all negotiations by email, and always let the other party place the first bid. Instead of answering what Avicii cost for one night, they would ask what the promoter's budget was. Either they were then offered more than the price really was or the bid was so low that they could immediately dismiss the question. The bookers had exposed themselves while At Night had not shown their cards.

At the beginning of 2011, they were able to squeeze out almost fifteen thousand dollars for certain gigs, and that price tag was rising quickly.

When something important was going on, everyone in the office was expected to be available around the clock. If they were to take over the world, they would have to work in several time zones at once. And Arash himself pushed harder than anyone else. He used to go home in the evening to have dinner with his girlfriend and daughter, but after a couple of hours he would return to the basement and stay well into the night.

'This will be fucking *mode*,' said Marcus Lindgren, who sat at his place and worked on a new video.

The expression came from Sebastian Ingrosso. Mode was to be pronounced as in English and meant that something was good, nice, powerful. *Meich*, on the other hand, was miserable or boring. *Pagir* meant money, and both *sönder* and *värst* were amplifying superlatives.

There was a lot that was *värst* right now. Lindgren finished editing something on a Tuesday and by Thursday hundreds of thousands of people had already seen it.

'Do-do-do-do-do-do-do,' Tim hummed for Arash in one of the latest clips, which was filmed on a train on their way to a gig in Gothenburg.

Tim had made a new tune, one that felt effective and big. He had laid seven, eight synths and acoustic piano chords on top of each other, until he reached a sound that was rich and distinct at the same time. Wet finger snaps, screaming sirens and a rumbling bass.

'Damn, that's cool,' said Tim.

'Yeah, it's fucking cool,' said Arash.

Tim also had a sample that would probably fit over the melody. The music was almost fifty years old, recorded in 1962 by one of his dad's favourite artists. 'Something's Got A Hold On Me', as the original song was called, was a love song where blues singer Etta James explained how her new love made her blissful and thrilled. Producer duo Pretty Lights had used the same part in the song 'Finally Moving' a few years earlier, that's how Tim had found the sample.

'Ooooh ...'

'What are you up to?' asked Arash.

'Trying to put it in the right key.'

While Tim smiled, Etta James's raspy voice echoed across the train: 'Ooooh, sometimes ... I get a good feeling!'

EMILY GOLDBERG FLOATED in the mornings. Being a student at George Washington University had been fun recently, and now, in the spring of 2011, she had only a few months left before she would finish her bachelor's degree in art history. Carefree and open, the twenty-one-year-old danced over to the next lecture. In her headphones thumped Skrillex's 'Scary Monsters And Nice Sprites', a high-octane song that was a sign of something new. Skrillex was a DJ from Los Angeles who took dubstep, the style that had been developed in London, and made it less murky, more efficient and crisper. Gently scattered trance melodies torn by a roaring bass – music that was shuddering like a chainsaw in quicksand, as music magazine *Spin* wrote in a report on what was happening in the United States at this time.

Because something was bubbling, there was no doubt about it. If David Guetta and the Swedish House Mafia had cracked the door for European house music a few years earlier, through their collaborations with American pop stars, it was now about to be opened wide. Rihanna had hired the Scottish producer Calvin Harris to get just enough of a screaming drop in her hit 'We Found Love' and even Britney Spears had made a song with a flickering sequence of dubstep.

Emily felt that the music suited her in some way. It kind of captured who she was, or maybe who she wanted to be.

It was not a particularly promising time to enter adulthood in the United States. A few years earlier, a severe financial crisis had begun. Banks had crashed, economists said the country was experiencing the deepest crisis since the Depression of the 1920s. In three years, the number of long-term unemployed people had gone from just under two million to over six. Rather than a secure job, the adult world seemed to mean short-term gigs for low wages. Rather than buying their own homes, Emily's peers took fast loans to pay the rent on sublet apartments.

There seemed to be a halt in development. Would the young people of today be worse off than previous generations?

But at least the house music was throbbing with energy and spoke of its time. Knife Party's song 'Internet Friends' was about when someone unfriended you on Facebook and you wanted to kill the idiot. In Skrillex's biggest hit, he had sampled a young girl from Portland who shouted out her joy at having managed to balance cups in a trick on YouTube.

Emily loved the warm, friendly atmosphere of the clubs and festivals that played house music. It was sweaty and primal, but since so many were tripping on Ecstasy, the atmosphere was also cuddly and cosy. The security guards received handshakes and homemade bracelets instead of threats.

And maybe no one was as hopeful and euphoric as Avicii, the young guy from Sweden whose music always carried a promise that everything would work out fine.

The song 'Silhouettes', for example, which Avicii now included in his sets – an optimistic coming-of-age saga in a few lines:

> *So we will never get back to*
> *to the old school*
> *to the old rounds, it's all about the newfound*
> *we are the newborn, the world knew all about us*
> *we are the future and we're here to stay*

Perhaps the most important thing wasn't the lyrics. The rock generation was obsessed with words and symbols, with deciphering the message of a lyric – the duller the descriptions, the more important it was considered to be. Self-pity and melancholy were deemed excellent qualities.

That was not a bit interesting for Emily Goldberg. What mattered to her was how the songs felt, what they did to her body. The lovely vibrations in her chest.

She had just discovered Avicii's latest song, which he had included in a mix broadcast by Pete Tong on the BBC a few months earlier. It was called 'Levels', a distillation of happiness, with a riff so instant that it was impossible to get out of your skull. And then that old blues voice, the raspy and full-bodied one that came in at the chorus and sang about how fantastic you could feel.

Emily Goldberg had noticed that Avicii was playing more and more in the US and saw that in the summer of 2011 he would perform in Washington, DC, at a club with room for three thousand guests.

Emily was familiar with the promoter and had made sure to be at the venue early. When she was hanging out backstage, she had shaken hands with the Swedish star, who seemed absent-minded and embarrassed.

But now they were standing on the balcony, she and her best friend, and Avicii played Swedish House Mafia's bootleg of a Depeche Mode song.

Emily looked out over the sweaty crowd on the floor below. Girls on their boyfriends' shoulders, the smell of perfume, sweat and alcohol.

Three-quarters into the set came the song everyone had been waiting for, the one that was gaining traction on YouTube. The whole club sang in 'Levels' synth riff.

DO-DO-DO-DO-DO-DO-DO-DOOO-DO-DOOO-DO!
DO-DO-DO-DO-DO-DO-DO-DOOO-DO-DOOO-DO!

After Etta James's chorus, the strings filled the room. Emily closed her eyes and without thinking about it, she brought her right arm in front of her, as if she was playing the violin herself. When she looked down again, Avicii had raised his arm up into the air. He looked so incredibly happy and as the synth roared again, the spotlights moved upwards and Avicii looked towards the balcony – right at Emily, it seemed – and she felt as if her chest was about to explode.

A few minutes later, when Tim had gone into a version of Adele's 'Rolling In The Deep', the star's tour manager came up. He took the girls with him, led them down the stairs and through the crowd on the dance floor. A red rope was pulled aside and suddenly Emily stood in the middle of the stage and was dancing right next to the Swede.

Tim made a transition to his own 'My Feelings For You' and handed Emily a shot glass.

A few hours later, they were sitting in a suite at the Donovan Hotel. Someone overturned a bottle of Dom Pérignon and ran to get a towel.

'You're a towel,' Tim laughed in a squeaky voice.

It was a reference to the *South Park* character Towelie, a living piece of cloth whose only interest was to constantly be as high and fucked up as possible. No one else in the room seemed to pick up the reference, but Emily shouted Towelie's second standard phrase in falsetto: 'You wanna get high?'

Tim nodded at Emily, impressed. He sat down closer and began to loudly discuss which *South Park* episode was the best ever.

Later in the morning, just before Tim passed out on the

couch, he and Emily had exchanged numbers and agreed that they should be in touch again soon.

The wave of house music that swept across the United States had indeed begun to be picked up by the established music magazines. But if you wanted to follow the development in close-up, you needed to look online. Newly launched sites such as We Rave You and Dancing Astronaut wrote ecstatic articles about the shockwaves that the music sent through their writers' bodies. According to the online magazines, virtually every track was epic, huge, a BANGER. Dutchmen such as Afrojack, Chuckie and Hardwell were described as the great masters of modern times, and when Swedish House Mafia sold out Madison Square Garden in nine minutes, it appeared to be a triumph for humanity.

In Las Vegas, one of the reporters for Dancing Astronaut recounted a weekend when the new song 'Levels' had been heard at every pool party throughout the city: 'Avicii is a god,' he wrote, and said that he did not know what to do with his joyous body when he heard the Swede's song. 'Should I embrace the person right next to me because I am so uncontrollably happy that I need to share the moment with someone?' he wondered, before finally deciding on another option – to spray beer all around him.

Las Vegas was perhaps the one place in the United States where the growing popularity of dance music was most evident. The casino city was rapidly evolving, from a place where fading musical stars ended their careers, to the epicentre of a new youth culture.

At the end of June 2011, tens of thousands of young people made a pilgrimage to a speedway stadium north of the city. They came from all over the continent, in buses and caravans and their mothers' Ford Explorers. The girls had sewn butterfly wings on their neon-coloured tops and glued feathers on their bras, the boys came with battle paintings on their chests and glow sticks like wreaths in their hair. Others wore panda hats, fox tails and luminous tulle skirts. Alongside the stages built inside the arena, roller coasters and swings flashed in all the colours of the rainbow as acrobats sprayed fire and walked on stilts.

Around seventy thousand people came every day to join this psychedelic event, the Electric Daisy Carnival, to make out to Swedish House Mafia's fireworks and pump their hands in the air to European stars such as Laidback Luke, David Guetta, Tiësto and Nicky Romero. In many ways it was like a high-pitched version of the raves outside London in 1988 – the same dizzying feeling of reality being elevated to something magical. The organisers had realised that the word 'rave' had become impossible to use in the United States, but when they hired enough security personnel and instead called the spectacle a 'festival', it all became politically viable.

Tim went on stage on the third and final night. From his place behind the decks, he watched the beautiful madness. From above, it was impossible to distinguish any single face, the bodies spreading out like a sparkling coral reef swaying on the seabed. It was easy to think that this huge production would put the nerves to the test, but it was actually much nicer to play here than to confront the scrutinising gazes at one of the small clubs in France or Germany. In the sea of glowing phone cameras, it was impossible to see if anyone was staring sceptically or choosing to go to the bar in the middle of a drop. Here was a riot fence and distance from the crowd. Besides, Tim had worked up a damn good set, he knew it himself. Apart from a Nicky Romero remix, a Dirty South tune and a song by the Swede Henrik B, he was now able to do an hour and twenty minutes with only his own songs.

The steady rhythm pulsed through Tim Bergling's jerking legs. Damp with perspiration, his upper body bobbed over the decks, behind him flashed almost a hundred screens that together wrote out AVICII in purple and turquoise. Tim put on a majestic hymn he called 'Edom' – simply the word mode spelled backwards – and looked out over the people who were crackling in red, white and blue. They had become a single body reacting at the same time, hovering in a state unlike anything else.

If there was ever a moment when Avicii conquered the United States, it was probably now, 26 June 2011. Tim did not think any more, he just raised his right arm and played the chords to 'Levels' in the air.

One of the people behind the rapid change in Las Vegas was Jesse Waits, a thirty-six-year-old with sparkling white teeth who was responsible for the evenings at XS, the latest addition to the giant clubs in the desert. One Friday afternoon, the managing partner showed Tim through a lavish entrance with gold-coloured textiles on the walls, into a hall shaped like a crescent moon with collections of soft, golden-brown sofas scattered on plateaus surrounding the shiny dance floor. These booths were the basis of the business model: eighty per cent of the revenue came from alcohol sales at the private tables. Here, an ordinary bottle of vodka could cost around four hundred dollars, a drink made from aged champagne and brandy went for ten thousand. The biggest players hugged champagne bottles as big as toddlers and would pay an average monthly wage for ice buckets filled with bottles of liquor and grog.

Jesse Waits himself was fairly new to house music. He had

been to Paris and visited the classic gay club Le Queen and David Guetta's own nightclub. The American had fallen in love with the fluffy compositions, the filter effects that made the music sound as if it was tumbling underwater. Jesse had come home hungover and inspired – if house music had worked in Europe, where Tiësto sold out arenas in half an hour and had received a medal from the Queen of the Netherlands, why wouldn't it in the United States?

In the spring of 2011, Jesse Waits had booked Deadmau5, a Canadian DJ who, in addition to his progressive beats, had made himself known for always performing in a bulky, globular mouse mask. Waits had received unexpected help to prove that house music attracted a coveted audience when a notorious poker player had offered $200,000 to get permission to go up on stage and jump to the tunes of Jon Bon Jovi's 'Livin' On A Prayer', a song everyone in the audience was ashamed to like. Having Deadmau5 in the booth had attracted three times as many guests as usual and drawn in around $400,000 in one night, which made Waits's managers open their wallets and ask him to book more house artists. Avicii was a given for Jesse Waits – it felt like 'Levels' was taking over everything at the time.

When Jesse picked Tim up at the airport, he noticed that the Swede was unusually nervous. He decided to try to soften up his guest by ordering sole at his favourite restaurant and tentatively starting a conversation. A little puzzled, he looked at Tim's frizzy and sprawling hair that didn't seem to have had a shower in more than a week, but instinctively Jesse felt that he liked the Swede. Tim seemed unrefined and sincere – it was far off from what you could say about most people, especially in this city. Maybe Jesse felt a special kinship with Tim because he, too, in a lot of ways felt like an outsider. Sure, on the surface, Waits was the city's nightclub king, the guy who was featured in fashion reports and showed off his Louis Vuitton shoes and cars.

Very few, however, knew of Jesse Waits' background. Since he did not want anyone to feel sorry for him, he avoided talking about growing up on one of Hawaii's most desolate islands, in a part of the jungle where there was a total of eight houses. His mother, father and uncle had been young and good-looking surfers who had left California and moved to Hawaii to play music as loud as they wanted. Quickly, the free-spirited life had been derailed by addiction and darkness. Jesse's father had started abusing heroin and his mother had committed suicide when he was just a boy. The only memories he had of her were some photographs and four cassette tapes where she had recorded small reflections for herself. Jesse had still not been able to listen to the recordings, he didn't dare hear his mother's voice.

Deep below the surface, he hid a vulnerability that he also saw in Tim Bergling.

From: Klas Bergling
To: Tim Bergling
Date: 29 September 2011

Hi Tim,

How's it going? Have just arrived in Skillinge, played some poker with the guys, it's fun. Tonight it's starry skies and refreshing fall in the air. Always the same when you come back here after having been away for a while, it's so nice, easy to forget.

Thinking about you a lot and hoping your inspiration is enough for this huge tour with gigs every day. I don't think it's such a great plan, one needs to be able to pause and breathe a little, but it's your choice.

Kisses and hugs and I hope it's going sooooo well!

Your old man

Without even being properly released by a record company, in the autumn of 2011 'Levels' had almost twenty million views on YouTube. On Facebook, Avicii had over a hundred thousand followers, and there were more each night, while Tim Bergling toured between the college towns in the US – that was where the young people were.

In this country, it was important to strike while the iron was hot, something the singer Björn Skifs had experienced four decades earlier. In the mid-70s, he had been on his way to becoming the first Swede ever to conquer first place on the singles chart in the US, with his cover of the song 'Hooked on a Feeling', but he blew it all due to his Swedish sense of obligation. The artist had been standing backstage, in full make-up, when the record company called from the other side of the Atlantic and said it was rumoured that the song was about to go number one! IN THE US! Hey, cancel everything, throw yourself on a flight! Skifs explained that it was impossible, because he was about to play a clown in a musical in Västerås. When he and the band Blue Swede eventually left for the USA, the temperature had cooled down and there was never any more chance of a career there.

Avicii would not make that kind of mistake. He would be touring intensively to take advantage of the momentum that 'Levels' had created. Malik Adunni and Felix Alfonso were two Americans who had been hired to act as tour leaders and production managers and to make travel more efficient. The crew zigzagged across the continent, at a pace that dissolved day and night. Just take this October week of 2011, which had begun on Monday in Covington, Kentucky. Then they went to Gainesville, Florida, before flying all over the country to San Diego, making a stop at Jesse Waits' club in Las Vegas and finally ending up in Bloomington, Indiana, where Tim had just done Saturday night's first gig. Now they were on their way to an arena in New Jersey to make the evening's second appearance.

As usual, Tim sat immersed in his screens, drinking champagne from a plastic glass.

He had started chatting intensely with Emily, the girl he had met in Washington, DC, a few months earlier. Via WhatsApp, they sent quotes from the TV series *Arrested Development*, shared pictures of cute sloths, discussed the *Game of Thrones* books and joked about Disney movies. One meme led to the next, the topics of conversation never ended, everything was intense and fun. They were from different parts of the world, but Tim already felt that he had found a kindred spirit. Emily was not only funny, she also had good taste – when she suggested the TV series *Archer*, Tim downloaded it immediately.

In tandem with this, unfortunately, the job never ended. Filip Holm at least had a sense of humour when he emailed all the new commitments.

Interview No. 7888444 URGENT.

Another interview request from another student magazine. It was not that Tim did not want to talk about his music, but to answer the same fifteen questions over and over again was more tiring than they seemed to realise on Styrmansgatan.

Did he drink his coffee with or without milk? Did he ski? What were his favourite songs when he cleaned? Those questions were meaningless but at least they were different. Most were far more generic:

Had you expected all this success?

Would you like to collaborate with Swedish House Mafia?

What kind of music do you play in the clubs?

It was a Slovenian newspaper that wondered about the latter. 'Fuck this, they should at least know that one,' Tim wrote to

Filip. Why did they want to write about him when they did not even know the most basic things?

Do you have any habits before you go on stage?

'I always take a shot of Jäger before I go on. I have Tiësto to thank for that ritual!'

Pancakes, waffles or crêpes – choose one!

'Crêpes.'

What makes a party perfect?

'I would say good music, good people and Jägermeister.'

What does the name Avicii mean?

'Fuck this one too, the answer is already found 5000x on Google.'

Production manager Felix Alfonso began to understand for the first time how uncomfortable Tim could become around people one Sunday in Boston. Before that night's gig, they had decided to see the latest *Transformers* movie.

Felix noticed that Tim was behaving differently as they walked towards the theatre. He seemed to not be in the conversation, walked quietly and stared down at the ground.

'What's up, bro? You good?'

Tim hurried forward under his hat.

'I'm okay. Just anxious. There's so many people here; feels like everybody is staring.'

Felix was a little put off, did not know what to answer. Of course, there were people who saw that it was Avicii – he was dressed exactly the same as in the press photos. The same T-shirt from American Apparel, the same check shirt, the same cap.

'No one is recognising you,' Felix tried. 'Just keep on walking and you'll be fine.'

Inside the box office, it was crowded with people.

Now the pressure spread across Tim's chest, his whole body feeling tense. He tried to persuade himself that nothing terrible could happen, he was just out with his friends for a few hours. He tried to focus on breathing deeply and quietly.

But the air did not come down his throat, it was too thin. He had to sit down.

'I think I'm having a panic attack,' he said.

From a distance, Per Sundin had watched as house music swept the US. 'Levels' was changing everything for Tim; it was visible on YouTube, where happy people sang along to the synth riff in club after club. The record company manager had been vying with Arash Pournouri since the spring to buy the rights to release the song – at the manager's thirtieth birthday party, Sundin had even agreed to be spanked by some burlesque dancers in the hope it would help him secure the deal.

In early autumn of 2011, he and Arash spoke again over the phone. Arash said that Virgin EMI in London was also interested, and that the competing record company had given him an offer that he couldn't refuse.

They had offered five hundred thousand euros.

Per Sundin was shocked. An advance of around five million crowns? It was a sensational amount of money for a single song. Furthermore, the offer went against all custom in the industry.

Record companies were basically venture capitalists. They evaluated the potential of an artist and invested in the hope of getting a good return. In Sweden, the usual advance would be around fifty thousand euros – for a whole album. And then the record company also got the right to release two more records. Even if a debut album did not go as well as expected, they would still have several years to build the artist into a star. Apparently, no such option was included here.

Per Sundin realised that, in practice, it meant a complete shift of power. Such an extensive advance would force any record company to work extra hard to get its investment back, and if it went well for Avicii, the company would have helped build a brand that was open for everyone else to fight over even with the next song.

They ended the conversation quickly and Per Sundin slammed the phone down on his desk. As he sat in his office, surrounded by gold discs, he tried to evaluate what he had just heard. Sure, there was clearly a lot of buzz around Avicii. But for the rights to release Tim's latest song, 'Fade Into Darkness', Sundin had paid around ten thousand euros. Now Arash wanted half a million. Surely no one was idiotic enough to offer that amount without even getting an option?

At the same time, Sundin knew that working with an imprint of Virgin EMI in London was Jason Ellis, the man who had signed Swedish House Mafia. Maybe Ellis saw even greater potential in Avicii than in the Swedish trio?

At the office of At Night, the excitement was palpable. Arash had not actually received as high a bid as he'd claimed. But what did it matter? He did not even see it as being deceptive. He could have got the money, he reasoned – the sum simply reflected what he thought 'Levels' was worth out in Europe.

Arash stood in the kitchen on Styrmansgatan and spoke about his risky move.

'I've hustled people to the ground with "Levels". I mean, hustled to the ground! I'm like a scam broker,' he smiled.

Filip Holm thought that it was one of the most stimulating things about working with At Night. No one cared about any of the guidelines, because none of them had done anything like this before. If you didn't know about the rules, it was surely a lot easier not to give a shit about them.

Per Sundin, on the other hand, continued to worry. By this time, he had been selling Avicii to his colleagues at Universal for months – this was the artist who would hopefully propel him as well to new heights. And then the carpet was suddenly pulled out from under him. Shameful and angry, Sundin started calling local executives around Europe, mostly to explain that he had lost out.

To Sundin's surprise, his colleagues seemed ready to come to the rescue. Patrick Busschots, a Belgian veteran in particular, said that they just could not miss this artist. See what was happening on the house music scene in the US, it was really simmering over there!

Arash had given Sundin a short deadline to change his mind, so Universal quickly constructed a solution where Sweden, Germany, England and the US office each took a quarter of the cost of 'Levels'.

Humiliated but relieved, Universal confirmed that they had matched a bid that did not actually exist. Arash Pournouri had got the giant record company exactly where he wanted. Now it was not only Per Sundin and the Swedish office who needed to work hard in order to not lose money on the song, the same applied to the other offices in Europe and the US. And if they did not deliver, Arash had every right to go to another label with the next song.

It was the record company that was in the shit, not him.

FILIP ÅKESSON STEPPED OUT on to the sidewalk on Sunset Boulevard.

The traffic was calm this time of day, the grainy autumn morning helped by the streetlights that coloured the roofs of the taxis a pinkish yellow.

He had just done another night as Philgood in the DJ booth at Hyde Sunset, a restaurant with lush wood panels and overly perfumed guests. Typical Hollywood.

Åkesson had moved to Los Angeles, determined to establish himself as a musician in his own right. The chaotic night in Miami a couple of years earlier had driven the first wedge between him and Tim, and it had not got better when Filip drank himself silly in France – he had found himself in a courtyard somewhere in Toulouse, having no idea how he would make it to the morning flight, or even where the airport was located.

As a duo, Avicii & Philgood were dead, but Filip had left Stockholm with a plan. He had contacts, he was a devil with bass and drums, the years with Tim had given him the ability to produce – now the United States would see who Philgood was outside Avicii's shadow. In five years, he would be on the biggest stage at Ultra, then he would secure a three-storey house up in the mountains of Hollywood, the ones that now lay hidden in the morning mist behind him. There he would have parties at Tiësto level, with girls coming and going and alcohol flowing. Maybe marry a chick with silicone breasts eventually.

Reality had immediately crashed into Filip Åkesson's

expectations and scrapped them. The Range Rover he had rented for the first three months in Los Angeles had been repossessed. He had released a couple of songs that no one cared about. Instead of over $10,000 a month, which he'd counted on in his calculations, he made around a quarter of that by playing records. Breadcrumbs in this town.

In the wake of Avicii, in the autumn of 2011, a bunch of other guys from the same Stockholm generation came instead, and they did so fast.

Otto Jettman had also gone to Östra Real and sat on the same stone stairs during the breaks in high school. Under the name Otto Knows, he had just made 'Million Voices' and several other songs that Tim had started playing in his sets. The Swedish House Mafia had created their own small stable of artists, where Alesso was a rising star. The twenty-year-old from Stockholm got to open for the trio and his song 'Calling' was about to become a big hit. AN21 was another DJ who got hotter and hotter, his real name was Antoine and he was the little brother of Steve Angello. Stockholm duo Dada Life were famous for their insane shows where they threw inflatable bananas and invited their audience into pillow wars.

In short, in 2011 the Swedes had begun to take the lead in the invasion of the United States, but absolutely no one was talking about Philgood.

Filip Åkesson set off along Sunset Boulevard on his skate-board. As usual after an evening of free booze in the booth, he was excited, eager for something to happen. He climbed a small wall to gain speed and jump out on the sidewalk but instead fell in the other direction, straight into the bush three metres down.

The next day he went to see a doctor who found that the meniscus was torn and the knee full of fluid. The recovery risked becoming long and gruelling.

Exhausted, Filip limped into his seedy apartment with a crutch and a bottle of medicine for the pain.

He had never seen this kind of pill before. OxyContin was on the label of the amber jar. He would take a maximum of two per day, for five days. Then the doctor would evaluate the situation, see how the healing was going.

Filip Åkesson sat down gently on the brown sofa, swallowed a pill and slowly felt how the butterflies began to flutter in his stomach. They flew out softly towards his legs and arms, bringing with them a warmth that was almost paralysing.

OxyContin was a relatively new drug, launched in the United States just over ten years earlier. But its active ingredient, what made the pills so pleasant and dangerous, had a much longer history.

Long before our era, man understood that it was possible to crush the seeds of the opium poppy and mix the flour with water to create a solution that had a calming effect on the body. Opium, as the mixture came to be called, stimulated the same receptors in the brain that reacted as with, for example, sex, exercise and laughter. The drug had a euphoric effect, and made the muscles relax and relieved pain.

In the early nineteenth century, a German apprentice pharmacist isolated the active substance in poppy seeds and created a substance so powerful that it was named after the god of sleep and dreams in Greek mythology, Morpheus. Morphine became popular in the American upper class, where doctors prescribed the strong pain relief for such common problems as menstrual cramps. But after the American Civil War, the disadvantages began to show – tens of thousands of war veterans who came home and got fever and diarrhoea as soon as they no longer had morphine in their blood. The withdrawal symptoms had turned out to be more extensive than that. People who became addicted could quickly suffer from palpitations, chills, anxiety and worry when the effect of the medication faded. The body's longing for more could, in the worst case, lead to overdoses and deaths.

Ever since then, doctors had been more restrictive in prescribing morphine to anyone other than recently operated patients and those who were already in the final stages of life or had acute painful illnesses.

The research continued with the goal of producing an opioid that possessed the positive properties of morphine but did not throw the patient into a life of addiction and withdrawal. One such experiment was, for example, heroin, originally launched as a cough medicine and aid against loose stool.

Another was oxycodone, an opioid that was fifty per cent stronger than morphine. Oxycodone began to be used in a number of drugs, such as Percocet and Percodan, but with five milligrams mixed with a much larger amount of over-the-counter substances, such as paracetamol or acetyl-salicylic acid.

OxyContin, the pill that Filip Åkesson had brought home – and which in the last decade had become increasingly popular among American doctors – was something completely different.

The tablets contained only oxycodone. The strongest was a numbing bomb of 160 milligrams. Despite the fact that the active substance was significantly stronger than morphine, Perdue Pharma, the company behind the new drug, claimed that their product was, on the contrary, less addictive than that of its competitors. They said they had developed a unique extended-release formulation that had a delayed effect. The system was claimed to be revolutionary in two ways: the pain relief lasted longer than before, and the slow effect made the pill uninteresting as an intoxicant.

Perdue Pharma had invited doctors on nice trips at the same time as hundreds of salesmen travelled around the hospitals and praised the drug's wide range of uses. Above all, the company had marketed itself in the American countryside, where many, after decades of physically demanding work in coalmines or car factories, had problems with chronic pain.

And finally, they had managed to change the attitude of American doctors – since the turn of the millennium, the prescriptions of opioids had quadrupled in the United States.

As the contours of the room became softer and softer, Filip leaned back and elevated his leg against a box he had placed on the coffee table.

The feeling of delight was thick and fluffy.

Never mind the money, never mind the failed DJ career, everything would be fine.

No, it was better than that. Everything was already all right.

Images of yesterday's basketball games played on the TV. Filip Åkesson turned his head towards the window, heard the heated commentators on the screen and thought about nothing at all.

IN THE MIDST of his conquest of the United States, Tim had, in November 2011, made a hectic detour to New Zealand, Australia and Asia. In less than a month, he had squeezed in twenty-three gigs in Auckland, Sydney, Perth, Melbourne, Adelaide, Brisbane, Beijing, Hong Kong, Singapore, Delhi, Pune and Mumbai, among others.

In Bangkok, he had almost bottomed out, refusing to leave his hotel room in the morning. The tour manager had to call an annoyed promoter in Manila and postpone the gig in the Philippines for twenty-four hours.

On New Year's Eve, he had played in Niagara Falls, Canada. Before they celebrated the clock turning twelve, he'd run off stage, been driven to Buffalo, taken a plane to New Jersey, and rushed to a car that drove him to a helicopter that in turn flew him to Manhattan. The car that took him the final stretch to the club had swerved up on to the sidewalk to get him there in time. But the New Year's show in New York had been a triumph, a sing-along to fireworks that never seemed to end.

Now Tim reclined on the bed at the back of the bus as it was rolling towards the next American city.

In the back there was a separate room that had become his and Emily Goldberg's refuge during the long journeys. The student from Washington, DC, had become his girlfriend in the autumn, and every time Emily got a few days off from school, she jumped on the tour. On top of the bedspread, which was adorned with a cartoon lion, Tim had built a blanket fort that he and Emily could snuggle in.

He was in an email discussion with his dad. With the money that had come in, Klas Bergling had helped his son buy an unfinished loft on Karlavägen, just a block away from the apartment where Tim grew up. The space had been gutted and was starting to be renovated, and father and son were sending pictures of lumber and appliances to each other. Tim had fallen in love with a black parquet floor and thought that the cupboard doors would match up well with the stone on the kitchen counter.

It was a relief to talk with Klas about something other than work. Having his father as a business partner was not entirely uncomplicated. When Klas was stressed, he could become neurotic, writing long emails about payroll taxes and accounting and the importance of keeping track of expenses versus income, and Tim thought one thing was more boring than the other.

'You. are. a. drama. queen,' Tim would write sourly. 'It's obvious that I need to get more involved in the companies, but I hardly understand anything at all, so it's difficult even after you have explained things.'

The questions about which showerhead looked best were more enjoyable. And would they have frosted glass in the bathroom? It was something that the aesthete Tim liked to think about. *DJ Mag* had just named him the world's sixth best DJ; he thought he deserved an apartment where he could chill out when he got home.

If he ever came home. Right now, it didn't seem like he would.

Since the New Year's gig in New York, it had gone on relentlessly: Detroit, Minneapolis, Milwaukee, Pittsburgh, Hanover, St Louis, Kansas City, Boulder, Reno, Tucson and Phoenix on the same day, Austin, San Antonio, El Paso, Houston, Dallas ...

The tour was to last throughout January 2012 and was called House for Hunger. That, of course, was Arash's concept. In a commercial on YouTube, the manager explained that in twenty-six days Avicii would perform on twenty-five stages across the United States, and that they themselves would not keep a single penny of the proceeds. Instead, they had started a collaboration with the organisation Feeding America, which ran soup kitchens and shelters for the homeless.

The charity would soon be combined with other initiatives. The clothing company Ralph Lauren had reached out and wanted to use one of Tim's songs in an online campaign. Arash had immediately understood the value of piggybacking off one of the world's largest fashion brands and put a lot of effort into convincing the company that the collaboration should be bigger than an online campaign. House music was a growing youth movement – a DJ would mean perfect exposure for a coveted customer demographic.

Arash worked to form a partnership with Denim & Supply, Ralph Lauren's newly released line that consisted of bohemian jeans and pre-washed tunics. Together, they would soon design a pin that was at the same time an MP3 player full of house music. 'Wear it loud – feed the world' was the message on the promotional button, which could be bought at Macy's. The small print in the ad stated that the purchase did not affect how much money was distributed to charity, but by wearing the button the customer showed their concern for the hungry.

Philanthropy and business in sweet harmony.

'Hey guys, this is Avicii and my radio is NRJ. Hey guys, this is Avicii on NRJ. This is Avicii and all my new hits are first on NRJ.'

Tim would also do stuff like this during the trips, recording jingles for different radio stations on a microphone. Tour

manager Malik Adunni was on hand with all kinds of junk –
Tim would make a birthday greeting for Tiësto's podcast, a
thank-you speech for the Swedish awards ceremony P3 Guld
and even more email interviews.

'Hey guys, this is Avicii and you're listening to *Shut Up
and Dance* with Tara McDonald on FG Radio! My favourite
Swedish city is Stockholm. My favourite Swedish food? I'm
gonna go with Swedish meatballs.'

Tim didn't say anything to those he was travelling with, but
he had started to worry. The panic attack in Boston a couple of
months earlier somehow lingered in his body. He increasingly
felt an unpleasant restlessness creeping in, as if he had drunk
eight cans of Red Bull and become on edge without actually
being more alert. Tired and hyper at the same time.

A couple of times he had started crying without understanding why. The tears had just come.

He had lived in constant disarray for a little more than two
years. Over 600 gigs, always ready to keep moving, never time
to stop or see anything. The caps packed, new club promoters
to toast with, new fans to take selfies with, interviews to do.
But Tim pushed forward, swallowed his tears, and thought that
this state of emergency would soon be over.

'It feels like I'm going to faint every single day now,' he wrote
to Arash Pournouri. 'And not just today and this tour but from
about the first time I mentioned that I felt worn-out ... pretty
regularly but I push it back down and chose to not bring it up
because there's nothing I can do about it.'

In Rochester, a university city on the border with Canada,
Tim had forgotten to close the door to his hotel room.
While he was taking a nap, someone sneaked in and stole
his suitcase. In it was his computer, and even just that was a

catastrophe. On it were sketches of new songs and sets prepared in Rekordbox.

But the worst part for Tim was that the red-yellow capsules were gone. Soon they would be travelling to Puerto Rico, and he had no idea how they would manage to get hold of more acne medication.

The thief turned out to be a fan who sent an email saying that he would gladly return the computer if he got to take a picture with his idol. The production manager Felix Alfonso pretended to be Tim when he answered, but after a lot of fussing back and forth, the idiot stopped responding and disappeared into thin air. What the hell was wrong with people?

When they landed in Orlando the next day, a group of teenagers were waiting in the arrivals hall. They ran up and surrounded Tim, screaming and gawking, the worst one was a guy who had a whole bunch of pictures with him and was not satisfied until Tim had signed his autograph on every single photo.

Felix pushed himself in among the fans and told them to back off. When the guy with the pictures started yelling at him, Felix shoved him in the chest so that he stumbled backwards. It was not nicely done, but somewhere he had to draw the line, didn't he? Did they not realise that Tim felt like shit?

They went on to Puerto Rico and when Tim then returned to the United States, he was finally able to get his hands on acne medication again.

He thought it was noticeable that he hadn't taken any for a few days and to be on the safe side, he immediately ingested three days' worth of doses.

Emily Goldberg had just returned from a lecture on Renaissance artists at school in Washington, DC, when Tim called. He was lying in a hotel room in Soho, New York, complaining of stomach ache. It felt as if the organs inside him had tied themselves into a knot and sent out a pain that radiated into his back. Did Emily know which American painkillers were the best? They were about to go on the road to Rhode Island, but if Tim was to play tonight's gig, he would probably need to stuff himself with some really strong tablets.

Emily heard how Tim's pain worsened with each passing minute. It just hurt all the time now, he said, particularly high up in his stomach.

She asked him to hand over the phone to someone in the crew.

'We need to take Tim to the hospital right now,' Emily said. 'He is literally screaming into the phone!'

'He has a show tonight,' said the man on the other end.

'I don't care! This is my boyfriend!'

Emily heard Tim grab the phone and put it on speaker, so that he could also hear.

'Tim, just lie down,' she said. 'We're gonna get through this. Just breathe calmly.'

After a while Tim no longer responded, he just moaned and whimpered. Emily was so angry that she hissed into the phone: 'Call the fucking ambulance. Now.'

Malik Adunni had been elsewhere when Tim was rushed to the hospital. When the tour manager arrived at Presbyterian, the hospital on the south end of Manhattan, Tim had been checked in and put in a single room, 404–2.

Malik looked at his twenty-two-year-old employer as he slept in the hospital bed. He had his beanie on, and was hooked up to a drip and a bunch of other wires and devices, that Malik didn't really know.

The final shows in the House for Hunger tour would not happen, that much was clear.

How did they end up here, anyway? How did the situation get so out of hand? As soon as Tim woke up, he grimaced in pain and was given a liquid morphine drug that dissolved the stomach cramps. He could not eat solid food; to keep his stomach going he instead got thin flakes of ice.

Emily Goldberg had come to New York and paced around the corridors and answered anxious emails from Tim's mother. Several times a day, Tim's father called, worried and restless, and wondered if it wouldn't be better if Tim flew home to get care in Sweden.

The guys on Styrmansgatan thought they should at least keep the audience updated, so Tim posted a picture on Twitter where the drip tubes could be seen hanging from his left wrist.

'Where I've spent the last 3 days,' he wrote and was showered with love from the fans, both there and on Facebook.

Get better Tim! ♥ *Take care, health comes first :)*
Hope to see you soon in Tel Aviv.
Come back to Pennsylvania when you're feeling better!
Take care of yourself. Your fans can wait ;)
We love you feel better Tim.

The pain came and went. As long as Tim got painkillers he felt okay, but once they wore off it immediately hit his stomach again.

The remarkable thing was that Tim didn't seem particularly depressed. Instead, he asked Felix and Emily to go out and buy a new computer for him. The upcoming shows in Israel, Austria and Italy had to be cancelled, the inbox got a little quieter, he could in good conscience try out a new game from Blizzard.

After almost a week, Emily turned on the old TV that hung

on the wall in the hospital room. On Sunday night the Super Bowl was broadcast, the final game of the American National Football League. Every year the game was one of the world's biggest sporting events, and now over a hundred million Americans were sitting down to watch the New York Giants face the New England Patriots.

The gang at the hospital was interested in something else.

During the first commercial break, Tim hushed the nurse who was in on her rounds, and everyone turned towards the small screen. First came a couple of commercials for cars and one for soft drinks. Then the ad they were waiting for.

Well-dressed office workers stood in airy rooms at a quiet corporate party. The camera panned towards the skyscraper's dark windows, and there, behind his decks, was a smiling Avicii playing 'Levels'.

Tim had filmed the commercial for Budweiser's new low-calorie beer a month earlier. It had taken a whole day, he had hated every minute of the shoot, but now it was over. A bigger penetration of the market was hardly possible – after all, a third of the country's population was tuned in to watch this.

Afterwards, Emily crept into Tim's narrow bed. They fell asleep tightly wrapped around each other, before the painkillers wore off and Tim woke up in horrible pain.

From: Anki Lidén
To: Emily Goldberg
Date: 2 February 2012

Hi got the photos of Tim, and you and Tim, so nice to see him and you there with him. Do you know if he's been scanned yet? Fever? Is he ok? Maybe you are asleep now, where do you stay and how long can you be there? Many questions …Take care of both of you and kiss him again! Anki

> **From: Emily Goldberg**
> **To: Anki Lidén**
> **Date: 2 February 2012**

> Hi Anki,

> Tim is doing better and is in good spirits. They did a cat scan yesterday and it confirmed he has severe pancreatitis. The doctors say he should spend at least 1–2 more days in the hospital. He had a small fever last night but it didn't last long. He's feeling much better, and the pain is not as bad.

> I will keep you updated.

> Emily

Anki Lidén was walking aimlessly through Malmö. At a theatre in town, she was acting in a farce about a mustard maker and his illegitimate children, but it was impossible to focus on comical intrigues and mix-ups on stage when her Tim-a-lim was lying in a hospital bed on the other side of the world.

The whole situation had felt quite unreal for a long time now. Her son, who had sometimes refused to leave his own room, was now standing in front of tens of thousands of new people every night. Upraised and worshipped and therefore alone.

Tim sometimes called at night, proudly telling her that he had figured out how to handle the moments up in the bright spotlight. It was important not to catch anyone's gaze. Just look out over the waves of heads, away towards the horizon. And look happy, laugh a lot. When he mimed along and really articulated the lyrics of the songs, the audience seemed to be satisfied. But being forced to be nice and approachable, to take selfies and do interviews and have dinners with club owners, it took effort. Each promoter wanted to invite him to a restaurant and then arrange their own small interview with which they could market their clubs or festivals.

Anki had tried to remind him that it was okay to say no to things. The next time someone came up and wanted to take a photo, he could, for example, say that he was on his way to an important meeting. That's what she used to do when she was recognised in town.

As she walked, Anki pondered how Tim was doing over there in the hospital. Really, she just wanted to cancel everything, take a taxi to the airport and board a plane to New York. But her son did not want that. It was completely unnecessary for his parents to fly over, he said. He was fine, he insisted – he had finally been given a few days off and would probably be discharged any day anyway.

Now the doctors knew what was wrong. The diagnosis was, in medical parlance, pancreatitis.

The pancreas sits high up in the abdomen and secretes a fluid that helps the body break down food. A large and continuous intake of alcohol can cause inflammation and lead harmful enzymes to break down the organ. Moreover, Tim's doctors had explained that, in addition to the alcohol, his acne medication was probably playing a role. The three-day dose that Tim had ingested just before the hospital stay had probably been a trigger.

For the inflammation to have a chance to heal, Tim would need to be sober for at least six months, probably more. If the stomach was not properly restored now, it might never be. In that case, Tim risked getting chronic pain for the rest of his life.

Anki ended up at McDonald's at the Triangeln shopping centre, among high school students and prams. While ordering her McFeast meal, she heard a piano loop she recognised. It was 'Fade into Darkness', Tim's song about running away from the darkness and into the light.

'That's my son who wrote this fantastic tune!'

That's what she wanted to shout out across the whole restaurant, to the mothers on parental leave and the snotty toddlers on this dull day in Malmö.

'Hey! Isn't it extraordinary!?'

But she controlled herself, quietly chewing her burger. She could become so anxious and full of emotions that she would almost shut down. She didn't want to end up there. It was still a consolation that Tim seemed to be okay in the hospital, and that Emily, Felix and Malik were with him. Tim's North American agent, David Brady, had also gone down there from Toronto.

Tim had been prescribed painkillers. Anki did not really know what kind of medicine it was, but it was good that there was help available.

Those days in hospital were the most anxiety and stress free days I can remember the past 6 years, those were my true vacations as depressing as it might sound. The relief of going from extreme pain to none, knowing that no one is expecting anything other than for you to wait it out (which is the only way of treating pancreatitis) and then recover was huge. It was an extreme relief considering the insane schedule I had kept up until that point.

'DO YOU LOVE ME?'

'Ya I said I love u more than u love me!!!'

'No way.'

Tim was lying on the black leather sofa in the apartment on Karlavägen and texting with his girlfriend, who was still in the USA. The pain wasn't as intense as it had been in the hospital, but on the other hand it was constant. As soon as Tim woke up, his stomach cramped. Then the pain was there, like an endless rumble in his body; it hurt whenever he moved.

But it was nice to be home in Stockholm again. The bathroom needed to be tiled, the new kitchen counter wasn't yet in place. But Klas had still done a good job, the old attic was almost exactly how Tim wanted it. Glittering black surfaces, minimalist and modern. Tim wondered if it would work to have a wine cooler built into the wall. And he wanted a plaster fireplace, one that always glowed with heat.

He had rested on the sofa looking for a place that he and Emily could rent during their holiday trip to Saint-Barthélemy. A couple of gigs in Malmö and Oslo had been taken off the schedule and finally he would be able get away for a few days and just chill on a Caribbean beach and turn brown.

The TV in the background broadcast the Grammis Awards, where the year's best Swedish artists and producers were celebrated. To the record company's annoyance, Tim had refused to attend the ceremony, instead lying here and watching himself be crowned artist of the year and 'Levels' being named the best song of 2011.

'Mah bebe,' wrote Emily Goldberg. 'Did u win????'

'Two prizes baby,' Tim replied.

'My bf is a star!!!!! You're like Brad Pitt.'

Accompanied by his father, Tim had gone to a doctor in Stockholm for a follow-up check on his stomach, and the message had not been very uplifting.

He would no longer be able to eat things like pizza and burgers: fatty food would irritate the inflammation in his stomach. He was not allowed to drink alcohol for several months. To relieve his pain, more painkillers had been prescribed.

Tim contemplated. The opioids he had been given at the hospital in New York had been a mixture of oxycodone and paracetamol, but these new pills seemed to contain only oxycodone. It should make them weaker, he reasoned – there was only one active substance in them?

He asked Emily over WhatsApp, but she did not really know either.

'Just be careful,' his girlfriend wrote. 'That stuff is really addictive.'

'Noo I'll be fine baby,' Tim replied, describing the miracle of the medicine. The cramps in his stomach were completely resolved. Instead, butterflies flew through his body, making him pleased and relaxed.

For the moment there was nothing he needed to do but find a kick-ass house in the Caribbean and chat with Emily.

'I love you baby.'

'I love you so much baby.'

He could not get enough of writing the words.

'I hope we'll be together forever.'

After a while, his girlfriend reacted.

'U don't love me,' she teased. 'U only talk to me when you are high on those pills.'

'I do love u. These pills haven't started working yet. My tummy doesn't hurt that bad but I'm taking the pills as a precaution.'

'Hahaha. Baaaby, that's what addicts saaayy.'

'Haha I know. Only difference is that I'm not gonna take more pills after this.'

19 May 2012

Tim Bergling

I'm gonna need more time,

still not done with set completely

Like 6.45 pickup

>**Felix Alfonso**
>
>Just pulled up

Tim Bergling

I'm just abt to jump in shower

>**Felix Alfonso**
>
>No can do
>
>We need to leave now

Tim Bergling

I can't

>**Felix Alfonso**
>
>Man we have an interview 7.45
>
>It takes 40 mins to get there

Tim Bergling

Gonna have to push interview

I think, not done with set,

I'm stressing out. I'll work in the car

Production manager Felix Alfonso rushed through the hotel lobby at The Standard and took the elevator to Tim's room. Forty-five thousand people were waiting in an arena in New Jersey, where the Electric Daisy Carnival had spawned.

Felix already knew on the way up to Tim's room what was going to happen. It was almost comical how predictable this scene had become. Tim was like a four-year-old who refused to put on his boots in the morning. For some reason, he would rather check the traffic on a hundred different sites than take a shower, pack his caps and get down to the reception. It felt as if half of Felix's job description was to drag Tim out of suites, despite his procrastination and trickery.

Felix knocked on the locked door. Of course, Tim didn't open it.

'Come on, Tim, we can't be doing this, it's not professional. We need to leave in a couple of minutes!'

'Is that *Tim time*? I was just gonna jump in the shower!'

'No, that's real, actual time.'

'Five minutes, bro!'

Tim time had become an inside joke, a kind of sliding scale which always meant that fifteen minutes ended up being at least forty-five. Forty-five minutes could, in the worst case, mean two hours.

It was hard to reason with Tim, because he was so charming in his foolish stubbornness.

'It's gonna be forty minutes to the venue,' Felix tried. 'I told you that.'

Triumphantly, Tim answered from the other side of the door: 'I googled it. It'll only take half an hour!'

They had just got one week in the Caribbean, Tim and Emily. There, they had eaten good food, Tim had tried out all of Emily's skincare products and after a few days they had even found a beach that was so isolated that Tim could sunbathe in peace. But even during the holidays, the mailbox had been buzzing – an Italian promoter who needed to book a new date because Tim had cancelled when he became ill, a song with Lenny Kravitz that must be finished. The guys on Styrmansgatan had asked if it was okay for some fans to take selfies with Tim before a gig, and could he print and sign a document so they could arrange a new visa to Australia?

After the short holiday, Tim had done a bunch of gigs in South Africa before moving on to Taiwan, Indonesia and Thailand, and now they just were just arriving from a festival in southern Germany.

At many of the gigs in the United States that spring and summer, Tim performed in a booth the shape of a man's head about five metres high, cast in hard white plastic. At the top of this strange colossus, the scalp was hollowed out and there was room for Tim and his equipment. With the help of wires in the ceiling, Tim was able to go out over the audience on a ramp from the giant's forehead. Lighting from below created the illusion that Avicii was floating in the air, and when Etta James sang the chorus to 'Levels', a giant singing mouth was projected on the face.

Perhaps such an escalation in the stage production was necessary. Swedish House Mafia had shown that some Swedes could sell out Madison Square Garden and turn the ice hockey arena into a hedonistic nightclub. It was not without reason that the guy responsible for their special effects was called Pyro Pete – he would set off such large flames that those closest to the stage had a hard time keeping their eyes open. The other artists also did their best to make a lone DJ feel like a full experience. Deadmau5 now dressed in a special costume that read his body movements and got a glowing skeleton to mirror his movements on the screens behind him. The long-haired Steve Aoki climbed the stage rigs and threw cream cakes in the faces of his ecstatic audience, who had started holding up placards that read 'CAKE ME'. It was this kind of bombastic experience that Tim needed to compete with.

But the large Avicii head required four expensive trucks to transport, took the stagehands half a day to assemble and was technically difficult to maintain. The first time they used the construction, at the Coachella festival, the computers broke down and Tim had to play the first songs in pitch darkness. It was a fucking monstrosity, quite honestly.

At the same time, the collaboration with Ralph Lauren had deepened. Now it wasn't just Tim's music that would be available in Denim & Supply's stores – he would be the face of their entire autumn collection. Recently, they had recorded a campaign film in which fashion models in khaki shorts and fringed vests danced as Tim played for them in a warehouse on Long Island. Tim hated filming. Sober audiences in such an artificial environment, where everyone also knew they were being recorded. It had felt stiff and uncomfortable.

They were butting heads more and more, the artist and his manager. Sometimes Tim felt disconnected from the decisions. Recently, when Arash had complained that Tim forgot to mention him in an interview, Tim had replied:

I don't like not being allowed in on the live shows at all, have asked several times to be involved precisely because I want it to be our thing and not just yours! Feel too much like a puppet sometimes, which in some cases I am but don't want it to become my image, and I am worried that I'll be kind of like a Korean boy band controlled with an iron fist :P

The crew would this summer start flying between gigs on a private jet; Tim had chosen a luxurious ten-seater Cessna. There would be two decals on the plane: Air Vicii and Ash

Alliance. Arash had also drawn up a new logo, which was now printed on the posters ahead of the gigs around Europe. It said Avicii just like always, but suddenly there was an addition: 'Avicii, part of the At Night family'. In silence, Tim had begun to get annoyed at Arash constantly putting his name next to his. It was Tim who paid for the plane, for example – why would his manager really have his name there? Tim felt that he really made an effort to highlight the importance of Arash in all possible contexts, and he was the person Tim trusted the most in the world when it came to music. But sometimes it felt to Tim like Arash never got enough of the spotlight.

It was probably also the situation itself that had become increasingly tense and unmanageable. There were thousands of things constantly in motion, an entire industry that Tim really only got a sense of from the contours of his inbox.

Out there, outside his hotel room, so much was going on that could no longer be controlled. Lawyers and advisers, press consultants and fall collections, riggers and drivers and pilots, rights disputes and agreements and draft contracts. One never saw what the other was doing, and eventually, it all ended up in Tim's lap. That's how it felt. It was him who had to perform, him who had to do the interviews and the jingles and be photographed and prepare new gigs and make songs so that the fans were constantly fed with something fresh.

What would they do without him? Would Felix Alfonso go up on stage? Would Filip Holm be a model for the autumn collection? The Avicii brand simply could not do without Tim, that's still how it was, in spite of everything. And he was not someone who could just be dragged along, nor did he want it to appear that way.

In his hotel room with light wood panels and a view of the Hudson River, it was him who was in control.

Felix and the others could certainly wait a little longer.

5 September 2012

Jesse Waits

What r u doing

Tim Bergling

I'm getting sick :s

Jesse Waits

That sucks

Fuck

Flu?

Tim Bergling

Dont know rly, flu like symptoms now

But feel rly exhausted mentally also

Jesse Waits

You are just burnt out

Even on your vacation you were working

U need rest

Tim Bergling

I know

But this year is booked solid

Jesse Waits, the nightclub king, stood shivering outside the royal palace and wondered why he had gone to Stockholm at all. And what the hell kind of country was this? How could people live in a place where it rained and was bitterly cold even before the summer was over?

Ever since Tim started playing at Jesse's club XS in Las Vegas, the club manager and his main attraction had become close friends. Jesse had given his old sports car to Tim as a birthday present, a 1965 Ford Thunderbird, and taken Tim and Emily to the Las Vegas desert to shoot targets with his rifles and pistols. Jesse and Tim now talked to each other quite intimately via text messages, discussing gossip and secrets. But now Tim was behaving in a way that made Jesse both annoyed and puzzled. They had decided to have lunch, but Tim did not show up. Jesse went to the studio on Styrmansgatan, waiting for Tim to finish his work.

When they finally got out on the street, Jesse saw how Tim secretly put a pill in his mouth. They went to a restaurant just below Tim's apartment on Karlavägen, and by the time they sat down to their pizzas, Tim's pupils had shrunk to pinheads.

Jesse recognised the look from his father. One day when Jesse was a teenager, his father had torn a tendon in his shoulder on a construction site where he worked and became bedridden. For almost a year, he had struggled with surgeries and rehab while on painkillers. When his father then found out that the woman he'd been seeing was unfaithful, he closed the bedroom door and pulled down the curtains. The painkillers had soon become too expensive and Jesse's father had switched to the drug that in its structure was most similar to the morphine pills and gave the corresponding pain relief. Heroin.

Jesse had, since then, learned to read the small signs, the changes in a face. That shiftless and absent-minded look, the satisfied and blank expression. Tim seemed to have slipped away in a similar way; if the restaurant had caught on fire it would not have bothered him.

'Tim, I can tell you're a little fucked up right now,' Jesse said. 'That's all right, but try to look at yourself from the outside a little bit.'

'What do you mean?'

'Just think about how tough it is for someone who earns $40,000 in a year. You get $150,000 per gig. You're living a pretty good life right now, try to take that in.'

'You don't get it, Jesse. I don't give a shit about money. I never cared about the money.'

'That's not the point. I'm talking about perspective. People struggle all their life for not even a fraction of what you have. Don't just throw that away.'

Tim was demonstrably uninterested, scraping the cutlery against the porcelain with an empty gaze.

'I told you I don't care about the money.'

A few weeks later, Tim was back in New York. He would open for Madonna at Yankee Stadium. As if to really emphasise which DJ was king of the city, the latest fashion campaign was on billboards all around Manhattan. Tim's face was watching over the pedestrians with a serious look, wearing a red-and-black check Ralph Lauren shirt and with a slender woman leaning against his shoulder.

Tim, Emily and production manager Felix Alfonso had been sneaked out through the back entrance when they left the hotel in the Meatpacking District, but still the paparazzi found them just a few blocks south, in Soho. The rumour spread fast, someone told someone else who called a third person and suddenly the photographers came raging through traffic on their motorcycles with cameras around their necks.

The clatter of the lenses caused Emily Goldberg's pulse to race. After almost a year as the girlfriend of a superstar, she too had become increasingly shy. A few months earlier, a gossip site had posted screenshots taken from her Facebook profile, which would prove that she was on tour with Avicii. She felt more and more under surveillance. At a club in New Jersey, a jealous girl had poured her drink of cranberry juice all over Emily; the slimy sugar had clung to her back under the clear blue dress with rhinestones, Emily's favourite.

And yet it was still nothing compared to what her boyfriend had to endure. Parallel with the success, the comments on the internet had begun to change in character. On Twitter, people dwelled on Tim's dress and appearance. Many compared him to a young Leonardo DiCaprio, or wrote about how much they would give in order to make out with him.

But it was the other comments that Tim got fixated on. For example, people pointed out his nose, which he had never had a good relationship with – they hit him right where it hurt the most.

Who is this Avicii, why is he so ugly, and why are people obsessing over him?

@Avicii ye were unreal tonight however the smell of acne off ye is scandalous.

I love Avicii and all, but he kinda looks like a pig

VIP for avicii? all u get to do is his ugly mug closer :/

Tim and the others escaped from the photographers and slipped into a pet store on Christopher Street. The production manager immediately understood where this was going.

'For fuck's sake, Tim, don't get a dog,' Felix pleaded.

Neither Tim nor Emily listened, instead moving purposefully

between enclosures of puppies, each cuter than the last. They had talked about it for a long time – a dog would give their lives a sense of calm and normality.

At the far end, Emily found some smaller cages, filled with fluffy tufts of fur that stood straight out from their small bodies.

'Oh, Pomeranians!' Emily shouted, picking up one of the puppies in her arms. It was sweet but wild and naughty, barking incessantly. When she turned around, Tim was standing across from her with another one of the puppies pressed against his chest. This one was completely still and silent, looking up at Tim as if he were the only person that mattered in the whole world.

'You guys get that this is a bad idea, right?' Felix tried again. 'You're flying to different cities every day, you can't buy a dog.'

Tim looked appealingly at Emily. For a moment she saw her boyfriend as if from the outside: a twenty-three-year-old who was constantly surrounded by chaos and noise and camera sounds. As if by magic, he was now content and relaxed, his eyes soft.

'You wanna hold her?' Tim asked, leaning forward towards Emily. She looked into the small eyes, stroking her hand over white fur and a beautiful brown little head.

'Oh, look at you two,' said Tim. 'So cute!'

'Yes. She's the one,' Emily said.

My procrastination.

It needed to be explained to me very logically and caveman-esque for me to truly understand its nature and how it was harming me. 'Ouch, pain. Why me pain now? Uncomfortable feeling. Future Tim deal with pain. Future Tim deal with pain better than present Tim because already there's too many present pains more urgent to deal with.'

IN NOVEMBER 2012 Tim went back to Stockholm.

Along the wharf on Södermalm, where tourists strolled in the summer, lay the dark mirror of Riddarfjärden bay, shiny and quiet at that time of year. In a yellow stone building right on the water, a former foundry, Salem Al Fakir had rented a studio.

Salem immediately saw that Tim was in high spirits when he came upstairs. There was a bustle in his body, as if he were a proud child who wanted to show off a shell he had just found.

'So listen to this,' Tim said, and asked Salem to pull up a song.

The room was filled with trumpet blasts, accordions and hand claps. The song was called 'Little Talks' and was made by Of Monsters and Men, a band from Iceland that Tim and Emily had been listening to continuously for the last few weeks. Tim had performed his own version of the song at his latest gigs – the ecstatic drive fitted perfectly in large arenas. At the same time, the music was distinctly acoustic, sounding like something performed by sailors with wooden spoons and tin plates while the sea rolled wildly outside the galley.

The mix of the rustic instruments and the rumbling cheers was quite irresistible, Tim thought.

'Wouldn't it be awesome to try something like this?'

In the room was a new acquaintance of Salem Al Fakir, a tall guy with blond Viking hair and a friendly manner.

Like Al Fakir, Vincent Pontare had been marinated in music since childhood. His father, Roger Pontare, was one

Tim Bergling was born in Stockholm in September 1989. His father Klas Bergling ran a profitable office supply store and his mother Anki Lidén was a successful actress.

Tim grew up in Östermalm, a prosperous neighbourhood where preschool and friends were within a comfortable walking distance.

Tim was born much later than his siblings. Anton and the other two half-siblings all moved away from home when their younger brother was still little, but often came to visit the family apartment on Linnégatan.

Tim spent large parts of his childhood in his room in the apartment on Linnégatan, where he drew, wrote poems and read everything he could about outer space and science.

Tim's thoughtful and somewhat reserved nature was already evident in his childhood, when he could become hesitant and anxious in new situations.

Tim's father Klas also had a big interest in music. He would put on blues songs that echoed throughout the apartment, while Tim sat engrossed in front of his computer games for hours on end.

Tim liked music from an early age, sang along with songs and messed around learning the guitar and piano. His mum suggested lessons, but for Tim it was important to find his way all on his own.

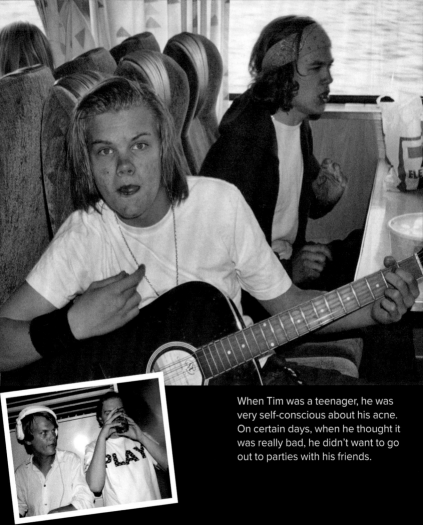

When Tim was a teenager, he was very self-conscious about his acne. On certain days, when he thought it was really bad, he didn't want to go out to parties with his friends.

One of the first people to be impressed by Tim's knack for melodies was the producer Laidback Luke, here in a mask. In March 2009, the Dutchman invited Tim and Filip to the US for their first performance abroad.

Arash Pournouri, on the left, was an ambitious club promoter on Stockholm's bustling House scene. He quickly saw the potential in Tim's beats. Pournouri became Tim's manager and saw to it that he made contact with stars like Tiësto, on the right.

2011				TRAVEL LAS VEGAS →	Blue Moon II Karlstad	STOCKHEL	Club Moments	Karlstad	
2011				Sweden TRAVEL AMSTERDAM →	STOCKHOLM				
2011				TRAVEL KARLSTAD → STOCKHOLM					
2011	Blue Moon B Karlstad								
2011							Siera Grand Club	Melle	FL
2011				TRAVEL STOCKHOLM	→		The Venue	Tampa	
2011				TRAVEL FRANKFURT → ORLANDO → TORONTO			Palace	Guelph	
2011				TRAVEL TAMPA → DETROIT → TORONTO			Area	Winnipeg	
2011				TORONTO			Playhouse	Ottawa	
2011				TRAVEL			Ultra Music Fest	Headline	
2011				TRAVEL			Ultra Music Fest	Prime T	
2011				TRAVEL OTTAWA → TORONTO → MIAMI			Ultra Music Fest	Headli	
2011									
2011				TRAVEL MIAMI → FRANKFURT					
2011				TRAVEL FRANKFURT → ATLANTA/STOCKH				STOCKI	
2011							Belgil Brussels		
2011				TRAVEL STOCKHOLM → Brussel Brussel			Luxe Luxembourg		
2011				Luxembourg Luxembourg Beach					
2011	Brussel Brussel		Belgium TRAVEL LUX →						
2011	Luxembourg Luxembourg		TRAVEL LUX → STOCKHOLM						
2011			Spain Otto Zutz → Barcelona						
2011	Otto Zutz Barcelona		TRAVEL						
2011									
2011				TRAVEL STOCKHOLM → FRANKFURT → ORLANDO → MIAMI					
2011				ORLANDO → MIAMI					
2011				TRAVEL MIAMI → LOS ANGE					
2011				TRAVEL LOS ANGELES → STOCKHOL					
2011				STOCKHOLM → TOULOUSE					
2011				TOULOUSE → OSLO			Nord Sensation	Oslo	
2011				OSLO → STOCKHOLM					
2011				atom → OSLO Sensation W Oslo					
2011				O → STOCKHOLM			Vain	Orlando	FL
2011				OCKHOLM → FRANKFURT → ORLANDO					
2011				ORLANDO → EDMONTON			EEC	Edmonton	
2011							Musicbox	Los Angeles	CA
2011				EDMONTON → LOS ANGELES			Pacha	NYC	NY
2011				LOS ANGELES → N Y C					

24	
25	
26	
27	
28	
29	
30	
1	
2	
3	
4	

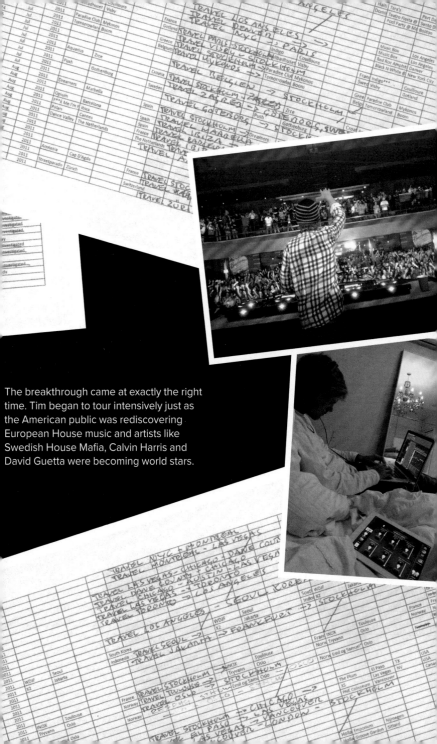

The breakthrough came at exactly the right time. Tim began to tour intensively just as the American public was rediscovering European House music and artists like Swedish House Mafia, Calvin Harris and David Guetta were becoming world stars.

The immediate synth riff in the song 'Levels', which became a huge hit in 2011, meant that Avicii was soon selling out arenas all over the world. Unlike the older generations of rock musicians, a DJ of his stature never stopped touring, and Tim would even do gigs in two different countries on the same night.

			USA	USA
Buchanan's	El Paso	TX	USA	USA
Stereo Live	Houston	TX	USA	USA
Palladium Ballro	Dallas	TX	USA	USA
Lavo	New York C	NY	USA	USA
House For Hunger Tour				to be investigated
House For Hunger Tour			unknown	to be investigated
Orpheum Theatr	Madison	WI	USA	USA
Paramount Thea	Seattle	WA	USA	USA
Main Street Arm	Rochester	NY	USA	USA
University of Ce	Orlando	FL	USA	USA
Coliseum Of Pue	Puerto Ric		Puerto Rico	Puerto Rico
House For Hunger Tour			unknown	to be investigated
Ryan Center	Kingston	RI	USA	USA
Mullins Center	Amherst	MA	USA	USA
				to be investigated

CANCELLED SICKNESS NYC HOSPITAL

In the spring of 2012, the hectic touring life, and the habits that came with it, had made Tim ill. With an inflamed pancreas, he crash-landed at a hospital in New York.

Tim's girlfriend Emily Goldberg, like so many other Americans during this time, loved the hopeful power of House music.

In the spring of 2013, Tim moved to Los Angeles to record his debut album. Swedish songwriters Salem Al Fakir and Vincent Pontare were partners in developing a sound that was groundbreaking. With influences from American folk music and bluegrass, they wrote songs such as 'Hey Brother' with Tim.

Avicii's stage production became increasingly colossal. Two of those responsible for the visual experience were the Brit Harry Bird and the American Charlie Alves, at the back. Robb Harker, in red, was the agent for the Australian and Asian markets.

Tim found an unexpected musical soulmate in Mike Einziger, guitarist in the rock band Incubus, who together with soul singer Aloe Blacc wrote 'Wake Me Up' – another song that with its acoustic character pushed the boundaries of how dance music could sound.

In the period preceding his debut album, Tim had made over three hundred shows a year. When *True* was released in the autumn of 2013, its songs were played by both pop radio and country stations in the United States, and the record cemented Avicii's name among the world's biggest artists.

of the country's big pop stars when Vincent was growing up; he himself had started playing metal guitar early in the guest house out in the Ängermanland forest. When Pontare moved to Stockholm, it was to establish himself as a rapper in the hip-hop duo Verbal 'N' Vincent, but after a couple of half-failed attempts as a solo artist, he had instead started to find his place as a songwriter in the background – a few years earlier he had co-written Swedish House Mafia's smash hit 'Save the World'.

It was Vincent Pontare who had rented out his studio space to Salem Al Fakir; they had noticed that they enjoyed each other's company and started working together.

Now they both looked at their excited guest.

It was not entirely easy to understand what Tim wanted to get out of this Icelandic squall, which Vincent mostly thought sounded like some kind of plastic wannabe-country. But he picked up his guitar and started looking for a melody.

Tim's search for a more rural soundscape came at just the right time. In recent days, Vincent and Salem had collaborated with Veronica Maggio, a singer who had become one of Sweden's most popular. The three of them were working on an album set in an atmospheric and hazy landscape. Salem hummed a small melody he had just composed for 'Hela Huset' ('The Whole House'), one of Maggio's songs.

Tim shouted right away.

'Yes! There it is!'

It was as simple as it was the last time Tim and Salem worked together while writing 'Silhouettes' in just one afternoon. Salem threw out the fishing line and Tim knew exactly when to bite. His ability to intuitively perceive that one second that sparkled, that could be built on, was astounding.

While Vincent Pontare was strumming his guitar, he began

to mumble sounds. For much of his teenage years, he had sat with dictionaries and studied English expressions to become a tongue-twisting rapper, something that had given him a gift for improvising words on the go.

'Bidaaaaaaaahh biii booooothaa!'

'Ah, there! There!'

Tim was even more excited now, when he heard a sound that formed a word.

'Shit, *brother*! That's good!'

They continued to work, now with a vague idea about brotherhood, loyalty, blood ties. First and foremost, it was a feeling they were going for, sometimes the lyrics then came second: '*Hey sister, know the water's sweet but blood is thicker.*' Water is sweet but blood is thicker? Could you say that in English? It didn't sound really smart when you thought about it, but what the hell – it fitted nicely with the melody.

After an intro that was dominated by Vincent's guitar playing and a driving bass drum, Tim drew up a drop that was clearly inspired by the Icelanders' 'Little Talks'. The cheering trumpet fanfare made 'Hey Brother' explode, Tim could already envision the rain of confetti at the gigs in front of him.

'This is going to be fucking sick,' he shouted.

'That's for sure,' laughed Vincent.

Tim left the old foundry with feelings of happiness in his chest. He was at home in Stockholm, in a couple of days he would see his favourite comedian Ricky Gervais perform at the Globe Arena, and now he knew in which direction he wanted to go musically.

'Folk-electronica, bro,' he wrote to Arash before contacting his father to tell him as well about his new creative direction: 'I think country music and house could be cool as hell!'

*

It was time to show the world who was really on top.

Tim and Arash had agreed that Avicii would not be yet another house producer who only made singles.

He would record a real record, a full-length album.

That's why Tim and Emily were in a taxi on their way to Universal's main office building in Santa Monica. Tim was nervous. He thought that the man he was about to meet would surely be pushy and presumptious, and he didn't really know what he was expected to say to a high-profile record label exec in the United States. Arash had assured him that Neil Jacobson was cool, but he was still one of the top decision-makers at Interscope, an imprint of Universal – a person with power.

Tim's concerns were immediately dismissed. Neil Jacobson turned out to be a noisy and talkative big-city man from New York who showed Tim and Emily to one of those corner offices they had seen in the movies, where the big boss putts golf balls across the carpet while making life-changing decisions on speakerphone. Jacobson had ramped up the cliché even more because, in addition to the putter and the balls, he had a basketball hoop mounted on the door. Now he threw himself into his chair, wearing worn jeans and a shirt, and immediately took command of the conversation.

Jacobson talked about the model for songwriting that he had started to use, one that he was convinced would make electronic music mature and reach its full potential as pop.

Back in the day, he had received a number of instrumentals from a producer, demos that he played for artists and then asked which song they would like to sing on. The beat had always come first, the topline melody and the lyrics had been an afterthought.

But because the production of a song – how the instruments sounded sonically – was so timebound, many house tracks had quickly become dated. A soundscape that was cool one summer could already feel painfully dorky the following year. Very few eternal classics had been produced in this way.

Neil Jacobson got the idea for changing the process from Will.i.am, producer of the group Black Eyed Peas. Jacobson had been the sounding board for the group three years earlier, when they sold platinum around the world alongside David Guetta, so Jacobson had seen the producer at work. Will.i.am wrote the melodies of the songs on his guitar. Only when the foundation was ready did he enter the sketch into the computer and start building the electronic costume around his stripped-down demo. In a way, he did a remix of his own acoustic song.

Tim Bergling listened intently. Neil put into words the philosophy he himself was already following. It was exactly this that had made the collaboration with Salem and Vincent so much fun – that the melodies, the beating heart of the songs, were at the centre.

This was exactly how he wanted to work.

Neil had now gone so far as to ask all songwriters who contacted him to remove the rhythmic instruments completely from their sketches. The song should flow regardless of which production they would later choose to put on it. He had his computer full of such demos, which he called backwards songs.

'Think about how it's done in Hollywood,' he said. 'Millions of dollars are spent to create a very specific screenplay before any other decisions are made. You see, without that fantastic groundwork there's no great movie, no matter how many tricks you're able to pull later on in the production.'

Jacobson noticed that film enthusiast Tim Bergling liked the analogy.

'You are the director. But we have to be careful which screenplays we choose.'

Tim already knew who he wanted to try this method with.

'I wanna work with Paul Simon,' he said. 'And Stevie Wonder.'

When they parted ways, Neil Jacobson tried to digest what Tim had actually said. Jacobson had been in the business for a long time by now, but the suggestions for collaborators still left him astonished.

So far, the European house scene had grown properly within the box: Swedish House Mafia had worked with Pharrell Williams, Calvin Harris with Rihanna, David Guetta with the Black Eyed Peas. Sure, those were collaborations across unspoken borders – from the club towards the slick pop world, from Europe to the USA – but they were still ties between colleagues who were contemporaries.

Tim had wanted musicians like Paul Simon, a legend who made smart ballads in the 60s. Did Simon even know what house music was?

The other requests Tim had made were not easy either.

Mick Jagger said no; Van Morrison's representatives were vague in their answer, giving a kind of half maybe. Neil didn't even manage to get in touch with Slash, the guitarist in the hard rock band Guns N' Roses. Nor with Stevie Wonder or Sting.

It was not particularly difficult to understand. Avicii certainly was on a fantastic run right now – 'I Could Be The One', a song he had done with Dutch producer Nicky Romero, had just gone straight to number one on the UK singles chart. But why would a rock veteran like John Fogerty care about that? For these contented men, whose career peaks were at least twenty years behind them, Avicii was at best an obscure Swede with a summer hit.

It was therefore on a pure whim that Neil Jacobson asked another old-timer. They were on the fourteenth hole of the

Bel-Air Country Club golf course. Neil's playing partner for the day was a seventy-year-old from Texas, an idol of Jacobson. In the late 60s, Mac Davis had helped Elvis Presley reboot his career by writing the songs 'A Little Less Conversation' and 'In The Ghetto' for the star. After that, Davis had had his own career as a country musician, became a movie star and performed in musicals on Broadway. He wrote low-key lyrics about love and heartbreak, and Neil Jacobson thought that Mac Davis, in addition to having a short game that was impressive for his age, was one of the great songwriters in the country.

'By the way, Mac,' Neil said just before teeing up, 'how would you like to work with Avicii?'

'Well, I don't know. Who's that?'

'A young guy making electronic music.'

Mac Davis looked at his younger friend in disbelief. Davis was a troubadour, a storyteller, a man who could spend days finding the right rhythm of a rhyme. Although his sons liked that hectic dance music, it hardly seemed to focus on the lyrics.

'Hey listen,' said Jacobson, 'this guy is twenty-three years old and made a boatload of money last year.'

'Okay,' laughed Mac Davis. 'Why not?'

Universal had its own recording studios in Santa Monica. Neil Jacobson showed the way to a room with dim lighting and a pair of deep leather sofas. On the floor was a thick Persian rug, by one of the walls stood the mixing table that Dr. Dre used when he completed *The Chronic*, one of the greatest hip-hop albums ever.

Jacobson introduced the veteran and the newcomer to each other before Mac Davis picked up his dark brown guitar and started singing 'Black And Blue', a sketch he already had, about a man who woke up hungover and heartbroken in his hotel room.

Tim Bergling listened with delight. He had received so many suggestions for lyrics in recent years that were full of breasts, buttocks and strippers. This was something completely different. Although this story was also about love and lust, it was characterised by bitter-sweet realism.

Mac Davis went on. He lowered the next demo a key, from D to C, to be able to play the melody faster and gradually build up to the higher notes. He had understood that this was how it would sound in this genre.

The second ballad he had named 'Addicted To You'. This too was a love story, of a person almost blinded by passion.

Tim entered the guitar sound into his computer and put on his headphones. He was working fast now, his fingers flying over the keys. Mac Davis was sitting behind Tim's back and saw his face reflected in the blue light of the screen.

After twenty minutes, the Swede took off his headphones and turned around.

'What do you think?'

From the speakers rippled music that sounded like a whole orchestra.

Not even by Elvis Presley had Mac Davis been so enchanted.

Tim and Emily had rented a house in The Bird Streets, the area in Hollywood's steep mountains where all the streets were named after little birds: nightingales, thrushes, orioles, larks and swallows.

Just a few minutes away from the noise down on Sunset Boulevard was a completely different world. Up here the blocks were closed off, the plots rested hidden behind eucalyptus trees and hedges. If, on the other hand, you entered one of the houses, the whole of Los Angeles unfolded before your eyes.

It was fucking *mode*.

The owners of the house they rented were Cameron and Tyler Winklevoss, a pair of twins who early on had co-operated with Facebook founder Mark Zuckerberg, only to be outmanoeuvred. At least that's how the story was told in the film that Tim had seen about the drama. The twins were fans, had asked Tim for lessons in the art of being a DJ.

Now Tim was sitting with Bear curled up next to him on the sofa. He had become extremely attached to the dog, who followed him everywhere he went when he was at home.

Tim wrote an email to Vincent Pontare. 'Just did this with Mac Davis,' he said, attaching the song about the newly dumped man in the hotel room. 'Thought about us IMMEDIATELY, those times we sat and tried to come up with lyrics etc. This guy is a fucking genius as a lyricist!'

Workwise, it was a treat to be in Los Angeles. Everyone was here, and the new acquaintance Neil Jacobson had already organised a meeting with childhood idol Mike Shinoda of Linkin Park while Arash had arranged for disco hero Nile Rodgers to be involved in the recordings. Even though most of the rock legends seemed to say no, it felt as if things were on the move.

This was exactly what Tim wanted to do: be in the same room as other talented people, get ideas and energy on the spot.

'Damn what fucking *mode* it is here in LA!!' he summarised for Vincent. 'So fucking much talent, have been in the studio for like 12h per day! Shiiiit would have been so much fun if you all had been here too – we could have done some sick stuff then!'

Another one of Neil Jacobson's golf buddies was Mike Einziger. The thirty-six-year-old was the guitarist in Incubus, a rock band that around the turn of the millennium had triumphed with Californian punk mixed with metal and funk.

Bare-chested and pierced like their contemporaries Korn, Slipknot and Limp Bizkit, Incubus had become big teen idols with music that was not always easy to categorise – but a house musician was probably the last thing Mike Einziger was.

He nevertheless said yes immediately when Jacobson asked. It was always worth trying out new creative paths.

Tim took an Uber out to the guitarist's house in Malibu and was taken aback that someone could have such a complete studio in his own home. Mixing tables, keyboards, guitars, everything you would need was there. But Einziger was not the only musician in the household – his fiancée Ann Marie Calhoun was a renowned violinist who during her upbringing in rural Virginia had played violin and banjo in her family's country band. It just so happened that a few months later, in February 2013, the couple would perform at a gala celebrating bluegrass, the folk music that emerged in the meeting between American blues and joyous Irish fiddle playing. Einziger was rehearsing traditional songs such as 'Whiskey Before Breakfast' and 'Groundspeed', and had realised how challenging the music was. Bluegrass required a different attack on the strings than he was used to, and would need to be played both quickly and cleanly.

He hadn't strummed his guitar for long before Tim pointed out a chord progression he liked.

'Oh! Keep playing that!'

Then the blocks were dancing up and down in Tim's computer, and Einziger was wondering what his guest was doing with a particularly screaming synth sound that he smeared all over the various parts. It did not sound elegant at all, just rough and annoying.

Tim explained that he was drawing how the vocal melody would fit. Mike had never seen anything like it. When they wrote songs in his band, the singing itself was always more loosely defined than the actual melody – the vocalist rather came up with a rough idea of the melody and went into the recording booth making his own interpretation.

Tim was much more precise, wanted every eighth note to be already determined in the sketch. It was as if he could see the whole song in his head and just needed to draw it for himself.

A few days earlier, Tim had first met Aloe Blacc, a singer who belonged to the Los Angeles alternative hip-hop scene and had a minor hit with his song 'I Need A Dollar', which was the theme song for a TV series. Tim thought that Aloe Blacc's dark voice would give the song a splash of soul and got in touch with him.

Aloe immediately got in his car and drove out to the coast. He arrived well prepared, with sketches of lyrics that he had recently scribbled down during a flight. Together they found some particularly beautiful stanzas that could be built on:

So wake me up when it's all over
when I'm wiser and I'm older
all this time I was finding myself
and I did not know I was lost

Tim motioned with his hand how he wanted Aloe to sing. Pointing up and down with his finger until it sat perfectly. It was quite funny really: a metal guitarist making bluegrass with a soul guy who was shown exactly how he should do it by a house DJ.

Around midnight, eight hours after they had met, Tim left Malibu and went home to Emily and the dog. In the taxi, he continued to work with his computer in his lap, already knowing that 'Wake Me Up' would be a world hit. There was no doubt about that.

*

150

The song 'Hey Brother', on the other hand, had been lacking a singer for a while. It was Nick Groff, a colleague of Neil Jacobson, who by chance found the man who would do the song justice. To find Tim's demo in his computer, he typed in the keyword 'brother' and then got the soundtrack to the comedy *O Brother, Where Art Thou*? People in general didn't know about the musician Dan Tyminski, but many recognised his voice – it was him who in the film gave voice to George Clooney's character when he sang 'I'm A Man Of Constant Sorrow', a song that had become a big hit on American radio. Dan Tyminski was a well-respected bluegrass musician, whose full tenor voice was perfect for Tim's song.

Tim began to realise that he might not need the biggest of stars – so far there had been even more surprises and excitement together with the slightly odd names, the ones you needed to be in the industry to know.

One restless night, he randomly emailed Neil Jacobson.

'U think anyone's up for a session tonight?'

Neil's colleague Nick thought of a singer from Oklahoma whom he had met some years earlier. She had played her latest project, updated folk songs accompanied by a stomping orchestra. It had hardly been anything for the radio, but her warm voice had remained in his memory.

When the record company called, Audra Mae was sitting in the car, on her way to pick up her sister at the airport. But the conversation sounded too strange and interesting to ignore – make some dance music with a Swedish DJ? Now, right now?

When Audra arrived in Santa Monica, she and this tobacco-chewing Swede started talking about blues music. Audra Mae was mesmerised by a documentary she had just seen about the mysterious singer Robert Johnson. According to legend, he had sold his soul to the devil to be able to play the guitar sharper than anyone else. While Audra was sketching lyrics about Johnson's fateful pact, Tim began working on a melody based on 'Take Five', a jazz song that, when written in 1959, had caused a stir because it went in a particularly complicated musical meter. It was one of his dad's favourites.

'Man, I wish we had a trumpet or saxophone player here,' said Tim. 'I could ask if Neil would be able to find somebody.'

'What if we whistle it?' Audra asked as she sat sunk in the brown leather sofa in the studio. 'Or you know, I brought my kazoo, if you wanna try that?'

Audra Mae pulled out a wind instrument from her purse. It looked like a very small flute and fitted in the palm of your hand. Tim laughed when he heard the nasal sound that came as Audra blew into it. But why not? There was something enticing in the simplicity of the instrument; it felt like something that belonged by a campfire one late night.

'Long Road To Hell' became the first song Tim and Audra did together, but not the last. Tim asked Audra to sing the vocals on Mac Davis's 'Addicted To You' and thought that she had exactly the voice he had been looking for. Adele may have been the immediate reference, but it was that underlying stuff that made Tim interested. In his ears, Audra had the bite and attack of Nina Simone or Etta James, voices he heard echoing on Linnégatan during his childhood.

'Listen to her voice, ohhhh mannnnnnn brooooooo,' he wrote to Arash. 'You get goosebumps when she starts vibing. Listen to the second chorus, it's totally sick.'

9 January 2013

Emily Goldberg

I think I might go home tomorrow

Tim Bergling

:(

Emily Goldberg

Babe, ever since we had that
talk I've started to notice how
uninterested you are, how ur
really tired and how your focus is
100% studio, in and out of it, and
I just get sad being around you
when I can tell ur not interested in
me anymore

Tim Bergling

I am.

Emily Goldberg

and I was prepared for the studio
to be 100 percent ur main focus but
I wasn't prepared for u not to be
attracted to me

Tim Bergling

I mean I can't talk abt this now

There was nothing wrong with the surroundings; on the contrary. Emily liked the coolness and shadows of Tanager Way. There were many rooms, the ceilings high. The best part was the two toilets connected by an elongated, shared bathroom. Finally, there was some personal space and mysticism after all the months on the tour bus and in hotel rooms.

But Emily Goldberg did not feel good in the late winter of 2013. She had begun to feel that she worked for Avicii rather than being Tim's girlfriend. When the guys over in Stockholm couldn't get hold of Tim – and they very rarely could right now – they chased her instead. Emails and text messages and phone calls that Emily could not sift through at all. In the flood of commitments, what was important and what could be opted out of? How could she judge that? Everything in Tim's world felt unbelievably important.

And while her boyfriend was making his big debut album, she had become almost completely insignificant, so it felt.

Tim sat in the studio all day, rarely coming home before three in the morning. He woke up late in the afternoon and immediately got into an Uber and drove back to Santa Monica.

He took more and more pills. Apparently, he had quickly developed a level of tolerance for the medicine he had started taking a year earlier. By now he needed extra pills to achieve the same effect of relaxation and relief as before.

That seemed to be what he needed to ease the pain.

In addition to the album, Tim would this spring make an advertising collaboration with the Swedish telecom company Ericsson. He had written a short chord progression to start from, then the idea was that fans from around the world would send in bass lines and drumbeats and effects that would be put together piece by piece into a single song. Ericsson wanted to demonstrate that their infrastructure made it possible for the whole world to be connected. At Night would be visible on thousands of people's social media: vote for my drums, my break, my effects!

Emily had learned Tim's pattern by now. When he was asked, he almost always thought that such a commitment was cool – he also wanted his music to be as widespread as possible. The assignment was often six months ahead of time and was still abstract enough for him to say yes.

When it later came to the actual implementation, it became more difficult. The commitments piled up the closer Tim got to them, until even basic things felt insurmountable. An email became impossible to answer, a phone call turned into the world's highest mountain.

The collaboration with Ericsson seemed to feel just like that for him. A couple of unfortunate Swedish advertisers had flown to Los Angeles to produce a film about the project – they wanted to follow Tim's work in the studio and do some short interviews. Tim avoided them like the plague.

More and more often, Emily Goldberg felt that she too had become a burden on her boyfriend, something he needed to tick off the to-do list. They never ate together any more. If Tim had anything at all, it was tacos or pizza, just what the doctors had advised against, before he sat down in front of the computer again.

Despite the intensive work on the record, the touring would continue. In mid-February 2013, Tim flew to Argentina, to where Ultra Music Festival had now expanded.

For a while now, there had been a couple of important staff additions to the road crew.

One of the new employees was Harry Bird, a young Brit

who was behind large parts of Swedish House Mafia's visual expression. His company Comix produced evocative film sequences that would make the audience feel Avicii's songs even more in their stomachs. On huge screens behind Tim, animated flames of fire, flashing cobwebs and winding tunnels now rolled. Harry himself stood in the so-called front of house, an enclosed section in the middle of the audience from where the sound was handled, and in real time matched up the various film clips with the songs that Tim was playing.

Also on the tour was the new production manager Charlie Alves, a big and blunt guy from Chicago who had toured with the performance group Blue Man Group and the crooner Michael Bublé. He ran around the huge lighting rigs and stage constructions and shouted in his headset, making sure that everyone in the production played together.

They were both welcome new acquisitions – Tim and Harry had quickly realised that they both loved *The Office* and developed a secret language based on facial expressions borrowed from Ricky Gervais's cocky boss character in the series. Charlie had been nicknamed Sergeant Bilko, after the talkative military commander in the 90s movie of the same name.

Forty thousand South Americans were watching Avicii bounce in the booth, illuminated by pyro and strobe light.

When Tim stepped off the stage, he was dripping with sweat, the adrenalin rushed through him. The tension of standing alone in front of so many people was impossible to get used to. When they got back to the hotel, he turned to production manager Charlie Alves.

'I don't wanna go to bed.'

'What you up to?'

'I'm gonna come by your room and we're gonna raid your minibar.'

Tim ignored the doctors' warnings. Sure, sometimes when he drank alcohol the stomach pains crept in again, but what the hell? He was twenty-three years old, when else would he be allowed to go and wind down if not after a gig in front of forty thousand people?

As the sun rose over Buenos Aires, they sat on the balcony of Charlie's room, opening small bottles of spirits and wine and talking about life and the universe. When the minibar was empty, they ordered champagne and, eight hours later, the lunch rush could be heard down the street.

Then it was off to Spain. At a gathering for the telecom industry, the song that had been made together with the fans would be presented. Filip Holm and Marcus Lindgren had sat on Styrmansgatan through the nights and listened to thirteen thousand entries, one bass line worse than the next. Since the components came separately, it had proved impossible to get a feel for how the pieces of the puzzle would sound together and, in the end, it had still been Tim who'd had to paste everything together into somewhat of a song. Nonetheless, it was now called 'Avicii X You'.

In front of the suits in Barcelona, Tim was interviewed by Ericsson's CEO Hans Vestberg, before they went and ate together with Arash, Per Sundin from Universal, and a sales manager at Ericsson.

Per Sundin was a little surprised that Tim had red wine with his meal – he had heard that Tim wasn't drinking any more – but didn't want to protest.

The next day, 27 February 2013, the plane took off for the Future Music Festival in Australia.

I had a hard time accepting never drinking again though strongly suggested from all doctors to wait at least a year before even having a beer. Of course I didn't listen to the majority of the doctors, I listened to the couple who said it was ok if I was careful.

I was ignorant and naive and touring the world, still on the never-ending tour – because once you've circled it once, guess what?

You start right back over again.

WITH THREE HOURS left until landing, it hit. Tim recognised the pain. The cramp that twisted at the top of his abdomen, the stabbing pains in his back.

He kicked the seat in front of him, focusing on not screaming.

The tramadol he tossed back didn't help; after an hour the fucking pancreas had his whole body in its grip. An ambulance was waiting at the airport to take him to the Royal Brisbane and Women's Hospital.

Robb Harker, an agent for Avicii in Australia and Asia, arrived at the hospital a few hours later and took the elevator to Tim's room. Harker had a hard time wrapping his head around the situation. He thought to himself that he might have heard about a hospital visit to New York a year earlier, but he didn't know what it had been about really. In any case, Tim was lying there, in hospital pyjamas and his red cap, surrounded by tubes and machines.

He looked so emaciated.

There was no question that they would have to cancel both Brisbane and Perth. But what about the other gigs during the week?

Tim woke up, squeezed out a half-smile and asked Robb for a Coca-Cola and a WiFi connection. He seemed surprisingly satisfied with being in hospital, having been put on a sizeable dose of painkillers.

'I'm hurting,' Tim wrote to musician Audra Mae, 'but I'm so jacked up on OxyContin here and Vicodin there so I can't feel anything haha ...'

Tim thought it was a great opportunity to continue working on the album. From the hospital bed, he made fine-tuned adjustments to a song that, due to its history, meant a little extra to him. When they were younger, Tim and Fricko and the others had for a while listened to S1, an obscure rapper from Örebro whose song 'Sommar' ('Summer') was popular among teenagers in Östermalm. None of them knew then that the intro was a sampling of the saxophonist Jonas Knutsson. Anyway, the melody was nice – Tim twisted it around and used it as a drop in 'Dear Boy'.

Those were the type of things he wanted to play and discuss when Robb Harker or someone else came into the room, rather than talking about his boring pancreas.

The record was gonna be so fucking insane.

He emailed Neil Jacobson to find out if there had been any progress with rock singer John Fogerty and discussed changes to 'Liar Liar'. He composed a new drop for 'Addicted to You' that he thought gave it a nice Daft Punk feel.

In addition to the usual road crew, a young filmmaker was on the trip. Levan Tsikurishvili had been hired to make a documentary for Swedish Television, which would focus on Avicii's and At Night's work for the Swedish charity Hungerhjälpen. Tim invited the filmmaker into his room, where the men in blue coats were examining their patient's stomach with an ultrasound.

Just like their colleagues in New York, the doctors pointed out that Tim should not drink alcohol at all – one of the reasons the pancreas had become inflamed again was undoubtedly drinking.

But they also saw that stones had formed in Tim's gall bladder. A gallstone could block the exit of the pancreas, in which case it would severely worsen the inflammation. Sooner or later, it was possible that Tim would have a problem with this. The doctors therefore wanted to remove the gall bladder with simple keyhole surgery – the gall bladder is one of the organs that the body, with a little adaptation, can do without.

Levan Tsikurishvili filmed inside the hospital while the men in coats explained their views on the matter.

'The conventional teaching is you normally take your gall bladder out before you go home from the hospital admission. The reason being that you don't get another attack in the meantime.'

'Yeah.'

'We understand your situation and that you're in the middle of a world tour and whatnot. We think at some point you need your gall bladder out – whether that be while you're here or on tour or when you're home, it's up to you really.'

Tim wanted to push forward, if only for the sake of the audience. On Wednesday, he therefore left the hospital without having any surgery. No fucking gall bladder would stop him. You had to work hard; he had learned that from Arash early on. If he only got enough painkillers to cope with the three remaining gigs in Australia, he should be fine. He just had to brace himself for a few more days.

Now he and Robb Harker were sitting in a car in Melbourne, Tsikurishvili's camera capturing the scene.

'Future is asking if there is any chance you could do a, like, phone interview,' the agent asked as he went through his emails on his mobile phone.

The festival organisers wanted to get the news out that their main attraction had left the hospital and wondered if it was possible to arrange half an hour when radio stations could call and do interviews.

'Would you be up for them in like two hours? Twelve thirty?'

Tim didn't answer, just mumbled something with an empty gaze before his eyes crossed and he went out with his head against the car window.

Production manager Charlie Alves met them at the hotel. He had never seen Tim like this before. Hollow-eyed and foggy, he stumbled up to the hotel room. The questions about the stage production would have to wait.

The youth radio station Triple J called, the host was keyed up and sounded rushed.

'Avicii is touring around Australia at the moment, with Future Music Festival,' he panted out. 'He had to pull out of Brisbane and Perth last weekend, cos he was taken to hospital. He's on the phone tonight. How you doing, man? Hello!'

'Hi.'

'How are you feeling?'

'I'm okay.'

'You're better now, right?'

'I am better now, yes.'

'Okay, cos that's the question on all of Australia's lips tonight. And that is: are you feeling okay, the tummy pain has gone away?'

'Yes.'

'Now, was this like stomach cramps?'

'No, I have to remove my gall bladder. It's ... It's ... very serious. It's one of the most painful things you can have. I was there for six days. Basically, I was scheduled to remove the gall bladder now but I was able to push that until after this tour.'

'You will be back on stage this weekend, right?'

'I ... I will. Yes.'

From: Anki Lidén
To: Tim Bergling
Date: 15 March 2013

Dearest lovely Tim!! Hope you're feeling better and better and that you can soon look forward to feeling healthy and strong and making your fantastic music and not feeling PRESSURE about anything!! You are so unbelievably talented at what you do and the MOST IMPORTANT thing is that you feel for yourself what you want – with the number of shows, when you want to be at home with friends in Sthlm and just have a normal life, YOU decide and don't even THINK about the money – it means soooo little compared to health, friends, love!! You know we love you wherever you are in the world.

Mum

> **From: Tim Bergling**
> **To: Anki Lidén**
> **Date: 17 March 2013**
>
> I know Mummy, love you more than anything else too! See you soon!!! Feeling better, haven't needed to take painkillers for three days and feeling better and better mentally too!
>
> kisses!!

Five days after the last gig in Australia, Tim flew to Miami, to perform once again at the Ultra Music Festival. Compared to four years earlier, when Tim was in town for the first time and played at Laidback Luke's party, the United States was a completely different musical landscape.

There was a new buzzword that suddenly appeared all over the country: EDM. The acronym stood for 'electronic dance music', and was now used by media and the record industry as a collective name for everything from progressive big room to techhouse. Deadmau5 graced the cover of *Rolling Stone*, Kaskade had sold out the Staples Center in Los Angeles, and the American audience had become acquainted with the young German Zedd. Dutch Afrojack and Hardwell were big stars by now. The fact that the business magazine *Forbes* had started publishing an annual list of the world's highest paid DJs was telling. According to the magazine, Tiësto, who led the pack, could now make just over $250,000 for each gig.

The scope of the scene was also felt here in Miami, where Ultra had booked over three hundred artists. Tim and Arash had discussed how they would succeed in standing out in such an enormous context. It required something that was on the verge of provocative – then even those who were not already devoted fans of house music would hear about the upcoming album.

Avicii would not be just one in the crowd, ever.

Therefore, on 22 March 2013, he and a whole crew of other musicians would do something historic. Tim was tense and impatient when they all gathered in the green room, which was housed on a luxury yacht moored at one end of Bayfront Park. Guitarist Mike Einziger had brought the drummer and bassist with him from his rock band, which meant that almost half of Incubus was present. That was big enough in and of itself.

Einziger's fiancée Ann Marie Calhoun would play the banjo and violin. In addition, Mac Davis, Audra Mae, Dan Tyminski and Aloe Blacc had travelled here. A motley and odd gang, but that was the whole point.

The plan was for Tim to start with a completely conventional set, which lulled the audience into peace. Then they would blow the minds of fifty thousand people with epic bluegrass played on acoustic instruments.

Record company manager Per Sundin had booked his own section on the festival's VIP stand and ordered buckets of Red Bull, vodka and sparkling wine. The northerner felt like a rooster with all the most important people at Universal swarming around him – here were execs from South America, the marketing department, and Neil Jacobson and his gang from Los Angeles.

Avicii had led the way into a new market for Sundin, who had now brought a whole bunch of Swedes on to the company's roster: Alesso, Otto Knows, Nause, Dada Life. In the record industry, EDM was talked about as if it were salvation – the first style of music that led to real financial returns after the dramatic fall in record sales a decade earlier. Internally, Sundin's star rose fast, he had become known as the Swede who knew what the teens wanted.

The dream of getting a number one in America with a discovery from the office in Stockholm felt more alive than ever when the gig started revving up on stage. True to form, Tim mixed wildly between genre buddies such as Nicky Romero, Bingo Players and AN21 and more unexpected bootlegs of, for example, rapper Pharoahe Monch's song 'Simon Says' and indie rockers Florence + the Machine.

The devotion of fifty thousand sweaty people was all-encompassing.

Then the last note in 'Levels' sounded out, the lights went out and darkness descended over the park.

The audience was puzzled. Was it over already?

Some tried to start a cheer, others just looked around confused and began to move towards the exit.

Suddenly a spotlight came on.

In the bright red light, a guy in an old man's cap was singing country music.

Feeling my way through the darkness
guided by a beating heart
I don't know where the journey will end
but I know where to start

Aloe Blacc's singing in 'Wake Me Up' did not get the response that the crew behind the stage had hoped for.

Out of sight of the audience, Audra Mae began to wonder what she had got herself into. Out on stage, the poor drummer banged for everything he was worth, the banjo melodies fluttered beautifully, but it did not lift off.

Not at all.

In the next song, Mac Davis stepped out on stage, his voice a little rusty and off, almost screaming his first few notes. When the gang reached 'Hey Brother', the audience began to boo and whistle.

Confusion filled the air; many spectators were outraged. So they started tweeting.

Avicii is so fucking shit at #Ultralive what is he even doing?

I'd rather shit in my hands and clap than watch this shit

Stop wasting time with these singers and play some banging beats!?

WTF is happening during Avicii's set? Seriously, banjos?

Afterwards, no one among the musicians really understood what had just happened.

'People may not understand it now,' Emily Goldberg shouted in Tim's ear as the squad moved towards the green rooms. 'But I promise you, all these songs are bangers!'

'But just look,' Tim answered, holding up his phone.

He read some of the comments on Twitter aloud.

Back on the yacht, he threw himself on to a sofa in the corner. He was furious. Arash was rather elated. Everything had gone according to plan! They wanted to send shockwaves even outside the house world, and they had succeeded with flying colours. In five days, public opinion would change, the manager was sure of that. Eventually, everyone would realise that Tim was the great innovator.

Tim frantically searched for recordings and clips from the audience. Maybe there had been a problem with the light? Or was the volume too low? Why was everyone so angry?

'Let's go for a cigarette,' said production manager Charlie Alves. 'You'll feel better if you move a little.'

They sat out on the foredeck and looked out towards the industrial area on the other side of the water. Tiësto's music thumped faintly behind their backs: he had gone on stage right after Avicii.

'I just don't get it,' said Tim.

Charlie reached for Tim's phone, tried to get him to let it go.

'Man, that's their fault, the crowd's. This isn't on you. You played some fabulous music, period. People just aren't used to acoustic instruments, that's all.'

It was easy to see the similarities with Bob Dylan's famous England tour five decades earlier, even though the situation was now the opposite.

In 1966, Dylan had become a young icon, hailed as the great

protest singer of his generation, a pacifist with pathos. That spring he went on tour. As long as Dylan was alone, accompanied only by his acoustic guitar, everything went well. But once he invited his backing band on stage, the audience changed. They booed and whistled, feeling betrayed by the roaring volume of the instruments. An electric guitar was considered out of place and superficial; playing the old folk songs with an entire rock band was blasphemous. Self-absorbed music, not to mention bourgeois.

'Judas!'

It was a man in Manchester who shouted, loudly and scornfully, before Dylan started the new song 'Like A Rolling Stone'. A camera captured how Dylan scoffed in response, before turning to his band and asking them to play the next song extra fucking loud.

It had become a classic moment in music history, something that was replayed over and over again in documentaries, precisely because the exchange over the years had taken on a deeper meaning.

Charlie Alves lit another smoke.

Who would end up on the right side of history? Who was the brave visionary in this context? It was not the backward-looking people in the audience, the ones who clung stubbornly to nostalgia.

Tim nodded.

'Yes, I guess it's all right,' he said. 'I know these are good songs. But I just wanna understand how this happened.'

Then he disappeared back into his screen.

The next morning, Emily woke up early. She went out on the balcony of the hotel room for a while, worried and frustrated, before crawling back in beside her boyfriend.

While Tim stretched out in bed, she hugged him as hard as she could.

'They just don't understand. Your music is outstanding. Don't doubt that.'

Tim was silent. When he met Emily's gaze, his eyes were glistening with tears.

He sat up in bed, with the computer in his lap, and continued to scroll.

Was that @Avicii's way of saying he wants to switch genres? . . . feel free. I'm not sure many of us would miss ya too much.

Is it me or is @AVICII really thin? Looks like he's not eating or on drugs.

Avicii you suck ass.

WHEN JESSE WAITS looked out over the pool area at his nightclub XS, he was proud of the kind of guests that the EDM wave had attracted to Las Vegas.

Four years after opening, XS grossed around $80 million a year, which was the highest sum for a nightclub in the entire United States. The place had become the prime hub for a mixed bag of fashion models, sports stars, gamblers and financiers from Silicon Valley. This was largely due to the fact that Waits had managed to attract almost every headliner in house music. When the two founders of Instagram sold their company to Facebook, it was here they went to take a selfie with Avicii and Deadmau5. Star actors like Leonardo DiCaprio and Tom Hardy were among the regulars, British Prince Harry had started taking DJ lessons and came here to party.

But in the spring of 2013, Jesse Waits was beginning to face competition.

He had already sensed trouble when the contracts for the spring season were to be written and the agent who represented the majority of the biggest artists had stopped answering his calls. In the end, it was the Scotsman Calvin Harris who had whispered that there would soon be a new challenger in the city.

With a pounding heart, Jesse Waits had driven to his boss Steve Wynn's house and told him about the rumours: the casino hotel MGM Grand would apparently start a competing club.

The really worrying thing was that in the background there seemed to be capital on a whole new level. Jesse didn't know much, but rumours were that a sultan or prince was involved. His boss made a few calls and they soon realised that behind the investment in the MGM Grand was a fund in the United Arab Emirates run by Mansour bin Zayed Al Nahyan, brother of the Crown Prince of the wealthy oil kingdom. Five years earlier, the same royal had been behind the purchase of the British football club Manchester City, and with new top players for hundreds of millions, the club had just won the English league for the first time in over forty years.

Now the sheikhs clearly wanted to enter the house music scene. Several of the biggest artists were rumoured to have been offered around $300,000 a night to play at MGM Grand's new club Hakkasan.

'I see,' Jesse's boss said when he hung up. 'Look, these guys don't give a fuck about money. They have enough not to care. It's all about ego, they just wanna win.'

More sharks had begun circling in the water. *Billboard Magazine*, the prime publication for the music industry in the United States, had recently graced its cover with an elderly man in a leather jacket and white moustache. Robert Sillerman was unknown to most fans, but this was a man who had fundamentally changed the music industry.

In the 1980s, he had bought over a hundred local radio stations in the United States before venturing into concert venues and booking companies with a similar strategy: take over, merge, refine and corporatise. By the turn of the millennium, he had resold his empire for almost $4.5 billion. The company was named Live Nation and became the world's largest concert organiser.

Now Sillerman said that he had around a billion dollars that he intended to invest in dance music.

'I know nothing about EDM,' the sixty-year-old said in the article, even though he had already sent out proposals to eighteen companies stating that he had an interest in buying them. 'But I sit in the meetings. I meet the people whose places we're buying. And I haven't a fucking clue what they do or what they're talking about. Not a clue. And I love it.'

It shocked the industry that someone was so casually flaunting his ignorance about what he intended to invest billions in.

Tim Bergling had mixed feelings about the rapid development.

Older men in suits competing to be the first to package a new youth movement was of course a sign of the influence of house music.

At the same time, the development affected the perception of him. The prejudice that a DJ was not a real musician lived on to a very high degree, not least in Sweden where the rock tradition still cast long shadows. In David Guetta or Tiësto or Avicii, critics saw driven businessmen without artistic ambitions. Beats created on speculation. Tim always dismissed that notion. He argued that he made exactly the kind of music he had fallen in love with in his bedroom – it was the financial interests that had come to him and the house scene, not the other way around.

But seen in that light, the gigs in Las Vegas could feel vulgar and tasteless. Nowhere was the shameless blurring between business and art more clearly expressed than at XS, where many of the visitors sought a social context rather than music. The price tag on the bottle was more important to some guests than who was in the booth.

At the same time, Tim appreciated his friendship with Jesse Waits, and it could not be denied that it was easy money. Before the 2013 season – while the new club Hakkasan attracted

173

several other performers – Tim signed a contract with XS: during the spring he would play in Las Vegas every Friday for around $325,000 per gig.

It was during such a weekend that Tim got a glimpse of his new girlfriend.

Racquel Bettencourt had flown in with a friend from Los Angeles, where she had moved a couple of years earlier to study interior design.

Racquel and her friend loved the new music from Sweden – Swedish House Mafia, Alesso and Avicii – and then there was no better place to party than Las Vegas.

For several years Bettencourt had worked as a bartender in her hometown of Toronto, and through her work at nightclubs she had got to know Jesse Waits. The two girlfriends therefore moved comfortably and relaxed in the Las Vegas nightlife, where female beauty was hard currency and girls entered the clubs for free or at a reduced fee. The newly rich men in the bar would never spend tens of thousands of dollars if there were no women to impress.

Around the stage at XS was a VIP area surrounded by ropes. There, the celebrities could party by themselves, while their presence made the regular guests feel that they were in the company of stars.

As David Guetta was playing upstairs, Tim's and Racquel's eyes met for a moment. It was just a brief glance, but Tim's interest was piqued.

The weekend before, he had ended up in a big quarrel with Emily, one of those when all the unspoken grudges came to the surface all at once. Emily felt that Tim took all his stress and frustration out on her and Tim felt that Emily didn't understand that the job with the album required his full attention.

Tim was hungry for a fresh start. But he did not dare to approach this stranger and say hi; he had always been too nervous for such things. Instead, it was one of Jesse Waits' colleagues who had to facilitate the connection, after which Tim and Racquel tentatively began to text each other.

When they were both back in Los Angeles, they began to see each other in a late-night restaurant on Santa Monica Boulevard, just below the house Tim rented. Most of the time, it was already midnight when Tim finished in the studio, and as the traffic began to lighten outside the window, Racquel talked about her family back home in Toronto. She had previously been an elite gymnast, but in recent years had become interested in interior design. The courses at the Fashion Institute of Design & Merchandising were her dream education.

In the early hours of the morning, they would take an Uber up to the house in the mountains where they popped popcorn and watched reruns of Jerry Springer's talk show.

Racquel was glad that Tim seemed to be living such a sensible life. A few years earlier she had been partying a lot – far too much, she now felt. She was looking for something quieter and to her great surprise seemed to have found it in a DJ.

Tim, in turn, was amazed at how quickly he felt safe with Racquel. That she was three years older was noticeable with some small things – sometimes he could laugh to himself at how bad she was at choosing the right emojis, for example, but maybe that's how it was when you were twenty-six years old?

The advantage of the age difference was that Racquel seemed to be done with her worst party years and was now looking for something else.

'She is great for me,' Tim wrote to Jesse Waits. 'Rly is.'

A MONTH AFTER the tough gig at the festival in Miami, the winds changed. On 10 April 2013, the guys on Styrmansgatan posted an hour-long file on the music site Soundcloud, with the simple name *Avicii – Promo Mix 2013*.

Here, Tim had collected the new songs in their studio versions, a much more recognisable form for the house audience, and the rumour spread quickly online.

The first song in the mix was a highly unexpected cover. A decade or so earlier, Antony and the Johnsons had made a name for themselves in New York's queer clubs with their fragile songs about demise and darkness. Their 'Hope There's Someone' was a prayer for a comforting life in the hereafter – hardly a song that Swedish House Mafia or Deadmau5 would choose to interpret. Tim had taken this gut-wrenching ballad and let the steady house piano and synths increase in a kind of border-crossing experiment that really shouldn't have worked, but that said a lot about where Avicii was headed.

Without any visible acoustic instruments that stole the spotlight, it was obviously easier for the audience to understand Tim Bergling's vision. All the ill-natured remarks were turned into cheers in the Soundcloud comment section and raised expectations for the album to the max.

It had turned out exactly as Arash Pournouri had predicted.

When 'Wake Me Up' was finally released as the first single in June 2013, the dividend was huge. The song went straight to number one on the influential singles chart in the UK and sold over a quarter of a million copies in one week – the fastest-selling single in a long time in the country. In the United States, the song ranked among the top twenty-five on the Billboard charts before it even started playing on the radio.

The light guitar strum that opened the song invited a whole new audience to Avicii's world. Even the rock guys who stubbornly claimed that a DJ just pressed buttons had to give in. The shift that a few years earlier had begun with David Guetta, Calvin Harris and Swedish House Mafia had now once and for all been confirmed by Avicii. Dance music was no longer seen as instrumental music with a sampled chorus. It had become pure pop, legitimate for all ages, even played on rock radio stations.

In this turbulent time, Tim Bergling was again travelling through Europe.

The road crew had started checking him in at hotels under the pseudonym Mark Walls. It was a security measure, but despite trying to move as anonymously as possible, chaos erupted wherever they went. Phone cameras in the air, people running, girls crying, people pushing and screaming and a newly hired bodyguard extending his body as much as he could to protect the star.

As Racquel Bettencourt was finishing up her final classes at the design school in Los Angeles, she followed the tour from a distance. At night, her new boyfriend sent messages that made her not only surprised but also worried.

Tim told how he relied on Red Bull to be able to work out the final tweaks to the album. Once he went to bed, sleep still did not arrive. It didn't matter, Tim thought, because he had in return got three new songs ready.

Racquel, who was completely new to this universe, thought the whole picture seemed off-balance. How had this destructive work ethic set in? Why did Tim not say no?

Over WhatsApp, her boyfriend described how he sat awake for two days in a row and then went straight up on stage, then ate a pizza and was finally able to fall asleep. His dreams were about the apocalypse: zombies attacking and a meteorite crashing down on Earth and wiping out all life.

Then he was jerked awake again.

'Almost 48h soon,' Tim wrote. 'Forcing myself.'

'You should sleep,' Racquel tried.

'Need 2 more hours.'

There was another problem of a more logistical nature. A large number of the gigs that summer had been booked before 'Wake Me Up' was released and had catapulted Avicii to a whole new level. The small beach restaurants on the Mediterranean had actually been overcrowded already last summer – for someone who had just become one of the world's biggest pop stars, the premises were far too small.

The French nightclub Le Bâoli was a good example. The space was intended for a few hundred people, at most a thousand. Now half of Cannes tried to squeeze themselves in, hoping to take a selfie where they appeared in the same picture as Avicii.

The mirrored roof made the floor and ceiling merge, and from his place in the booth, Tim felt crammed in from both above and below. Arms in the air, flashes from phone cameras, suddenly a hand on his head from someone who reached into the booth.

Racquel had joined the tour and reacted to how much her boyfriend was sweating. That he did it while performing was no surprise, but even when they slept, Tim woke up soaking wet and anxious. When Racquel tried to crawl closer to hold him, he turned dismissively to the other side of the bed.

During the day, Tim complained of a splitting headache.

In addition, his appetite seemed to have disappeared. Racquel tried to ignore her fears. She was probably just imagining things. After all, this was a completely dry tour – Arash had made sure that no promoters served alcohol and even the minibars in the hotel rooms had been cleared out of spirits and wine bottles in advance. The manager had given strict instructions to everyone who worked with the stage production not to drink near Tim.

But the longer the summer went on, the harder it was for Racquel to ignore her concerns.

Tim had told her that he had been taking strong painkillers before they got to know each other, pills he had got after his hospital stay in Australia. He had stopped taking medication, he said, but still he kept complaining of migraines, continued to sweat. He seemed down. Racquel, who had been so relieved that her boyfriend did not drink wine or party, began to suspect that there was something else beneath the surface.

An evasion that she had not previously felt.

Something was weighing on Tim, something shameful and secret.

In the beginning of August 2013, the couple went on a quick visit to the small Swedish town of Sunne. In the summer heat of Värmland stood a barn dressed up for a party – Tim's brother Anton was getting married, and the wedding was to take place in the bride's home district. Her mother and sisters had sewn white covers for the chairs and hung up tablecloths that floated under the roof. Anki Lidén had borrowed a folk costume that was several sizes too small, but with the yellow apron on, it still looked traditional and fitting.

When Tim came walking between the ash trees and birches on the gravel road that led up to the homestead, he appeared almost like a mirage to his mother. He had arranged a break of a couple of days between Marbella and Ibiza, had his suit on and Racquel by his side, the girlfriend that Tim had already sent pictures of to show Anki how beautiful she was.

A bell rang from a tower and the bride and her maids came thundering in a military jeep, Anton rode in with one of his best friends in a sports car with the top down.

Rose petals and cheers, before the skies suddenly opened.

As the guests ran back and forth looking for umbrellas and covering up the audio equipment, Klas Bergling felt his son squinting at him.

A stolen glance, barely noticeable.

What did Tim want to say?

A couple of days earlier, they had fussed via email. After a promotional stunt in Hungary for the energy drink Burn, Tim had a stomach pain once again. He had been examined by a doctor in Belgium before he was given painkillers and went on stage again. They had argued about that. Klas knew nothing about drugs, but was worried that Tim was constantly getting new pills for various reasons.

After the spring hospital stay in Australia, Tim had hired a private doctor in Los Angeles. The system was completely different from what Klas was used to in Sweden, where healthcare was still largely public and tax funded. Instead, they paid the physician in the United States a large sum of money in annual premiums, and the doctor in return promised to be able to quickly help Tim and prescribe the drugs that were deemed necessary. But maybe there was too much medicine?

Tim had shrugged off the objections. That he was put on pills at the hospital in Belgium was nothing strange, he was in pain.

In the rain, Klas tried to read his son. He looked insecure in some way, searching.

Klas dismissed the discomfort. Today was Anton's big day.

Anki only reacted when they sat down at the table. While the groom's friends gave funny speeches, she looked sideways to the party on her right.

Suddenly, Tim's head fell straight down to his chest. He closed his eyes for a moment before straightening his back and picking up the cutlery.

What was that?

Right after dinner, Tim came over to his mother and gave her a long hug. He was so tired, he said, just jet lag. He and Racquel would go to bed.

The party continued, Anton and his friends performed celebrated versions of Swedish classics such as 'Gyllene Skor' ('Golden Shoes') and 'Jag vill vara din, Margareta' ('I Want To Be Yours, Margareta'), it was an enchanting wedding night.

But Anki had a hard time being fully present.

Had Tim really fallen asleep there at the table? In the middle of dinner? And if so, why?

The next day it was as if nothing had happened. Tim was alert and clear-headed, in the back seat he cuddled with Racquel as they all drove together towards the airport. Later that Sunday night, Tim had two gigs booked in Ibiza.

Klas and Anki checked into a hotel in Karlstad and talked about the previous day. It was difficult to take in what they had actually witnessed. The worst thing had been the eyes. That attentive and curious look that Tim used to have was gone. Instead, he had been dim and absent.

His parents did not become much the wiser by talking about it, after a while they even doubted if anything had actually happened.

Could they have been wrong?

After all, Tim had been in a great mood when they'd waved him off a few hours earlier. Playful and lively.

Maybe he'd just needed a good night's sleep, especially now that he was rushing around between all the summer festivals?

A week later, Tim and Racquel were lying on a hotel roof in Mallorca; Tim wanted to get some sun before the night's work.

Since the wedding, he had done Mykonos and Marbella once more; he had pulled off a festival in Portugal and then one in Denmark. Maybe he had been to Italy too? Everything blended together.

Tim spoke to Arash on the phone. Racquel didn't understand what they were saying, but heard the irritation in Tim's voice. He was tired of the insane flying, here and there across continents: Israel on a Thursday, two gigs in Las Vegas on Saturday, the following week London and then back to the United States.

'I'm starting to hate this,' Tim said when he hung up. 'I hate performing. This wasn't what I set out to do in the beginning.'

'So, what is it that you want to do?' Racquel asked.

'I just wanna make music.'

WHEN AUTUMN CAME, Tim walked through the pale-yellow aisles of Trader Joe's in Los Angeles, past coolers filled with pre-packaged burritos, organic tofu and large pieces of papaya. He found the pickled salmon and picked up a couple of packets of cream cheese.

He could barely remember the last time he'd been in a grocery store. Now such a simple thing as buying breakfast felt like an act of resistance. After a few gigs in Germany and England, there was finally some room in the schedule, and he had time to have breakfast with his girlfriend.

By mid-September 2013, the album *True* had at last been released, and it had been well received, sometimes exuberantly, even by newspapers that normally didn't care about dance music.

The rock critics liked the playful wink to the glam rockers Sweet in the song 'Shame On Me' or the bouncing organ in 'Liar Liar'. The vast majority seemed to see Tim's sincere intentions behind the cross-genre hybrid, perceiving that there was no calculation in his way of borrowing. On the contrary, with his sense of melody, he injected new power into old traditions.

'Don't see *True* as the album in which dance music imports the sounds of the American heartland into the club in hopes of digging up new audiences,' the *New York Times* wrote in its appreciative review. 'See it as the one in which country takes its place front and center in global pop.'

Even the Swedish newspapers had finally woken up: 'Avicii

is on his own level in commercial house music. In fact, he has already left it behind,' wrote *Aftonbladet*.

'The guy is completely unique,' it said in *Expressen*.

And now it was not blogs and giggly radio hosts who got in touch, but reputable outlets such as *Rolling Stone, Billboard Magazine* and the *Guardian*, who booked interviews for major profiles of the brave twenty-four-year-old who dared to take acoustic instruments into an increasingly uniform dance world.

Tim picked out more food and tossed it in the cart. He had become fond of toasting bagels and eating them with black caviar, which he scooped right out of the jar with a spoon. He and Racquel had rented a fully furnished apartment across the street from the grocery store, in the outskirts of Beverly Hills. It was quite sterile and dull really, but still something that resembled a fixed point. The last few weeks had been full of little discoveries – Racquel had taught Tim how to refuel a car, she had cooked both cauliflower and seabass and it had tasted surprisingly good. Their favourite recipe was oven-baked salmon with chilli sauce, maple syrup and coriander. Who knew that fish could be so good!

They had gone to The Valley to look at some dogs, and of course come home with a little puppy. Like the previous one, this was a Pomeranian, but Oliver's fur was as red as a fox. He walked around on the floor, pooping everywhere, chewing on pillows and clothes, but still gave the place a feeling of home.

One morning Tim was dancing around the kitchen in his Björn Borg underwear and a T-shirt. For the first time in a long time, Racquel saw the guy she had fallen so in love with six months earlier.

'Baby, we need to try to stick to this now,' she said.

'What do you mean?'

'You should look at the touring schedule and see how many days you need between each show. You have to speak up about how you feel, not just to me but to everybody else.'

Tim nodded. He had seen more and more clearly how even people around him had suffered from the state of emergency that never ended. The last time he was in Stockholm he had not seen any of his siblings, and his big sister Linda had got pissed off. Who could blame her? Living like he had been, being awake all night, buried in thirteen projects at once, no longer only affected him. In fact, Tim barely knew his nephews. Even if it was hard to admit, he was not a good uncle. Racquel was right. He had to stop pretending that everything was fine, it must not be like this again.

He spoke with the guys at the office in Stockholm and they agreed in 2014 to focus only on the festivals that made the biggest impression and that Tim liked the most. Ultra in Miami, of course, Stereosonic in Australia, Tomorrowland in Belgium. Maybe Lollapalooza. Just over ninety gigs were booked for next year, it felt manageable. Tim declined to be on Jimmy Kimmel's talk show during the autumn; he declined even when Jesse Waits contacted him with a lucrative offer to play at his twin brother's newly opened club in Miami.

It actually felt great saying no, even when it was Jesse who asked. 'Just wanted to say I do appreciate you as a friend and you looking out for me,' Tim wrote to the club manager and continued:

It's just been a crazy fucking year with a lot to take in both with my physical health and career etc and I've had such a crazy pace and haven't rly had a home either so even though I've been working so much and the career's been going great sometimes it just feels like it's work for nothing and never-ending. I already feel better after just a couple days here in LA and it's just temporary. I'm not gonna let the schedule get to this again and finally I feel like everyone in my team are on the same page when it comes to that.

That same autumn, singer Chris Martin was sitting at home at his piano. It was a special and somewhat tumultuous time for the Englishman, who had recently moved to Los Angeles with his wife Gwyneth Paltrow and their two children. Now the ten-year marriage was about to end.

For a couple of months, Chris Martin had been recording new songs with his band Coldplay, all of which were unusually melancholy and intimate. Slow farewells, changed feelings, the realisation that life did not always turn out as planned.

This evening he was thinking of a song title.

'A Sky Full Of Stars.'

The words had been there for a while; they seemed to fit together, creating a beautiful image. Chris Martin often worked like this: a phrase could live with him for months, or even years, waiting to find a home in the right tune. Now the music poured out of him. He immediately felt that the song had potential, it could become a warm and open door into an otherwise rather sore album about lost love.

At a festival in Scotland, Chris Martin had discovered what a grip house music had taken on the world. He had been standing on the stage and singing a sparse ballad when he suddenly perceived a familiar melody in the distance. It took a while before Martin understood what he was hearing – from another stage, Swedish House Mafia were simultaneously playing their version of Coldplay's 'Every Teardrop Is A Waterfall'. Very confusing altogether. But the moment had made the singer curious about dance music, it seemed to create exactly the feeling of community that Chris Martin himself strived for in everything he did. Coldplay was often criticised for just that, that they made such universal music that the personal aspect was erased. On the other hand, it was for the same reason that they had become one of the world's biggest groups. They were a distinct arena band, one that shone most brightly when the music became a collective experience.

Chris now needed someone who could give 'A Sky Full Of Stars' a modern feel and so they met in the studio The Village – Chris Martin and Tim Bergling. From the street, the place didn't look like much to the world, but here everyone from Etta James to The Beach Boys and Aerosmith had recorded.

Chris Martin played his naked demo, with only piano and vocals, and then Tim started to colour. That's how Chris thought of it – Tim not only added a beat, he rearranged the song, made it blossom. Who needed dozens of studio musicians when Tim had his imagination and a sound card?

The magical thing in Martin's eyes was how Tim managed to make the song so pumping and contemporary and yet still kept the heart of it, that fragile thing. There was no doubt for any of them: Tim had taken a simple home demo and turned it into a number one smash.

That same night, Tim had a gig at XS. The plane there had to wait while Tim finished his sketch. When he landed in Las Vegas shortly after midnight, just an hour before the show, he was picked up by production manager Charlie Alves.

Tim threw himself into the back seat.

'We won't have time to eat, we just gotta go straight to the club,' Charlie said.

'That's fine,' said Tim.

He leaned forward, smiled at Charlie.

'You might wanna know why I was late?'

Tim asked for the cord for the car's speaker system and plugged it into his computer. Charlie heard the unmistakable Avicii sound, that swoosh in the beginning. Then came a voice that he first had a hard time placing.

After a while, it was impossible to miss who it was.

'Holy shit, Tim. Is that Chris Martin?'

Tim sat contentedly playing the piano in the air.

'Yep. I just made this for Coldplay.'

One evening, Tim and Racquel were on a house tour of The Bird Streets in the Hollywood Hills, where Tim had rented a house with his ex-girlfriend.

Just a few blocks higher than that property, on Blue Jay Way, stood a house built almost entirely in glass.

When Tim and Racquel went out on to the balcony, it was as if they were floating in the air. The boundaries between outside and inside, sky and earth, were dissolved. Down in Santa Monica, the mountains melted in the pink evening sun, on the other side of the huge city they saw the Pacific Ocean.

The house had been built from the ground up five years earlier, with dramatic angles and steps, commissioned by a Brit who had made a fortune on Toni & Guy's haircare products. The property was divided by a long narrow pool that created a ravine between the two ends of the house. To get from the bedroom to the kitchen, you could walk over a kind of stone-paved bridge – just the kind of fun effect that Tim loved.

And then there were the neighbours. Down to the right was the house of actor Keanu Reeves, you could see his roof from here; and a little further down the hill Leonardo DiCaprio threw his parties. Singer Robin Thicke had moved into the same street, as had eccentric Instagram celebrity Dan Bilzerian.

Tim looked around. Six hundred square metres that he could put his touch on. Surrealist paintings by Salvador Dalí and René Magritte on the walls, he envisioned, and a totally decked-out studio. He could invite both his sister and Mike Einziger here without being ashamed. Here he could start a family eventually and maybe even begin working as just a producer.

Life would be calmer now, they had all agreed on that.

'Tim, this is crazy,' Racquel said. 'We're gonna need to do a lot of work to get this place looking right.'

She looked at the red and white decor – beyond the house itself, the shampoo billionaire obviously had no taste. Did it really make sense to buy a place for over $15 million and then tear everything out?

'We should look for something smaller,' she tried.

Tim was lost in his thoughts, his eyes fixed on the greenery of Beverly Hills. Far down there, life was buzzing, silently.

'This is the most beautiful view I've ever seen,' he said.

It could not be so difficult to get the money, could it? By this time, 'Wake Me Up' had climbed to number one on the charts in sixty-three countries. The song had garnered over 160 million views on YouTube and sold almost six million copies.

'I'm getting this house,' he said.

Even women who's been through childbirth describe the pancreatitis pain as much more intense and severe. Everyone around me understood that this was not a choice I made, they were indeed concerned – particularly my father – and so was I.

I hated being on oxycodone to hydrocodone to tramadol. I can remember a couple of nice experiences with pain medication when I was hospitalised the first and second time – but then again it was rather the fact that I got a real proper break with everyone's support and care that was the nice sensation I remember. Not the headaches/ lack of appetite/nausea/lack of control that I got from the pain medication.

AS 2014 APPROACHED, Tim Bergling was lying in bed upstairs in the apartment on the edge of Beverly Hills. The heat passed through him in pulsating waves, the sheets wet with sweat. But he was still shivering, clenching his knuckles until they turned white. He grabbed another blanket, but was still freezing.

The most unpleasant thing was that creeping sensation in his legs. It tingled and itched, as if it was coming from the inside.

By now Racquel understood what was going on – Tim had told both her and his family.

Throughout the summer and autumn, he had been taking opioids. He did not really want to, but every time he tried to get off them, the tremors had returned, the sweating, the discomfort, the pain in his stomach.

So he would take another pill.

Even though he knew it wasn't sustainable, it had been impossible to quit, especially on tour. He couldn't be on stage with withdrawal running through his body.

Now he would soon go on tour in Europe and play the songs from *True*. Before that, Tim had decided he would stop taking each and every pill.

To help, he had been prescribed a type of antidote by his American doctor. Suboxone was developed to manage and get out of an opioid addiction and did not give the same euphoric feeling as the painkillers he had previously taken. But buprenorphine, the active ingredient in Suboxone, was itself an opioid, only milder than oxycodone. The doctor had explained that it was therefore important to slowly taper off this medicine as well. Tim's body needed to gradually get used to not having the drug in the system, otherwise he risked suffering from vomiting, fever and severe restlessness.

But Tim had a hard time sticking to the recommendations. He was impatient and wanted to get rid of every pill, including the antidote, and phased them out as quickly as he could possibly manage.

After five days in bed things were at their worst, the headache cracking in his skull.

'Have this gnarly feeling and wanna punch myself almost,' Tim wrote to guitarist Mike Einziger. Still, it felt worth it. 'I'm very agitated and stuff but I'm sure it'll all just get better and better from here.'

And finally one day, when Tim had finished sweating and being tormented, he came downstairs with colour in his cheeks and a spring in his step.

He had made it, he felt invincible.

With great energy, Tim now began to look into decorating the house they had done a viewing for and which he had decided to buy. Bookcases, baths, office furniture and ottomans. Different types of mirrors, fixtures, wallpaper and a solid wood chair shaped like a rhino. Everything was in white and black, with smaller accents in steel. Together with Racquel, he went to the industrial areas in The Valley to look for the right material for the kitchen island. Tim fell in love with a marble that had been quarried in Spain, with white veins winding through the pitch-black stone. It would be perfect as an accent wall at the short end of the pool.

*

Now, at the beginning of 2014, Tim Bergling thought that most things were exciting, now that he had finally broken out of his pill habit. Even when *American Idol* got in contact and wanted to have him as a guest coach in the TV talent show, he reacted positively. He wanted to go to the People's Choice Awards when he was nominated. He himself suggested that he expand his commitment to Ralph Lauren.

He already wanted to start planning participation in various radio shows to promote the next album, which he wanted to release exactly a year after *True*, in just over six months.

He had picked up steam and was eager to continue to prove that he was not just a DJ who happily waved to the audience. He was a songwriter, a composer, someone Chris Martin asked for advice.

And after all the successes, the door was suddenly open to more idols than the singer in Coldplay. Tim had Sting and Jon Bon Jovi try out 'No Pleasing A Woman', a song he wrote with Mike Einziger. He worked with Billie Joe Armstrong from the punk group Green Day and Serj Tankian from the metal band System of a Down.

No song turned out quite as well as he had hoped. Not until Alex Ebert hovered into Jim Henson's classic studio, which had become Tim's favourite hangout in Los Angeles.

Alex Ebert's chest was full of the kind of heightened sensitivity that could only be created by fulfilled dreams combined with a resounding hangover. Just a few hours earlier, the singer had been on stage in Beverly Hills and received a Golden Globe Award for his score to the film *All is Lost*, a drama starring Robert Redford. The night had become surreal. Alex Ebert, a sensitive thirty-five-year-old who usually kept to himself in New Orleans, had said cheers with Matt Damon, received praise from Jim Carrey and partied with rap mogul P Diddy until five in the morning.

The feeling of unreality seemed to be continuing, now that he was sitting at the piano in front of Avicii. Alex Ebert usually made psychedelic hippie rock with his band Edward Sharpe and the Magnetic Zeros, but Arash had suggested a collaboration, and now Ebert was playing the skeleton of a tune that had been lying dormant for a few years without him really knowing what to do with it.

It sounded like a sad psalm.

Tim immediately threw the computer off his lap and rushed off the couch. Bent over Ebert, he waved his finger in the air.

'Play that again. Is it aaa-daaa-da-da-daaa-da or is it a-da-da-daaa-daa?'

'Shit, I don't know,' said Alex, unused to someone who was so incredibly meticulous already at the demo stage.

Ebert, thinking in pictures as he wrote lyrics, saw a faint shimmer from a streetlamp in front of him. A lone man there in the light. The wind was blowing.

Tim wanted to squeeze the very best words out of him, even here he was exact.

'What kind of wind?' he asked.

For Tim, the song marked a shift. 'For A Better Day', as he and Alex Ebert named the piece, meant a break with the relaxed and sweeping tone that had been present in many of the songs on *True*.

This song was more thumping, had a minimalist bite, was sharper at the edges.

'Trust me, this one's a monster,' Tim summed up to Arash.

Racquel looked at her beloved boyfriend as he sat on the couch with the dog Oliver next to him. He was working on an instrumental song that he had named after her, 'Raqattack'.

Somehow Racquel had always known that he would be able

to get off the medications. Yet she was taken by his strength. That stubbornness that was often Tim's most exhausting trait was also his most beautiful.

Just before they were to leave on the spring tour of Europe, it turned out that Tim had kidney stones. At the hospital, the assessment was made that no intervention was needed, he would probably just pee them out. But he was given two morphine tablets – good to have if he had problems during the trip and did not have time to see a doctor.

Tim put the pills in his pocket and decided to keep them there. He wanted to prove to himself that he could control himself. Could tour with a couple of pills burning in his pocket that he would never take.

They started the tour in Frankfurt, with a show that was well oiled and massive. Charlie Alves pulled out all the stops with dry ice smoke and flames; Harry Bird had outdone himself. Gone were the bouncing circles and winding tunnels; now Tim appeared in front of fabulous tableaux – a roaring lion on the savannah, panning images of a magical forest, burning eagles. The laser beams formed powerful prisms that extended all the way back to the rear seats.

On Valentine's Day, they were in Paris. Tim surprised Racquel with a walk to the Pont des Arts, the bridge where couples in love fastened on padlocks with their initials to eternalise their love. When they got back to the tour bus, it was filled with buckets of red roses all the way along the corridor towards the bedroom.

In Amsterdam, Tim's brothers Anton and David turned up and wanted to watch ice hockey – Sweden was facing Canada in the Olympic final. Tim's crew pulled up a sofa and two armchairs which they placed in the middle of the arena floor. The sound from the game thundered through a speaker system built for tens of thousands of people, and that Sweden lost didn't really matter because the brothers for the first time in a long time got to hang out and goof off. Tim loved it when his brothers laughed.

In Anton's hotel room, Tim recounted how proud he was to have finally overcome the pills.

'That is under control now,' he said. 'I never really wanted to take the shit anyway.'

After a couple of weeks touring, they arrived in Stockholm, where Tim filled Tele2 Arena two nights in a row. He played bootlegs on Swedish classics such as Latin King's rap song 'Snubben' ('The Bloke'), and the final number, 'Wake Me Up', was magnificent: flashing lights from tens of thousands of mobiles as Charlie Alves pushed out a waterfall of fire sparks swirling down from the ceiling.

At At Night, many changes had taken place over the last six months. The largest was physical. Arash Pournouri's management company had moved from Styrmansgatan to one of the capital's most fashionable addresses. Ever since Stockholm had industrialised, Strandvägen had been the majestic connection between the alarming city and the disciplined nature away at the island of Djurgården. Here stood Sweden's national theatre Dramaten, next to exclusive interior design shops, real estate agents and fine restaurants. Here was also a yellow-plastered property covered with cherubs sculpted in French sandstone. In the autumn of 2013, new signs had been put up on the arched façade. Next to the logos of a British law firm and a long-established paper manufacturer, AT NIGHT now shone.

Nothing was missing in the new premises. Next to a tastefully lit reception desk adorned with mirrors stood striking brass tables. A chromed elevator led straight down to the dining room at one of the city's finest restaurants. The crowning glory was the three recording studios, the largest of which was decorated in collaboration with Ralph Lauren. Heavy curtains in burgundy velvet, floor-to-ceiling speakers.

The Swedish business magazines took notice of the new tenant and Arash Pournouri confirmed to the reporters that the 500-square-metre premises had been chosen with care.

They had taken Avicii to the top, now Arash would use the achievement to develop a gathering place for so much more than music. Creators of all kinds would have space here – the outside world would see how significant the Swedish creative industries were.

Arash had started his own record imprint, PRMD, and signed Cazzette, a Swedish duo who, on the manager's advice, always performed with masks designed as cassette tapes over their heads. After Arash got to know Spotify's founder Daniel Ek, Cazzette had become the first in the world to release an album exclusively on a streaming service – their debut album *Eject* had perhaps received more attention for the launch itself than for the music. But that's where he was a champion, Pournouri. He no longer wanted to be called a manager, he told the newspaper *Veckans Affärer*, but an operator. He gave Coca-Cola advice on how to reach a younger target audience and had invested in a Swedish company that had big plans for its vodka brand.

It happened that people from Universal came by with a framed gold disc and a bottle of champagne, eager to celebrate one of Avicii's new sales records. They found the entire At Night office deeply involved in phone calls and emails.

Here they would not celebrate any milestones, here they would run after the next.

Still satisfied by the two triumphant gigs in Stockholm, Tim came to the new premises on Strandvägen in March 2014.

There sat Salem Al Fakir and Vincent Pontare waiting, eager to compose new material together.

As reference points for the next record, Tim had two albums in particular – Pink Floyd's concept album *Dark Side of the Moon* and Michael Jackson's twisted pop on *Thriller*.

These were works with certain points of contact.

The Brits in Pink Floyd had, in the early 70s, been in a break-up phase because their significant member Syd Barrett was feeling worse and was forced to leave the group. Inspired by his mental illness, the remaining members experimented with new synths, recorded clunks from coins and cash registers and played with the bass drum so that it sounded like a beating heart. The lyrics revolved around greed, stress and insanity, a dark contemplation of modern life.

Michael Jackson had of course moved in a completely different genre, but his *Thriller* had been innovative and epic as well. The former child star had reached the age of twenty-three in 1982 and was disillusioned and alone. In a bid to free himself and show his integrity, he had written lyrics about obsessed fans and desperate love for unparalleled pop compositions.

The biggest common denominator between the two records – and what Tim was most impressed by – was the self-confidence. Both albums were absolute classics, by artists who had the courage to create their own universes both acoustically and visually. Without hesitation, Pink Floyd dove into a four-minute nightmare in which a breathless man escaped distorted laughter and growing discomfort. In one of his videos, Michael Jackson turned himself into a werewolf and chased his girlfriend through the night.

In addition, both records had of course sold in unimaginable quantities, broken historic records, and were easily counted as two of the most important albums ever.

That's what Tim Bergling wanted to achieve.

However, he did not talk much with Vincent and Salem about this. It was not necessary. They had come prepared with a riff that was just to build on.

Tim loved the chord progression; 'The Days' immediately felt like a tune made for a sunny afternoon on an American highway. It was a song about celebrating life, one that matched the freedom he felt from finally being rid of the opioids.

THE PROJECTOR ON the other side of the street illuminated the white façade of the SLS Hotel. Outside, a sign as tall as a man was flashing in large letters: AVICII.

Six golf carts were lined up along the sidewalk on South Beach in Miami. The speakers blasted songs from Tim's new remix album, young women in white Avicii tops and leather shorts handed out ice cream to passers-by. Once inside the lobby, the visitor was greeted by black-and-white framed pictures of Tim Bergling – even in the bathrooms his face was plastered on to the mirror wall, so that those who peed could, for a short while, feel like a superstar.

The most expensive double room cost almost $900, but that included a pair of headphones, slippers and a bathing suit, all emblazoned with the Avicii logo.

Filip Holm wiped the sweat from his brow. It had been a hell of a struggle to get the hotel in order and at the same time his inbox continued to scream. Holm, who had toured with Tim for the first few years, was now working on the development of PRMD and LE7ELS, the record imprints that were run out of the office in Stockholm and released the work of other house musicians from all over Europe. Avicii was the springboard, but expansion was just as important. And since the entire industry was in Miami in March, the meetings had come thick and fast. Filip Holm had not slept much in the last twenty-four hours and now it was Thursday evening and At Night's party by the pool had been going on since eleven that morning.

The night before, Ibiza veteran Luciano had been spinning, proving that At Night still was in touch with the ground levels of the culture – Luciano was one of the respected pioneers in house music. Now the main attraction was the Swedish DJ duo Rebecca & Fiona, who were bouncing up on the stage by the pool, one with pink hair, the other with blue. It had ended up just as Filip and the others had hoped for: Paris Hilton was in the audience, the line was winding far down the street. Now they were just waiting for Tim's plane to land. Avicii would close out At Night's party this evening, show that he had arrived in town and was ready for a new triumph at Ultra Music Festival.

Arash Pournouri suddenly told Filip Holm that none of that was going to happen. Tim had gone to hospital.

Again.

Filip's body physically reacted to this information. He went into a secluded room and felt the nausea pour over him. What the hell was going on? He hurried over to the hotel across the street, ran up to his room, into the bathroom, and fell to his knees.

What came out of Filip's throat was a thick mass. Like sticky coffee grounds, solid red against the white toilet porcelain. Clotted, viscous blood. After a while, he lay exhausted on the bathroom floor. He dug for his cell phone and called one of the members of Cazzette.

'Hey, I need help. I think I'm going to die.'

Cazzette's tour manager arrived and lifted Filip off the bathroom floor and dragged him down to a car. The hospital was not far away.

The next day, Filip woke up with electrodes taped to his chest. The doctors had initially suspected that he had an internal bleed, it had been quite chaotic when he came in. Now they had agreed that it was just a massive stomach ulcer. Stress related, apparently.

'Do you know where Tim Bergling is?' Filip asked the doctor. 'He's lying right above you, one floor up.'

For Tim it was nearly a reprise of what happened in Australia one year earlier.

The knives had started stabbing into his back and stomach. He had been rushed to the hospital as soon as they landed and had been anaesthetised with something that made his eyes go out. Racquel had run out of the room crying.

Now she drifted back and forth on polished floors while waiting for the next doctor's rounds, cursing the whole situation. They had actually taken it easy for the majority of the autumn. It had felt like everyone around Tim understood the severity of the situation. And he had been so proud that he had managed without the opioids.

The stress had begun to overwhelm him again a couple of weeks earlier, when he was, together with Salem Al Fakir and Vincent Pontare, working with Madonna. There had been a whole bunch of Swedes in the Henson studio – Madonna posted pictures on Instagram and called them her Viking harem. They wrote and produced the singer's thirteenth album, but it was a collaboration that Tim was not so keen on. Sure, Madonna was always Madonna, but the co-writing had become difficult nonetheless. Tim felt that he had to sit through the nights and work through everything the others had come up with during the days. They did not agree on what style the songs should have and Tim had started to get careless with his diet again, drinking copious amounts of Coca-Cola.

And now he was lying there, with the drip hanging to the right of the bed, next to the bland landscape painting on the wall. The gig at Ultra was cancelled, his appendix had ruptured. That was the most urgent. But the doctors had discovered another complication – Tim's gall bladder was swollen and heavily inflamed.

The fucking gall bladder, Racquel thought. The one that the doctors had already warned him about in Australia a year earlier. Now it needed to be removed once and for all.

After the surgery, the doctors wanted to give Tim painkillers. New opioids.

Tim sat in the hospital bed and tried his best to argue against it. He had managed without these fucking pills for two months now. He had even gone through Europe with a couple of tablets in his pocket, just to prove to himself that he could finally resist them.

He did not want to go back to the creeps, to the cold sweat, did not want to fall asleep at more weddings. Had no desire to slip up again.

Was there really no other way to relieve the pain?

In retrospect it's very obvious, I was too eager and unequipped at the time, we all were, and I just cold turkey'd off the Suboxone, causing severe psychological and physical withdrawals which in itself became a trauma and a sense of emptiness and anxiety, or lump, that would remain still to this day.

IT WAS SUMMER 2014 and Filip Åkesson was pacing around Stockholm with a stinging pain in his arms. He had gone home to be protected from himself – at his parents' house in Bromma, it was impossible for Philgood to go as hard as he used to.

But instead, his body responded by sweating and his head wanted to explode. His mood swung in all possible directions, but most of all Filip was angry. At himself and his parents and at the ugly bastard next to him on the subway.

A couple of years earlier, the pills had made life comfortable. Åkesson, who had otherwise been so revved up, had got into step with life, landed softly on the brown sofa in Los Angeles. When he went out in the sunshine, he had done so with a confidence that made him float across the sidewalk on Sunset Boulevard.

What separated the opioids from everything else Filip had ingested was that only the body felt affected. His head was clear as a mirror while the wonderful butterflies whizzed around in his chest. No one could have guessed that he was high.

The discomfort had only begun when the bottle was about to be emptied. After a while, he did not even have to look but intuitively knew exactly when the ration began to run out. A few days later, the restlessness would creep under his skin. Then the pain in his muscles, the unpleasant twitches in his legs. The disgusting loose stool. The vomiting. An ordinary lunch with his buddies felt forced and annoying and Åkesson started angrily hanging up the phone on people.

One morning he found himself standing outside a strip club at dawn and explaining to an acquaintance that he had to get another fix – right now, immediately. When his friend tried to get him to grab a taxi home, Filip replied with a resounding slap.

The carpet in the apartment in Los Angeles was by now full of sooty holes from cigarette butts. The plates had been smashed when Filip threw them in the bin rather than do the dishes. The clothes lay in a single pile, he lived his days in a musty smell of sweat and dust.

He understood that he had problems with the opioids.

To his surprise, this realisation did not change anything at all.

It had been a long time since he took the drugs in order to be enveloped by the warmth. He now took them only to escape the nausea that was raging in him at this very moment. The pills had taken him hostage, made him an aggressive and moody person. Just the thought of feeling like this one more day was unbearable.

The phone buzzed in his pocket. Filip Åkesson was surprised that it was Tim and that he too was in Stockholm.

It had been a long time since they had seen each other and as they both happened to be in town, they decided to watch a movie, talk shit like before.

It might help him to forget the withdrawal for a while, Filip thought as he took the elevator up to the penthouse on Karlavägen.

It was not a big apartment, but well-planned and stylish. Lacquered black surfaces that gave a feeling of luxury. Tim seemed happy to see his old friend, proudly showing off a tattoo he had just got on his right forearm. It was a reworked motif by Banksy, the British street artist. Silhouettes of a boy and a girl opposite each other – behind the boy's back a bouquet of flowers, while the girl hid a gun.

Tim thought it was so damn cool.

They sat down on the black leather sofa and immediately started talking about music again, quickly agreeing that the house scene had recently become quite dull.

Robert Sillerman, the older businessman who a couple of years earlier had boasted of his ignorance of dance music, had by now acquired ID&T, the Dutch event group behind the legendary festivals Sensation and Tomorrowland. The booking company Live Nation had taken over Electric Daisy Carnival and British Creamfields. The festivals became increasingly impersonal spectacles and even much of the music was stuck in a rigid form. Same filters, same shrill synth sounds, same kinds of drops. The clearest example was a drum beat that was used so much that it got its own name: the Pryda Snare. Producer after producer had sampled Eric Prydz's hard-compressed crash cymbal, or straight up copied it, to achieve the same powerful effect that the Swede had in his song 'Miami to Atlanta'. The theatrics in house music had become so over the top and the audience so bombarded with colourful explosions that they seemed to have to count down to New Year's Eve fireworks every ten minutes to feel anything at all.

Frenetic and banal marching music, Tim thought.

The monotony had made the genre easy to make fun of, like when the comedy show *Saturday Night Live* in the spring had made a sketch about Davvincii, a brainless DJ who had so little to do in the booth that he fried eggs and played with his model train set while a hypnotised audience waited for the epic drop. For the hassle, Davvincii was rewarded with the audience's jewellery, credit cards and showered with money bags from smiling financiers in suits.

Tim had responded to the parody with a self-ironic picture on Avicii's Instagram account, but really, he just wanted to leave EDM completely behind, not be associated with the scene at all. He was seriously tired of the image of a DJ who just went up on stage and pressed a button and did not work for the love of the audience.

If they only knew how much he worked. If they only knew how much he cared about songwriting and the colours of a composition.

That's what they talked about, Tim and Filip. Music and life, a little bit of everything.

Suddenly Tim wondered: 'Hey, could you help me get hold of some stuff?'

The question came from nowhere.

'What kind of stuff?'

'Xanax. And Sub.'

Filip was completely taken aback. Four years earlier, Tim had gone crazy when Åkesson smoked a joint. Now he wanted Sub? That was some really heavy stuff, that's what scarred-up old junkies did.

In a way, Filip was happy. Maybe Tim had come down from his high horse, maybe they had something in common again.

But in his friend he also suspected the contours of himself. A person who really didn't want to be around others, who sanded down the edges until almost nothing was left, someone who longed to return to his cocoon.

Filip knew it was not good. But then again, he too was craving.

He called an old buddy from Östra Real, a slick bastard who could always take care of it.

A couple of weeks later, Tim strolled out on to the lawn next to the pool and teed up a ball. He had bought professional clubs at a hotel with its own course, and thought that golf might be a way to relax during the summer weeks in Ibiza. His big brother Anton played quite a lot; it could be a fun way for them to hang out, if nothing else.

Tim grabbed his club and took his stance, thundering the ball straight out among the pine trees on the hillside outside the house he was renting.

'Fuck, now you try,' he laughed and handed over the club to Fricko Boberg.

Childhood friend Fricko had got a call from Tim a few months earlier. They had kept in touch constantly, ever since they sat up through the nights playing World of Warcraft and watching movies. But now Tim had a new idea. He missed his teenage gang and had suggested that Fricko and three of the other old bros start travelling with him. He earned enough to be able to afford to pay for their travel and expenses, and that would make the time between gigs so much more enjoyable.

It wasn't a given that Fricko would say yes. He had recently graduated from the Calle Flygare theatre school and had just landed a role in Goethe's classic play *Faust*. He had a girlfriend in Stockholm, where his family and comfort was.

But Tim had insisted, explaining that such a chance would come only once in his life. And that was probably true. So Fricko and a couple of guys from the childhood gang had started working for their friend a few months ago. The job descriptions were really an afterthought – it was Tim's father Klas who had wanted it to at least feel like there were real tasks now that they signed contracts and started paying salaries from Tim's company. They had agreed that a couple of friends would help with Tim's music production, and eventually produce their own music. Another childhood friend would document the tours and Tim's everyday life with his camera.

For lack of anything else, they soon began calling Fricko Tim's personal assistant. Despite the fact that, in the group of friends, he was known for being forgetful and a little distrait, it was he who was given the responsibility for ensuring that Tim's things made it to the next festival and that those on the guest list enjoyed themselves.

The guys' illusions that Tim was living a wonderful jet-set life had quickly come to an end. In theory, of course, it sounded cool to travel around the world, but in fact they barely had time to register which country they were in. They would arrive in a new city, hurry to an arena, sleep a few hours in a hotel, continue on early the next morning. Fricko had met so many people in recent months that his brain was already exhausted.

Racquel sat and watched as her boyfriend slammed another golf ball straight into the woods, hoping it wouldn't hit a neighbour's house.

Tim had rented a villa on the same slope where he had lived with Tiësto four years earlier, just higher up the mountain. From above, they had an incomparable view of Ibiza. The planes swarming above the airport runway, the salt basins in the distance, and down on the beach the outdoor club Ushuaïa pulsing in red lights to the music. The place had opened up a couple of years earlier and quickly became Ibiza's most powerful house establishment – Avicii was booked on the club's stage every Sunday for a couple of months, until September 2014.

Racquel understood why Tim wanted to surround himself with his friends. They gave him a sense of security, a feeling of home back in Östermalm. But it was clear that the hospital stay in Miami had meant a major setback. Tim had been prescribed Suboxone again, the antidote with buprenorphine, which the doctors had explained would not have the same euphoric effect as the previous medication. It was possible that the medical staff were right, Racquel thought – maybe her boyfriend needed help to slowly taper off again. But after only a few weeks, it had been noticeable how his body had become addicted to this narcotic as well. He had started to lose his appetite and weight, made sure to always have access to tablets even when the prescription was out.

Tim's mood swung suddenly and erratically, and for the first time in their relationship Racquel saw him as combative. A spark seemed to have gone out, now that he was on a medication that did not even give him the euphoric and warm effect of the previous opioids. His hygiene had begun to suffer. For long periods, Tim didn't brush his teeth, and when the couple had a rare dinner together, he fell asleep at the table.

'I think that you have a problem,' Racquel finally said. 'This is a mental pattern that you have to break somehow.'

Tim got angry. He certainly knew what he could and could not do. He had read up on it, and he didn't want to be in this situation either. You couldn't abuse something you hated, could you?

'This is a physical thing,' he protested. 'My body is dependent, not my head, though.'

It got messy in a way it had not been before. One morning in mid-August, Racquel tried to get Tim out of bed. Drowsy and angry, he refused. When his girlfriend shook him there was a fight; Racquel threw a pillow at him, Tim slammed his fist straight into the wall.

He calmed down immediately, and cried. It was just so much, so much pressure, so much of everything. Sometimes it simply boiled over.

Tim tried to smooth over what had happened by booking the entire dining room in a restaurant on the same beach as

Ushuaïa, a place that boasted of being the world's most expensive restaurant and described its cooking as a gastronomic performance. There they sat alone and ate a tasting menu full of smoke, laser beams and effects, Tim with his right hand wrapped in a bandage. The blow to the wall had caused a fracture and he would have to DJ with only three fingers on one hand when he performed for the next few weeks.

He hated these fucking pills and what they did to him. Everything had felt so good in February. It had given him such a powerful sense of control to have freed himself from the medication on his own.

Now that gnawing anxiety came again. The feeling that he wanted to punch himself.

And even worse – inside he felt something grow. It had been a dormant discomfort at first, contourless, easy to brush off. Eventually more and more defined. It felt like a lump, which had begun to grow after he reduced his medication last winter, and had grown larger after the surgery in March.

Maybe it was a tumour?

He needed to find a new gap, a time when he could torment himself through the hell of detoxification again. He knew what it was like by now; last time he had been debilitated for nine days straight. The chills and fever required at least a week of rest and relaxation.

'I have looked at the schedule forward and back,' he wrote home to Strandvägen. 'If we take off TomorrowWorld then it would be a perfect time for me to get over this shit! Do you have any better suggestions for cancelling?'

Tim needed to do Norway, the UK and Spain at the end of August, then a promotional show in Germany.

Afterwards there was a week in the beginning of September when he would be able to be in his apartment in Stockholm and fight his way through all of this crap. It had to be then, because there wouldn't be another chance until the end of October, after a tour in Asia. He couldn't stand waiting so long.

'I am so damn close now and I just want to be done with this stuff.'

Klas Bergling and Arash Pournouri agreed. They had dinner together at a fish restaurant on the cliffs in the port area of Ibiza. Seeing Tim in the hospital bed in Miami had been tough for Arash – Tim then weighed no more than fifty kilos and was so obviously drained of energy.

They agreed that the situation was now unsustainable. Tim might be the headliner at the Storm Festival in Shanghai and in October he had gigs planned in Japan. A festival in San Bernardino and TomorrowWorld in Atlanta were also planned for the autumn, in addition to nine gigs in Las Vegas, all worth around $400,000 each.

But to hell with the money. The important thing was that Tim got better once and for all.

IN THE AUTUMN OF 2014, Tim got home to Stockholm, where the rain was pouring down. After a hot summer came a storm at the end of September that turned the city into a grey, floating chaos. Masses of water leaked into hospitals, paralysed parts of the metro system and caused the bicycles down on Karlavägen to tip over.

Anki stood by the stove in her son's apartment, frying yellow onions and lots of garlic with whole tomatoes. When the vegetables had turned brown, she carefully pulled off the tomato peel and poured on the cream and curry. She finished with shrimp and seasoned with a little cayenne pepper and salt.

Anki was worried about her son, who was lying on the leather sofa behind her. He had lost so much weight over the summer and she hoped that her pasta dish would get him to eat a little.

She was here for another reason too. The idea was that she would be responsible for Tim's antidote medicine; this had been agreed with a Swedish addiction doctor.

Gradually and controlled, Tim would taper off, not as hectically as last time. Twice daily he got his dose of the mild opioid buprenorphine, four milligrams in total. By slowly decreasing his dosage, Tim would hopefully be completely free from his addiction by Christmas.

Anki was not convinced. Tim was so quiet and closed off, he seemed depressed. He got up, went to the bathroom, said a few words, went into the bedroom again.

On his twenty-fifth birthday, *Billboard Magazine* had reported that Avicii had cancelled all gigs indefinitely. Fans on Twitter did not show much understanding. Sure, some thought he deserved a rest – the wish for a speedy recovery from Switzerland, a woman in California who promised to pray for him – but many seemed to think mostly of themselves.

If @Avicii doesn't show at tomorrowworld I am going to be so depressed! Don't do this to me again!!

How many festivals/shows has Avicii cancelled in the last year because of him not being able to control himself partying? #Toomanytocount

Avicii is so pathetic hahaha

fuck avicii right in the pussy

Even though Tim himself had wanted to go to Stockholm to ride out the withdrawal, he was now conflicted and sullen. He had a hard time coming to terms with the feeling of being controlled. He felt like Klas and Anki and the doctor and Arash and everyone around him suddenly didn't trust him.

'I'm gonna take what I'm told to every day, but I want to be in charge of it myself,' he explained to Racquel through the computer screen.

His girlfriend was in her mother's house in Toronto, not sure if she really should record the conversation. But Tim probably would not remember what they'd said when he sobered up in a few hours, and she wanted to show him how he slurred.

'I wanna be able to . . . not have other people . . . handling my pills. I'm not gonna wake up every day and go, "Hi, can I have my dose now?"'

'So what? What's the problem?'

'I wanna take my dose whenever the fuck I wanna take my dose.'

They just sat quietly for a long time.

'So you don't think that the medication has control over your body whatsoever?'

'Well, yeah. Of my body, not my mind.'

'I think they both go hand in hand.'

'I don't think so. Because if they did I wouldn't be taking four milligrams a day. I'd be taking more.'

In early October 2014, 'The Days' was released, the song that Tim had done with Salem Al Fakir and Vincent Pontare six months earlier, when everything had felt so much more fun. It had been hard to find a singer for the track. Brandon Flowers, frontman of the group The Killers, had recorded a version – but he and Tim had started arguing over text messages and it had petered out. In the end, it was Robbie Williams, the old pop star from Take That, who sang about the wonderful days you would never forget.

Tim's goal of releasing his album in the autumn of 2014 hadn't come through, so this song together with the sibling tune 'The Nights' served as a temporary thirst quencher for the fans.

But the single did not seem to take off. On Twitter, people were unsure about the sun-bleached radio rock, they complained that the song had no drop, and after only a week, it fell out of the Billboard charts.

That was not the reception Tim had become accustomed to. He was lying in bed watching the counter on YouTube – seven million views in about a month. Just a few years ago that would have been exhilarating, now it felt like a big failure. It was a song about living, really celebrating life – and here he was, bedridden and impatient, awake until seven every morning. It felt much more daunting to get off the medication this time. Especially when he felt monitored, it was difficult to summon the same fighting spirit that he had felt six months earlier.

And the lump he seemed to feel in his stomach did not disappear. On the contrary, as the effect of the pills diminished, it grew larger and stronger. Sometimes it felt like it encompassed his whole being.

Tim had started to be convinced that it was a tumour, that was all he could think of now. His father had arranged for Tim to have a gastroscopy and colonoscopy at the end of November, to have the problems investigated once and for all. Arash argued that Tim should stay in Stockholm and go to a dietitian.

But Tim felt restless, increasingly humiliated and restrained. He longed to get away.

A few blocks away from his son, Klas Bergling was also sleepless.

He cursed himself for being naive for so long.

With a rising sense of guilt and anger, Klas read about the opioids his son had taken. In Sweden, opioids were still mostly used in acute cancer cases and palliative care, to reduce the suffering of an already dying patient. The painkillers could also be prescribed for shorter treatments, for example after surgery.

In the United States, it was different. Just that autumn in 2014 a protracted lawsuit was pending in the southern parts of the country. The state of Kentucky had sued Purdue Pharma, the pharmaceutical company whose drug OxyContin had started what had by now grown into an epidemic in the country. It was the company's stubborn marketing a little over a decade earlier that had changed American doctors' views on opioids, so that they began to prescribe morphine drugs much more generously than before.

By this time, it had turned out that Purdue Pharma's marketing was based on misquoted studies, sponsored surveys and false premises. In addition, patients and misusers who had become addicted had quickly understood that it was enough to crush the tablets to put the much discussed extended-release formula out of action and shoot the euphoric feeling straight into the bloodstream. That OxyContin was less addictive than its competitors was downright bullshit, and the pharmaceutical company had been forced to retract all such claims.

The unfortunate thing was that the ball was already rolling, nonetheless. The pills had quickly slipped out on to the black market, and when they became more difficult to obtain, many who had already become addicted had switched to the street drug that provided the most similar pain relief – namely heroin. Kentucky was just one of the places where the effects were palpable: children who lost their parents in overdoses, law-abiding workers who became thieves and jailbirds, pharmacies that were forced to install bulletproof glass in their stores.

That autumn, another wave of opioids was rolling over the United States. Fentanyl was sometimes one hundred times stronger than morphine, manufactured illegally and very easy to overdose on. A Mexican cartel, led by the infamous mafia boss El Chapo, had become the largest distributor of fentanyl to the US market.

Klas sat in front of the computer and read about this gloomy development. Over two million Americans were now addicted to some form of opioid, a public health crisis that was having dire consequences for society.

For the first time in a very long time, the average life expectancy of the American population was declining.

Hell.

What kind of pills was Tim really taking?

EVENTUALLY, TIM ESCAPED back to Los Angeles, against the will of Arash and Klas.

What the hell could they do about it? He was an adult and had been uncomfortable lying on the couch in Stockholm and detoxing. The longing for redemption, a way to get rid of the fucking anxiety ball in his stomach, had only grown. After a tearing quarrel with Klas, he had simply boarded a plane.

Again, what the hell were they going to do?

Racquel and the dog Oliver received him up in the mountains of Hollywood. The renovation of the house he had bought was still not complete – it was still just a construction site with bare beams and knocked-out walls – but while Tim was gone, Racquel had unpacked their belongings in a house they would rent in the meantime. It was on the same street, Blue Jay Way, just a few hundred metres up the steep hill. Racquel had put the furniture in order and sorted her boyfriend's shirts and trousers in the wardrobe. Finally, Tim would get a real home studio where he could complete his second album. He was excited to get the record ready, he said, it was already delayed.

After a couple of days, Tim went down into town. Later in the afternoon, as Racquel was tidying up the largest of the house's bedrooms, a message pinged on the couple's shared iPad. Tim had long ago linked his phone messages there, so it was not uncommon for Racquel to also receive his text messages. That was one of the things she appreciated about Tim – he never minded when she happened to see something he wrote on his phone. Tim had secrets in front of many, but no longer her.

This message was different.

'I need to see somebody about my hand that I hit in a wall. It's still hurting and looks crooked.'

Racquel soon realised that Tim was writing to his private physician.

A new ping.

'Gets stomach pain again.'

The doctor replied that he could arrange for a colleague to see Tim the next morning. The patient was not satisfied with that response.

'I'm in 10 out of 10 in pain and it's freaking me out. Can we get some pain management for now to deal?'

Racquel felt her heart sink. Even though it had been a long battle with Tim's addiction, he had always seemed up front. Now he was unfaithful with his fucking pills. Was that why he had returned to the United States? Not to see her and the dog but because he knew he could easily get more medicine prescribed by his doctor?

In one fell swoop, everything changed. For the first time, the icy insight sank all the way down into Racquel's belly. No matter how hard she tried, she could never help Tim realise the seriousness of his addiction. She was afraid of who he had become and who she herself was. What the pills had done to them as a couple and as friends.

It was also the surroundings that Racquel couldn't cope with any more. The road crew, the agents, the doctors: everyone who affected concern when a crisis hit but then steamed on just like before. Besides, how could the doctor prescribe drugs to a patient he had not seen in months? Racquel had to control herself not to call and berate him.

This had become a sad tale now, one she had seen in documentaries about Kurt Cobain and Amy Winehouse. She did not want to be the girlfriend in that story, the girl who was afterwards blamed for letting it happen, the one who just said yes, who did not put a stop to it. For there would be an afterwards, she was convinced of it at this moment. Tim would die young. After New Year he would go on tour again and everyone would pretend that everything was fine and she refused to be a part of that lie any more.

To save herself, she had to leave Tim.

Racquel called some of his friends and told them about her suspicion – Tim had got new medicine prescribed, was probably on his way to a pharmacy any moment now. She rummaged through some stuff, got in the car, and drove towards Orange County, to a friend who was the only one who knew the extent of what was going on.

After a couple of hours along the highway to the south, one of Tim's friends called back.

Tim had drunk wine and taken too many pills and they were on their way with him to the emergency room.

Unaware that Tim had been in hospital and had his stomach pumped, Jesse Waits a few weeks later suggested a trip to Mexico, as he and Tim had not seen each other for a long time. Jesse rented a private jet and they left with some of the bros.

Tim had a terrible sore inside his mouth, which he said was due to an infected wisdom tooth. Waits didn't really believe that explanation, it looked more like Tim had bitten straight through his tongue and cheek. But it would surely get better if he could just lie on the beach and relax for a couple of days. They could talk it through then.

They landed in Cancun and headed for a spit of land in the Gulf of Mexico, surrounded by turquoise water. Here, Americans celebrated graduations and honeymoons or, at this time, that the Christmas holiday in 2014 was approaching. The first day was wonderfully lazy – they were chilling on the beach and Tim talked about how great it was to have got away from cold and rainy Stockholm. Tim was eating poorly, said it hurt his mouth, but wasn't getting drunk like before. When they went to a small club in the evening he drank only a few glasses of bubbly, took it easy.

After a couple of days, Jesse and some of the others were hanging out in the lobby, on their way out for lunch.

Suddenly, Tim came hurrying through the foyer past the elevators. He looked completely gone, could barely walk.

'What the fuck, Tim? Are you okay? What's going on?'

It was impossible to talk to him, he just mumbled something inaudible. His gaze was blank, he was somewhere far away.

This wasn't going to work. Avicii could not be wandering around unreachable in a tourist hotel in Mexico, any second now covert photos would start being taken.

While someone was calling a doctor, Jesse led Tim up to his room and laid him on the bed. Tim disappeared further into the fog; no matter how they shook him he did not react. When the doctor came, Tim seemed almost unconscious.

'Do you know what he's on?' she asked.

'Not a clue,' Jesse replied.

'Could you find out?'

When the friends went through Tim's stuff, they found pills everywhere: in the lid of a tobacco box, in his pockets and suitcase, hidden in his toiletry bag. Pills for panic disorder, a pack of opioids and a muscle relaxant. There was a bottle for the treatment of ADHD and yet another morphine drug.

Apparently, Tim had been to a pharmacy during the night and bought whatever he could find.

'This combination could be deadly,' the doctor said. 'We need to bring him with us.'

Afterwards, when Tim had had his stomach pumped and was back at the hotel again, the mood was heavy.

Jesse and the others wanted straight answers to what Tim had actually taken. And why so damn much? Tim was annoyed and didn't want to discuss it; he instead thought that someone could go to a pharmacy and buy him new pills.

'We don't trust you right now,' said Jesse. 'You need to sleep and have some food. You gotta do normal things.'

'But where's my stuff, though?'

Tim wouldn't budge. He needed painkillers for the wound in his mouth, sleeping pills to doze off. He'd go to the pharmacy himself then, he said, and set off towards the door. There stood one of his friends blocking the way, refusing to let Tim out.

'This is a problem,' said Jesse. 'You could have killed yourself.'

Tim just glared at him. Finally, they negotiated a compromise that allowed Tim to keep his sleeping pills and any of the other medications that did not seem directly life-threatening.

The situation calmed down.

For Tim, there was one thing that was more important than any other. Under no circumstances could his parents know anything about this. That put Jesse in an awkward situation. The incident felt so serious that Tim's family should know what had happened. But at the same time, Jesse was afraid that Tim would immediately break contact with him, see him as a traitor.

He decided to be loyal to Tim. He would not rat him out.

11 February 2015

Anki Lidén

Well hello you damn kid who doesn't respond or send any updates!!!!! What's going on in your head, what makes you just not give a damn about staying in touch, just even a few lines, to us – your family and above all ME – your MOTHER?

> **Tim Bergling**
>
> But I have been responding and texting jeez! You haven't been responding.

Anki Lidén

Huh?????

…but I just wonder how you're doing – maybe that's too tough to tell your Mum.

But you have a father who you're completely ignoring – HIM you're not responding to. I understand 0 0 0 why you're not answering your dad????? Are you afraid of smth? Do you think it's hard somehow?

Time passed slowly. The sun crept across the bright horizon while Anki Lidén waited for a phone call that never came. It had been so long since her son had called and wanted to talk.

She stood on the balcony above the boardwalk in Las Palmas, gazing out over the tourists playing down in the water. Together with Klas, she had taken a charter flight to the capital of the Canary Islands several years earlier and fallen in love with the slightly outdated city. It was not so fancy and tidy here – a carafe of the house red wine with steak, and boutiques that sold cheap blouses next to the tattoo parlours. The couple rented an apartment at the north end of the beach, where the waves never got too high to take a dip.

But now Anki was left there alone, as her husband had travelled to Los Angeles to help Tim renovate the expensive house their son had insisted on buying.

This spring in 2015, Anki began to feel a distance that was not just physical. More than ever, she felt that Tim was in a world to which she lacked access.

Every time they got in touch, Tim pretended that nothing was up. He talked mostly about what amazing songs he had made, what cool tattoos he had got. Everything was fine; his dear mother did not have to worry. But both parents now understood how devastating a prolonged use of opioids could be. And Anki was convinced that there were parts of the picture that were being withheld from her; she felt it intensely.

All that was invisible, everything that she could not grasp, grew in the darkness. What if Tim overdosed? What would happen to her then? What was she even without her son?

When the thoughts became too many, Anki went across the stairwell to the apartment next door. An older couple from Gothenburg lived there. She and Klas had got to know them during one of their previous trips to the Canary Islands.

A couple of decades earlier, the old man's daughter had committed suicide. The girl had been unwell for a long time and they hadn't known how to help her. Every bit of progress had been followed by setbacks. The discussions out on the couple's balcony became long and in a strange way comforting. With people who had felt exactly the same crippling powerlessness, Anki could still relax for a moment. Drink a few glasses of wine, cry, be redeemed.

When she went back into her own apartment again, darkness descended on her. The beach down there was emptied of people, the waves of the Atlantic turned dark blue.

Anki counted the hours – what time was it in Los Angeles now? What was Tim doing? Why did he not answer his father? Being on her guard all the time required so much energy, made her totally exhausted. Still, she could not fall asleep.

At the same time, Klas Bergling was sitting on scaffolding and rubble in Hollywood. Another eternal meeting with the craftsman who led the renovation of Tim's house had finally ended.

Klas felt that they were overdoing it. The kitchen could be nice with just a few minor interventions, there was already a large walk-in wardrobe in the bedroom, a balcony with a glass floor was not necessary. But Tim wanted to blow everything out, put his own stamp on the rooms and the decor. Yet he never showed up at the meetings. Klas did not stay at his son's home, but in a hotel below the hills, and Tim was virtually impossible to get hold of. Instead, one of his friends came to the construction deliberations and acted as a middle man. Supposedly, it was difficult for Tim to cope with these meetings, because he had been sleeping so poorly.

He would sit up all night, and then not wake up until late in the evening.

Klas made notes on the reports in his almanac:

2 February: Tim woke up 9:00 p.m.

3 February: Tim didn't sleep.

4 February: Tim fell asleep at noon today.

Across the inside cover: *Zoloft that makes you not sleep.*

Klas had nothing against the attempts of Tim's friends to act as mediators, but the whole situation felt unworthy. After all, he had been in Los Angeles for several days now, and Tim was still reluctant to answer when his father called. Klas felt like the enemy, someone who was interfering, someone to rebuff.

The house that Tim rented and where he lived with his friends was only a few hundred metres up the ravine but it had turned into an impenetrable fort.

What had really happened in Mexico, for example? Why did he suddenly have to seek an audience with his own son?

Tim, on the other hand, thought that Klas should understand his mandate. He knew he could be hard to deal with. But that was why they paid a whole lot of people to handle situations. Above all: did his father not see that Tim himself wanted to get away from this stress? Especially recently, Klas had started talking about Tim having put financial pressure on himself with the house purchase – he needed to continue working if he wanted to afford to renovate and buy furniture and at the same time maintain the standard of living he had grown accustomed to. There were expenses everywhere; not even one of the world's most successful musicians could burn through $15 million on a whim.

Added to this was the nagging about Tim's friends not being allowed to drink or, basically, do anything else around him.

Completely unnecessary, Tim thought.

'I just wanted to say that I can't stand you calling my friends all the time and dictating how I should live my life and what they should do and what their responsibilities to me are,' Tim wrote to his father. 'Everyone is afraid of you and Ash. That they shouldn't drink near me, that everything must be reported, etc., when no one understands why we don't just talk directly about your concerns.'

The distress also set in over Stockholm. In the beautiful properties on Strandvägen, the silence had spread.

Filip Holm came to the office in the mornings, hung up his jacket and sat down at his desk without a word.

What had happened to At Night? They had had so much fun in the basement on Styrmansgatan just a few years earlier. They had been a team; they were the underdogs who surprised the industry with their sharp teeth. They had played demos for each other so loud that the neighbours could hear, hugged each other every morning, laughed.

Now Filip Holm felt like he worked in a shipshape workplace with a receptionist and a bad mood.

In fact, it should be the other way around. Dance music had taken over not only the United States but almost everywhere. In 2015, more than two hundred festivals would be held around the world, all focusing on what was now well established as EDM. On the one hand, there were old-fashioned brands in new markets: Mysteryland exported from the Netherlands to Chile, American Ultra in Bali, Australian Future Music Festival in Malaysia. But those who wanted to could also see Skrillex and Laidback Luke on a cruise ship in the Bahamas, Hardwell and Tiësto on a beach in Estonia, Fatboy Slim in a Gothic castle in Transylvania.

The fact that some unrealistically rich sheikhs had entered

into the competition on the Las Vegas club scene had done its part to force the festival managers to sweeten their offers as well. The pay for a gig was by now astronomical, and the power lay with the main attractions like Avicii – those who could rightly say that they carried these enormous events on their shoulders. For the event companies, a few names could make the difference between thousands and hundreds of thousands of tickets sold.

Arash Pournouri was now featured in distinguished Swedish business magazines and would this summer host an episode of a hugely popular show on Swedish Radio – to be able to tell his life story on there was equated in the country's cultural sphere with being knighted. Together with Daniel Ek, the founder of Spotify, Arash was also putting together Brilliant Minds, an annual conference where they planned to gather international dignitaries from the IT sector, such as Twitter and Google. The first meeting was to take place at the beginning of the summer and Arash had used his network and was able to invite, among others, Wyclef Jean, Ericsson's CEO Hans Vestberg and Björn Ulvaeus of ABBA. He moved comfortably among the bigwigs.

But concern about what was going on with Tim way over in Los Angeles affected everything. Arash became more and more worried and annoyed. Tim was soon going on tour in Australia, and a big sponsorship deal with Volvo was underway, but the star himself didn't seem to care.

Tim, on the other hand, had long thought that Arash was giving less and less time to feedback on songs, and they hardly talked on the phone any more. Instead, sporadic communication took place via email, where their quarrels could become harsh and childish in tone. The distance did not make their relationship better; often there would be weeks without any contact.

The tense atmosphere in the office on Strandvägen overpowered Filip Holm. Ever since the stomach ulcer in Miami a year earlier, he had felt a paralysing tiredness, and now he was unable to get out of bed when he was off work. His girlfriend tried to get him out – a short Sunday walk at least? – but Filip just wanted to stay in the shadows behind the blinds.

One day when he had once more forced himself to work, he could no longer cope. He sat down in one of the recording studios, in front of the velvet curtains and the big speakers, and cried. It was nice, at least, to let the tears out.

His cell phone vibrated. Arash had noticed that Filip was not at his desk. Filip made up a lie, saying that he had gone into the studio to make a phone call.

He sat alone and thought for a while. Then he wrote a text saying that he was not feeling well, maybe he had become ill, he had to go home.

A few days later, in March 2015, he left At Night.

From: Tim Bergling
To: Neil Jacobson
Date: 11 April 2015

I think we can make a real impact like we did with *True* but on steroids this time around. I think this album is far beyond, being frank, much of the EDM bullshit that's going on and I want every fucking song on the record to feel timeless and great – and I want it to be a double album.

Despite everything, Tim Bergling wanted to focus on what was actually working. In the spring of 2015, for example, he had started training with a guy that Vincent Pontare had recommended.

Magnus Lygdbäck was a former ice hockey player from Småland who had moved to Los Angeles and promoted himself as a personal trainer for the stars. He had just been to London, where he had made sure that the actor Alexander Skarsgård did not eat more than two handfuls of food at each meal during the filming of the upcoming blockbuster about Tarzan.

Now Lygdbäck came to Tim's house in the mornings and pulled him out into the sunlight. Initially, the goal was modest: to oxygenate the body, let Tim breathe fresh air and get some colour in his cheeks.

They would usually go up the steep hill of Blue Jay Way and stop at the lookout point at the top. With their eyes fixed on the greenery of Beverly Hills, they talked about the plates lying unwashed on Tim's bed and the smelly takeaway boxes that no one bothered to throw away. Tim lay isolated in his room for days on end, watching *House of Cards*.

Eventually, the more physical training began. Dumbbells and barbells were set up in the garage and Magnus Lygdbäck came almost every day and trained Tim when he did his lifts.

It was not easy, because when Tim pushed himself, his body reacted instinctively. The fast heartbeats were confused with panic attacks. Suddenly Tim would feel faint, be forced to put down his dumbbells and catch his breath.

But he was still working out, and he was proud of it.

Tim also made progress with his music. By this time, he was at home in Jim Henson's classic studio, sitting through the nights in the same room where the classic song 'We Are the World' had been recorded.

One night Tim needed fresh ears and called a couple of new acquaintances to listen to the material he had recorded so far. He had over a hundred song sketches to choose between.

Albin Nedler and Kristoffer Fogelmark were two twenty-five-year-olds who a couple of years earlier had co-written songs on the boy band One Direction's album *Take Me Home*, which topped the album charts in over thirty countries. With this success in their armoury, the two young Swedes had started commuting between Stockholm and Los Angeles to write world hits. They were on their way home from the studio when Tim called just before midnight.

'Hey! I'm in the studio working and need feedback on some things,' said Tim. 'Come by, it's gonna be awesome!'

Albin Nedler sat down on a chair in front of the redwood panels as Tim restlessly began to jump from sketch to sketch. Flowing from the speakers were tunes flirting with new wave from the 80s and the hard-hitting 'City Lights'. Tim had made a reggae song that he liked with rapper Wyclef Jean and singer Matisyahu. He wanted to fill the record with full-bodied strings performed by a real symphony orchestra.

On one of the songs, it was Tim himself who sang. He had actually imagined Chris Martin's voice on 'True Believer', but when the Coldplay singer heard the demo, he had persuaded Tim to sing – the lyrics of the song felt so personal. Instead, Tim asked Chris to be a backing singer, a rather cocky way to use one of the world's most famous artists. That the album itself had become increasingly fragmented with each collaboration was not something that worried Tim. On the contrary, he thought it showed the breadth of his ability.

'Damn, I kind of feel like now is the time to make that big album,' he said. 'You know, something that defines the decade.'

Through his tour manager, Tim had discovered the British

group Cherry Ghost, whose old song 'Roses' had inspired a melodic progression in 'Waiting For Love', a song that gave Tim goosebumps. In the spring, he had invited the band's singer Simon Aldred to the house in Los Angeles, where they had recorded another song, 'Ten More Days', one of Tim's favourites.

Around dawn, Albin Nedler played a sketch that he and Kristoffer had made a few weeks earlier. It was basically a hip-hop song that consisted of raging hi-hats and a bass so heavy that it felt more like a pull to the stomach than an actual sound. Albin had laid down a synth loop inspired by Daft Punk over the drums.

Tim loved what he heard.

A hip-hop song could open the doors to a new audience; it was exactly what Tim needed to point him in a new direction. In addition, there was a melodic figure in the demo that Tim immediately became attached to. It was a cute little lick reminiscent of something a jazz saxophonist could have done in a solo. Many would think that that little trick was far too pretty, would see it as overkill. On the contrary, Tim thought that it gave the track life and lustre and showed that Albin Nedler knew what the hell he was doing.

'Shit, I love these kinda things. That is exactly my mode!'

Such finesse should characterise this project. The record may have been delayed, but in return it would be a real show of strength. In fact, Tim thought he had so many great songs that it should be a double album. A complex work brimming with self-confidence.

To Neil Jacobson at Universal he wrote:

As long as we have the singles to carry the album, which I finally think we do, I think the rest will follow. I want it to be

BAM BAM BAM BAM like I remember '21' from Adele was. Single on single on single. And then when the critics and industry listen to the album my hope is that they will see the different layers of the songs because I feel like a lot of the songs on the album are growers in a good way.

I'm not saying this is def it and this album will be that – but what I'm saying is that it should be our ultimate goal – something that we've all been a part of and can be proud of in 30 years' time when we're sitting all together in fucking lounge chairs smoking cigars and sipping whiskey, reminiscing about how we made this album happen.

DESPITE TIM'S OWN HOPES and promises, in the summer of 2015 it was difficult for those around him not to notice how quickly things were going downhill. Tim was certainly productive, but at the same time he was pale and thin. The dark circles under his eyes gave the impression that he had not slept for several days.

Albin Nedler continued to visit the studio and reacted to the sweet cannabis scent that always hung heavily between the speakers. Back in his teens, Tim had got feelings of unreality from weed and became angry every time Filip Åkesson smoked, but since then his perception had changed. Nowadays, he considered marijuana to be something soft and pleasant – compared to the tablets he had taken before, cannabis felt like a trifle. He had also hired a new American doctor, who instead of painkilling opioids prescribed a huge amount of sedatives and anti-anxiety drugs, as well as antidepressants and sleeping pills.

The fire-yellow jars of pills stood on a table in the studio, next to an ice bucket and a bottle of Jack Daniel's. Tim mixed drinks, sucked in another joint and got entangled in long monologues about what kind of voice was needed for the different songs.

Albin reacted to Tim repeatedly losing his train of thought, but he didn't know Tim well enough to object.

The team that travelled with Tim observed the deterioration too.

On the tour in Australia, he had locked himself in hotel rooms and looked for doctors who could get him sedatives, instead of preparing his sets. In Las Vegas, he had suffered a rupture of his cruciate ligament after trying to kick in a door and shortly afterwards performed on stage significantly drunk. Amused, he had played 'On My Way' with Axwell & Ingrosso three or four times in a row.

It was not like Avicii to be so careless. The audience also reacted to the fact that the artist seemed to be about to lose his footing; for example, he had started arguing with people online. The tabloid *Daily Star* had done an interview with a sensationalist headline: 'Madonna ruined my track: Avicii slams the Queen of Pop', whereupon Bergling took a screenshot of the article and posted on Twitter: 'Or maybe your shitty interviewers ruined what could have been a good interview', before tagging the reporter: 'What a slimy phoney c*nt u are my friend.'

It became fucking turmoil, with new articles in the press and lawyers who called from London and Tim who refused to take down the attacks unless he received a personal apology from the reporter.

At the airport in Los Angeles, a paparazzo came up and fussed about, wanting to provoke a reaction from the star, and Tim erupted. With a sunhat covering his face, Tim towered over the photographer, scornful and threatening.

Immediately afterwards, he called Neil Jacobson at Universal.

'These people don't know who the fuck they're fucking with. They haven't got a clue. I'll fucking kill all of them.'

'Tim, what are you talking about? Calm down. Just relax.'

Jacobson and Tim had talked quite a bit about how he should handle the media, but this was something new.

'People don't know how fucking strong I've become; they don't know what they're dealing with.'

Neil listened for ten minutes while Tim rambled on.

'You know, I'd fuck that guy up easily.'

'Tim, you're not going to fight anybody. That's freedom of the press; it's the price you have to pay for being famous. In fact, you're too rich to fight. Even if you could win the fight, you'd lose.'

After half an hour Tim was forced to board the plane and end the conversation.

Neil Jacobson found himself with a rising feeling of discomfort. It was not the anger, the belligerence that had frightened him, but something else. The feeling that Tim was not fully aware of what he was saying, as if Neil had not really reached him. He sensed something wild inside Tim, a glimpse of the shadows.

Harry Bird, producer of visuals, sat in the seat behind Tim on the plane and heard him expand on his revenge fantasies. He wanted to hire a private detective to spy on the photographer who had filmed him. Find some shit on him, make him suffer.

It basically never ended this summer, Tim's babbling. The clock could reach four in the morning and as soon as they landed, Harry would be moving right on to the next arena to prepare for the night's gig – he really needed a couple of hours of sleep. Instead, Tim showed pictures of a coat in luminous reflective material that was designed to ruin paparazzi pictures. Would be cool, Tim thought, but he was not content with just that. He wanted to create a jacket that made him completely invisible.

'Fuck, wouldn't that be awesome? I'd walk around everywhere and no one would see me at all.'

The next idea was an bracelet that Tim would invent. When his hand was raised against a photographer, an alarm would sound and put the paparazzo out of action while laser beams shot out at the camera lens.

Once Tim finally fell asleep, the others rolled their eyes and signalled to each other to be quiet so he wouldn't wake up again. Harry Bird had always marvelled at Tim's brilliant brain, but now he was just weird.

And so it became late summer, and time for the 2015 gigs at Ushuaïa. Tim had rented a new house this time, a magnificent white villa in a mountain village on the southern tip of Ibiza.

The cliffs slipped down into the Mediterranean, and through the panoramic windows yachts could be seen anchored in the water. The sticky evening mist made the green hills on the other side of the bay look like moss over the horizon.

Tim didn't notice any of it. He sat hunched over with his headphones covering his cap and listened to the same loop over and over again. The plate of food that the house chef had placed next to the computer was left untouched for hours. They had built a small studio in the living room, with guitars, electric bass and a couple of synthesisers, even a studio microphone had been brought to Ibiza.

Tim's eyes were foggy. He'd been working the shit out of himself for the past few weeks.

Alongside fiddling with the album, he had done festival gigs in France, England, Belgium and Romania, and performed every Sunday at Ushuaïa. Sometimes it felt as if his stubbornness was the only thing holding him together. He took amphetamine-based pills to be able to sit through the nights at the screen, sedatives to deal with the pressure. When he was going to sleep, he needed yet other pills.

Now he turned up the volume and drummed his arms into the air. The very last song was about to be finished. 'Pure

Grinding', the hip-hop track that Albin Nedler and Kristoffer Fogelmark had presented to him, now had a bridge that was a nod to the house singer Crystal Waters' 90s classic '100% Pure Love'. Tim loved the heavy bass and the sharp drums and fought with Universal to release 'Pure Grinding' as the first single, along with 'For A Better Day'. Both songs were such clear examples of his development as a composer, he thought. At the record company, they were more hesitant, but above all, the discussions right now were about marketing.

For this launch, it was especially important to adhere to the rules of the game, according to the record company people. Nowadays, Tim was up to a level where he competed for attention with the biggest pop stars, artists like Taylor Swift, Justin Bieber and Kanye West. The conclusion was simple – Tim would have to fly to London and do radio interviews, something they had postponed for far too long.

Tim refused. Not another fucking press tour. It was too lame, too predictable and pathetic. He wanted to do a single grand press conference in a seaside resort in England where the graffiti artist Banksy had built a dystopian amusement park, a satire on capitalism that included book bonfires and warped robots. It was a context that would fit Avicii hand in glove, Tim argued. The marketing manager at Universal, on the other hand, thought it less likely that a bunch of street artists devoted to critiquing consumerism would host one of the world's best-selling EDM artists.

After an intense fight, the record company won out and Tim boarded a plane to London. The interviews were not successful. The BBC had prepared a quiz where Tim would guess who had the most followers on Twitter – Martin Garrix or Swedish House Mafia? Zedd or Tiësto? Tim did his best to be nice but slurred his answers with a blank stare. When they arrived at the radio station Capital FM, the host asked the usual questions about how psyched Tim was over his new single. Tim barely answered before he completely changed gear and instead rattled on about his plans to buy a castle. He had been up all night looking for some sick palaces in Slovenia, Mozambique and Morocco.

Universal's representative in London thought it felt uncomfortable. Tim seemed to mean every word, that wasn't the problem. But the thoughts were difficult to understand, Tim was hollow-eyed and had tobacco in his mouth.

When he refused to come down to the hotel lobby the next morning, the record company decided to cancel the remaining interviews. In this condition, the artist would do more harm than good to his upcoming record.

Tim needed competent care, and fast.

THAT SAME AUTUMN, Laidback Luke received an invitation to open for Tim at Ushuaïa.

Lucas van Scheppingen was surprised by the request. He had tried to get hold of Tim several times, but his old friend had been elusive, not responding to emails. Lucas had hoped that they would now have the opportunity to sit down and talk again in connection with the gig, but Tim came to Ushuaïa at the last second and they barely had time to say hello before he went up on the club's outdoor stage.

The performance was magical. But when Lucas stood at the edge of the stage and watched, he still had a hard time shaking off his fears.

In the thin body up there, Lucas saw himself. Only a few years earlier, he too had been on the verge of capsizing completely.

The years after the first panic attacks, when van Scheppingen had been in his home studio paralysed by stress, had become intense. He had got some new songs out of it in the end, and with them came the touring. At least four new cities a week, every weekend shows where everyone he met was drunk and happy. He could certainly start indulging in a couple of drinks himself, just during the gigs? It would elevate them to pleasant exceptions from the hectic travel.

For a year it had worked, then two drinks had become three and three had become four and soon Lucas was hungover wherever he went. Up in the booth, he chose a song and found himself wondering if he had not already played it twenty minutes earlier. In the end, he lived on alcohol: sitting in Miami and pouring vodka in with cranberry juice for lunch, ending with Jäger shots at eight the next morning, before he started over again after snoozing for a few hours in the a.m.

Discussing his problems with someone else was still out of the question. He wasn't a wimp. He was a DJ, a fucking star, a name. He would deal with this in the same way as the previous crisis: simply work harder until the doubt subsided.

The turning point had come on a rare free Sunday at home in Amsterdam. Lucas's father had invited him to dinner in the sleepy suburb where he lived; Lucas's two little sons were playing with each other on the floor. As usual, Lucas was hungover and restless, his pounding head still in yesterday's job. That was probably why he got so annoyed by his sons' noise and screams. Still, in retrospect, he had a hard time understanding where the raging anger came from. Suddenly Lucas lifted his younger son by the shirt and threw the two-year-old on the floor.

Two good things had come out of this terrible event.

First, it was easy for Lucas van Scheppingen to stop drinking. Every time the craving for alcohol came over him, he saw his son's incomprehensible gaze as he looked up from the floor with his face full of blood.

Second, Lucas completely changed his view of what strength and courage were.

It was not keeping it together, not shutting up.

There was no shame in admitting that you were feeling bad.

Or rather – it shouldn't be.

As he stood at the edge of the stage in Ushuaïa, Lucas thought of Amy Winehouse. Four years earlier, the British singer had been in the middle of a dazzling career when she was found lifeless in her home in Camden, London, dead from acute alcohol poisoning. Winehouse's death had placed her in a mythical group of musicians who had all died when they were twenty-seven years old: guitarist Jimi Hendrix, Nirvana singer Kurt Cobain, Janis Joplin and Jim Morrison among others. Miserable fates romanticised by music consumers – when Amy Winehouse sang that she refused to be treated for her addiction, the audience had happily shouted along. That was also part of the problem in this industry – the audience did not always want to see that there was a real person behind the artist, they were happy to use their idol as a surface on which to project their own dreams and fantasies. Laidback Luke had felt the loneliness that came with being exalted.

At the edge of the stage, he counted, came to the conclusion that Tim was just turning twenty-six, and was filled with evil suspicions. Tim would be that artist for house music. The talented and young one who in a short time had given the scene and the audience so much, only to be snatched away from them too soon.

Luke was so disgusted by his own thoughts that he had to leave the club.

Underneath the dark evening sky, far back in the audience at Ushuaïa, an addiction therapist was also watching. John McKeown had come to the club not so much for the sake of the performance, but to try to understand the world that surrounded his future client.

It was McKeown and his staff who had been entrusted by Tim's family with trying to help the artist who was now bouncing behind the decks up there on stage.

A few weeks earlier, Klas Bergling had visited the therapist's newly opened clinic, which was located in an old farm on the island. Klas had been clearly worried. No attempts they had made so far to bring their son out of his addiction had worked, and now professional help was needed.

McKeown had also spoken to Tim's manager and tour manager, and by this time had got a picture of a young man who had become undiscerning and self-destructive. A person who lay in bed for hours even though he knew that others were waiting in the room next door, who had recently been in a car accident because they were in such a hurry getting to one of all these Ushuaïa gigs. Before one landing this summer, Tim had passed out on the plane; several in the crew thought he had died.

It would certainly not be an easy case, McKeown thought. Addicts were always difficult and demanded patience; he knew that after a long and successful career back home in England. During the 90s, John McKeown had been involved in developing a treatment programme for the country's prisons. It had started with eleven prisoners in Surrey – when John asked for a urine sample, it had turned out that all but two had drugs in their bodies. After a couple of years of regular therapy, the difference had been clear. The upset cell blocks settled down; the inmates started to greet the prison staff. The most important thing was that the number of repeat offenders had decreased.

After that, McKeown had worked as a therapist for football star Paul Gascoigne, who for a few years had been a favourite of the British press. Together they had written a book about Gascoigne's path away from addiction, which for the therapist had led to consulting assignments for several of the major football clubs in the country.

An aircraft on its way in to land thundered over the audience at Ushuaïa, Avicii mixed over into a new song.

John McKeown thought about how the confrontation with

the artist would go. He had written a form for Tim's friends and family to fill out. He wanted to help them remember specific events that made them worried about Tim's health. From experience, McKeown knew that it was important that everyone had formulated their thoughts before the meeting took place. When emotions ran high, it was so easy to lose heart and become discouraged, especially when you tried to convince someone you loved. Usually, you only got one chance to persuade, so it was of the utmost importance that everyone knew what to say.

Now there was at least a plan. They were to confront Tim after his final gig in Ushuaïa.

KLAS BERGLING BECAME UNEASY when he looked around the living room in Tim's villa in the mountains of Ibiza. Arash Pournouri had arrived, Tim's bodyguard and tour manager were there, and Tim's big brother David had also come to attend the meeting.

They all seemed to feel equally tense, as they restlessly went and picked at the snacks that the chef had set out in the kitchen. Now was the time that it needed to happen, they all knew it. Still, Klas could not let go of the feeling that he had betrayed his son, that they had conspired against him.

Throughout the afternoon, they had sat in a conference room in the hotel part of Ushuaïa with John McKeown and gone through the form the therapist had asked them to fill out. Several of the guys had cried as they spoke, but the rehearsal had also prepared them.

At six o'clock in the evening, Tim came down the stairs as the girl he had slept with crept away behind him. A rush of discomfort ran through Klas when he met his son's some-what uncertain gaze. Tim must have noticed that something was going on because he greeted John McKeown so appre-hensively – he had never met the man before and did not understand who he was.

They went and sat on the chairs that stood in a semicircle in front of the speakers, the synthesisers and other instruments. Tim took a seat in front of the stairs leading out to the pool, the therapist made sure that he ended up directly to the left of Tim.

It was Arash who spoke first.

'So, we're here because we have some concerns about you. And we've asked John here to come and facilitate.'

Tim's facial expression changed.

'Wait a minute,' he said. 'Is this an intervention?'

John McKeown tried to sound as calm and secure as possible.

'Yes, Tim. This is an intervention. We do this out of love and care; hopefully you'll be able to tell.'

Tim nodded warily. At least he did not rush out of the room; that was a good sign.

'If you don't mind, we're just gonna go around and share some examples,' McKeown continued. 'You'll be able to give your point of view in a minute, so please just try to just listen if you will.'

The friends followed their script from the rehearsal a few hours earlier. They talked about when Tim became ill in Belgium two years earlier. About the weight loss in Stockholm last autumn. About the overdose in Mexico and the outbursts of anger that came with withdrawal.

'There hasn't been a day in the last couple of years when I haven't lied about your addiction,' said one of his friends. 'What scares me the most is the fact that nothing surprises me any more.'

Tim was pissed off and started fighting back. One after the other, these people were declaring that they were worried about him.

'Why are you confronting me? You have been a part of it all. You should all get treatment.'

At least he performed; he had just finished his album, he'd delivered. Wasn't that what everyone wanted?

'I've noticed that your curtains are drawn,' McKeown said.

'Yeah?'

'Do you keep them closed a lot?'

The room fell silent. Tim was on his guard. The therapist

saw the confusion in his eyes – why did this old man talk as if he knew him?

'Tim, I've spoken to the others already,' McKeown continued. 'I've got to know you from a distance. And I've learned that the real Tim wouldn't keep his curtains closed. Especially not with this view.'

Without warning, a window opened. Thunder and lightning lit the rocks outside the panoramic windows. The staff started running around in the rain to secure the outdoor furniture.

Tim seemed almost unmoved by the claps. John was amazed at how stubborn this guy was. They had been sitting for several hours and energy was running low. John felt that there was a risk that they would not succeed. He asked everyone except Klas, Arash and some of Tim's friends to leave the circle. While the others went up to the guest rooms, the protracted negotiation continued. They sat there for several hours more, while Tim defended himself and declared that he was not an addict. He did not even like drugs!

'All right,' McKeown said when it was around two in the morning. 'We might have to end here. And it's a shame because you're really missing out on quite the opportunity.'

Then one of Tim's friends spoke. He would be willing to go to the clinic to keep his friend company, he said.

Tim finally agreed.

'Okay then. I'll go.'

The house exploded in cheers and applause and as Tim's other friends came running downstairs, Klas patted the therapist's back. Filled with a tingling rush of happiness, he went out on the wet porch and hugged his son.

'I decided several hours ago.' Tim smiled at his father. 'I just wanted to see how long you lasted.'

THEN THEY DROVE on rain-washed roads, past olive groves and quince trees and through the small village of Santa Gertrudis before the car turned off on to a gravel road. The forest hid a white-stepped stone mansion, the dwelling house of an old orchard.

Tim had been assigned the clinic's finest room. In the ceiling above the bed the timber frame was visible; next to the small desk was a fireplace. On the whole, the old farm was carefully renovated, and in the common rooms wooden chairs and clay pots remained from the time when the farm was one of the mainstays of the village.

The garden and the houses were divided into two levels. At the top was a screened and, in practice, private part of the facility. In front of the terrace, the lawn spread out, full of colourful trees and shrubs. A gardener cared for palm lilies, cassava and hibiscus bushes. Tim's room was up here.

Stone stairs led down to the main part of the rehab centre. The other clients lived there – including, at this time, a woman who had been on detox fifteen times and a British man whose heroin addiction had driven him to steal from his children. There was also a shared kitchen and a room for group therapy where tissues were always ready in a container on the floor.

On the first morning, the clinic's psychiatrist had examined Tim Bergling and found that he was suffering from fatigue syndrome. It was a straightforward diagnosis to make – he was easily irritated, had difficulty concentrating and could not

The inflamed pancreas had made Tim dependent on painkilling opioids. He would keep pill bottles in the studio as well as at his home in Los Angeles, where Pomeranian Oliver often kept Tim company on the sofa.

Racquel Bettencourt, a Canadian student whom Tim had met at a gig with David Guetta in Las Vegas, was now on the tour.

Tim felt he was growing as a songwriter and composer, and wanted to create an album that would make an impression in music history. The single 'For a Better Day', co-written with singer Alex Ebert, marked a shift towards songs with a more minimalist bite.

At the same time, the painkillers had made Tim moody and irritable. In the summer of 2014, he punched his hand into a wall and had to do the rest of the season's gigs with his hand bandaged up.

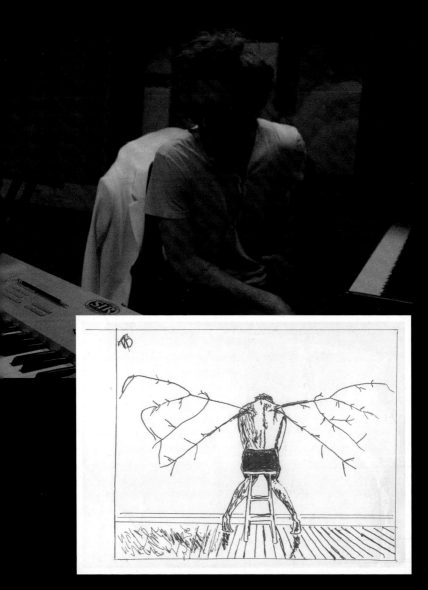

In the autumn of 2015, at the same time as the second album *Stories* was released, Tim was admitted to a rehab centre in Ibiza. After a few days of talking with the therapists, Tim made a drawing that depicted how he felt after the years of pills and constant overwork.

In the clinic, Tim started exercising at the outdoor gym down by the pool. Many new insights came to him during this period. Among other things, he tried practical techniques to be more in the moment and listen to his body's signals.

Soon after the months of rehabilitation, Tim embarked on a bus ride through national parks in the United States. Together with, among others, Swedish songwriter Carl Falk, he wrote songs like the freedom-seeking 'Without You'.

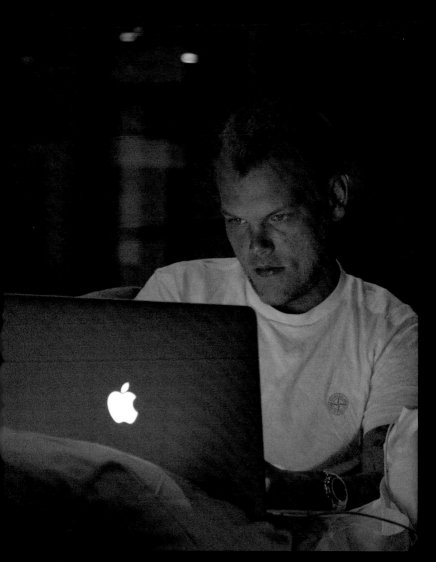

After a particularly stressful gig at the Ultra Music Festival in Miami, Tim decided to fundamentally change his life. He wrote a letter to his fans, in which he explained that he would no longer tour and perform. 'I have too little left for the life of a real person behind the artist,' he wrote.

Tim's new life meant other priorities. He continued to travel, but no longer as a busy superstar – now he was an ordinary tourist taking selfies with llamas or hiking with his childhood friend Fricko Boberg and Jesse Waits on Table Mountain in South Africa.

Jesse Waits, one of Las Vegas's biggest club promoters, had become a close friend. In the summer of 2017, he went with Tim and some other friends to the rainforest of Peru to get rid of stress and participate in indigenous ceremonies.

One of Tim's travelling companions was his new girlfriend, the Czech-born Tereza Kačerová. In the autumn of 2017, she had stormed into Tim's life with unbridled energy and her son Luka, whom Tim became very fond of. He felt more and more that he himself wanted to be a father soon.

The trips were interspersed with lazy days in the glass villa in Los Angeles, which after a long period of renovation was finally just as Tim wanted it.

After a time of musical drought, Tim's creativity returned in the spring of 2018. He invited a whole bunch of Swedes, including Albin Nedler and Kristoffer Fogelmark, here in yellow, to his house in the Hollywood Hills to record new songs. This time, Tim focused on the lyrics, and in songs like 'Freak' he dealt with topics such as addiction and shame.

In early April 2018, Tim went to Oman. He immediately fell in love with the breathtaking views of the mountains and the desert, but also sought freedom through long hours of meditation. In retrospect, many of his collaborators and friends wonder if he may not have been feeling as well as he himself wanted to believe.

Tim Bergling's death shocked the music world. His musical courage, the playful way in which he brought together different styles and elements, was praised in the press. At the same time, millions of fans testified to the importance of his music in their lives. Tim's melodies and lyrics, characterised by light and hopefulness, were a strengthening force when life was tough.

Tim Bergling was 28 years old.

After Tim's death, his family founded the Tim Bergling Foundation, to support organisations that combat mental illness among young people.

wind down even though he was so tired. They discussed how they would reduce his medicines. These comprised an extensive list of painkillers, anti-anxiety medications, antidepressants and sedatives that Tim had been using over the past year. Most patients tried to negotiate to make the process as slow as possible, but Tim had the opposite attitude. He wanted the detox to go quickly, like tearing off a plaster. He had been through it before, he explained, had got through withdrawal all on his own.

The treatment director Paul Tanner had his office in the lower part of the garden in a farmhouse facing the lemon grove. Here stood heavy furniture that smelled of wood and shelves swelling with leather-bound books.

Just like the founder of the treatment home, Paul Tanner was from the United Kingdom, but he had worked for a long time on the Spanish island. He had started the local branch of Narcotics Anonymous here and later became the organisation's representative for all of Spain.

Freshly awake and somewhat reluctant, Tim strolled into the room late one afternoon. The treatment director moved his chair to the side of the desk, leaning forward towards his new client.

'Tim, I need to tell you something. I've never heard of Avicii. I've listened to a couple of your songs now, but I'm not gonna let your job come into this room with you.'

Tanner hesitated. It was difficult to read Tim's reaction. Perhaps he had started off too hard?

'That sounds right,' said Tim.

The director described what he had heard. Stories about a selfish person who held meetings lying in bed, who kept his co-workers waiting for him for hours, who had recently disappointed his audience with sloppy performances.

'I don't believe that's who you really are, Tim.'

'No, it's not. But that has nothing to do with my medication.'

'So what is it, then?'

'Everybody's just on me, wanting me to do stuff. And I have a hard time telling them no.'

As Tim saw it, he was not here because he needed to be, but so that everyone around him would stop fussing: his father, Arash, his friends, everyone who had been at that intervention.

Paul looked at Tim, who was now sitting on the edge of the chair, gesturing wildly. A smart guy, he thought. Verbal, intelligent, interesting. Not at all in touch with his emotions.

One afternoon, Paul rolled in a whiteboard and placed it in the middle of the room. He started by drawing a sea with billowing waves and then a small yacht bouncing on the horizon.

Then he sketched a large, pointed triangle whose top protruded above the water's surface.

'This iceberg represents the behaviour of addiction,' he said. 'The withdrawal, the outbursts, the egotism, the betrayal of one's own ideals.'

This bit, the top of the iceberg, was the part that was simple to discover, what those around an addict usually reacted to sooner or later. But this was really just a symptom, Tanner continued, a sign of something else.

The real problem always lurked deeper.

Paul Tanner pointed to the larger part of the iceberg that lay below sea level in his picture.

'What's really interesting is what's hidden here,' he said.

To understand destructiveness, and thereby be able to put an end to it, one needed to understand the iceberg: why a human being wanted to numb themselves, what norms society had instilled.

Paul Tanner started talking about his own journey. It was

usually a good way to build trust. He told of his upbringing outside London in the 60s, how his father had died in a plane crash in the military and the long shadow his death had cast over the family. His mother had been ashamed of living on her husband's Air Force pension and had become increasingly blunt and mean, drinking sherry in secret at night. Her hugs had begun to feel sloppy and theatrical, as if the movements had been rehearsed. A strict stepfather, who also thought the family's circumstances were embarrassing, had entered Paul's life. But neither of the two adults had acknowledged or processed his mother's drinking and mood swings, instead they had all adapted to them.

Everything they stayed quiet about grew stronger in that silence. Reality became distorted while the adults were pretending that everything was in order.

The young Paul learned to do the same: to keep it together, to never show weakness. To suppress and hold everything in.

He had been ashamed of so much, he said. Ashamed because his reactions felt wrong, ashamed when he got angry, ashamed because he was ashamed. Subconsciously, he developed methods of coping with life, a false sense of self with which he soon fully identified. All people used coping mechanisms like this, he explained, and they could look very different. Some worked until they crashed, others diverted attention from their hardships by always joking, some wanted to save the world, many drank. They were all lying to themselves.

The behaviour was passed down from generation to generation. It did not happen out of malice, but parents who were unable to deal with their own emotions eventually influenced their children to do the same.

Paul had dressed his addiction in a romantic and rebellious costume – he had started smoking weed to protest against the traditional British middle class, he had tried heroin because he wanted to broaden his horizons.

But at the bottom of it all was shame. The heroin had become a soft embrace to relax in. The lust that shot through his body during the high, the pleasant distance from the outside world. Getting a fix was like sinking into a hot bath.

Tim Bergling got some help carrying a couple of deckchairs up on to the roof. In one direction he overlooked the garden, the pink bougainvillea that climbed along the white stone wall. On the other side ploughed fields stretched far and wide, and Tim could see all the way to the coast.

Paul Tanner had given Tim a blue notepad and asked him to write down what his life had been like up until now. At first he found it difficult to write, so instead he started drawing.

He sketched a figure with his back to the viewer. The young man was sitting on a stool, his upper body bare, the back hunched over, his head bowed. The body looked tense, the man closed in. Pierced into his back sat dark, gnarled tree branches.

Like spears skewered into the canvas of his flesh.

BY THE REHAB CLINIC'S gravel driveway was a staff room. Inside was a safe. The therapists took the clients' mobile phones, tablets and computers and locked them away. One of the most important rules here was that most of the days would be spent without access to a screen.

According to managing director John McKeown, this was significant for several reasons. Sitting in therapy sessions while withdrawal was ravaging the body was a shaky process in itself; in such a situation no phone ringtone should begin to sing. It was about a basic respect for the seriousness of the situation.

That was one thing.

But there were also other reasons, more worrying tendencies, recent surveys that seemed to say something about what effects this little device in the pocket had, not least on young people.

It was worth recalling how rapidly the digital shift had come about, and how revolutionary it had been. When John McKeown started working as a therapist just over a decade earlier, no one knew what a selfie was. YouTube did not exist, nor did Facebook or Instagram. The news came in small doses a few times a day; photographs were looked at in albums after sending in a film roll with twenty-four pictures to be developed. An anxious person did not sit and hyperventilate in front of Google, but simply went to the doctor.

In tandem with all the new ways of life, mental health issues had increased dramatically among young people. In the United States, studies had shown that depressive symptoms among high school students had skyrocketed since 2011, among both boys and girls. For girls, the increase was on its way to fifty per cent in just a few years. Even among college students, the dismaying curves pointed straight up, and soon more American students than ever suffered from symptoms of depression.

The role of smartphones in this development was still controversial. Of course, having the internet constantly in your pocket meant fantastic advantages – powerful protests could be started online, where people also could have direct contact with politicians or artists in a way that had previously been unthinkable. But one could also get caught up in destructive patterns of jealousy and anger. The collective behaviour scared McKeown – if there was nothing to be dissatisfied with, then social media would surely create something.

On the internet, one was often either perfect or useless, and if someone made a mistake, not only the actions but the individuals themselves were attacked, something that was especially true for public figures.

Above all, McKeown thought, the line between work and leisure had been almost completely dissolved. Many of his clients had jobs where they were expected to be reachable virtually around the clock: answering emails from bed, having appointments on the subway or on the bus. The noise of information never ceased, and stress-related conditions were on the rise. Prolonged stress, by the way, was the most common cause of depression.

Unsurprisingly, Tim Bergling thought it was a relief to turn off intrusions from the outside. No emails to deal with, no deadlines, no phone calls or text messages about where he would be and when. Instead, Paul Tanner pulled out a book from the shelf and handed it to Tim, who hesitantly began to page through it. *The Power of Now: A Guide to Spiritual Enlightenment* was written by a spiritual self-help author named Eckhart Tolle. In the preface, he said that he had long been plagued by depression and suicidal thoughts before he found the way to his inner peace.

Tolle said that we in the Western world too easily got caught up in demands and expectations. We all had an involuntary inner dialogue with ourselves, with a voice that judged, compared, attacked and complained. This demanding voice was our ego, and the only thing that mattered to the ego was what we had accomplished in the past and what we needed to do in the future. The present did not exist. But beyond that constant self-torture, on the other side of stress and deadlines, Tolle promised that it was possible to find the real self.

Tim read with increasing interest, felt how the message spoke to him and began to try out Tolle's thoughts in practice.

According to the author, the first step towards true inner peace was to learn to be present in the moment. The reader was encouraged to try to pay attention to even the smallest everyday actions, such as taking each step up a flight of stairs in peace and quiet, or observing your breathing. 'Or when you wash your hands,' wrote Tolle, 'pay attention to all the sense perceptions associated with the activity: the sound and feel of water, the movement of your hands, the scent of the soap.'

When Tim reached the last page, it was as if he had been punched by Mike Tyson. He put it that way in a message to his friend Jesse Waits when he, after three weeks in the clinic, felt ready to again make contact with the outside world.

22 September 2015

Tim Bergling:

Still learning

But I'm aware of things now that I wasn't before

Coping mechanisms

It can be drugs alcohol medication – even healthy stuff like working out, overworking. Shit that society will praise you for but in the end that anxiousness will still be there

My two biggest insights about myself are powerlessness and procrastination. I've always known but I've never realised how it all fits together

Take me being late as an example

Which has been a problem for abt 4 years. Coincidentally I've felt completely powerless and overwhelmed by the machine that is Avicii – never-ending touring etc etc. I've never felt like I had a choice – because the alternative was presented to me by Ash as disappearing as an artist overnight basically. So ofc I've always had a choice but in reality not rly

Jesse Waits:

Makes perfect sense

Tim Bergling:

So connecting this to me being
late – that's the only real thing I've
felt like I've been in control of

So it's been a coping mechanism
for my anxiety

Jesse Waits:

Wow

Makes it easy to understand

IN THE BEGINNING of October 2015, Avicii's second album, *Stories*, was finally released. The major music magazines were reserved in their reviews. 'It's time to stop calling Avicii EDM,' wrote *Billboard Magazine*, describing a record designed by a skilled pop musician. Although Tim Bergling was consciously looking away from the narrow confines of electronic dance music, many critics thought he had lost his way amongst power ballads, rap songs and mainstream rock. As if the artist now shunned the howling loops that had always been the hallmark of his own genre. A collection of completely ordinary songs with a splash of house, said the harshest critics, who thought that it was in classically filtered house tunes such as 'Talk To Myself' and 'Touch Me' that Avicii came into his own. 'Too bad that *Stories* brings so little to the EDM conversation,' *Rolling Stone* concluded their sour review.

The opinions of the critics, however, did not really matter right now. Mentally and physically, Tim Bergling was somewhere else entirely.

At night, he made excursions into the forest that surrounded the rehab centre. In amongst the pines, where the wild rabbits slept in their underground tunnels, it was completely silent. The only thing Tim could hear was his own steps on earth and grass.

In the afternoon sun, he would usually be working out in the lower garden, where there was a simple outdoor gym: some old dumbbells and barbells, a couple of exercise balls and mats, a punching bag on a rope. His feet danced against the tiles as Tim listened to the muffled sound his hands made when they met the packed sand.

It felt almost unreal to start taking everything in again, as if his brain was rusty. His whole body had received chemical help for so many years that it hadn't worked on its own. After twenty minutes, the bag was covered in blood from Tim's knuckles and he loved it.

He thought about what treatment director Paul Tanner had said about coping mechanisms.

Tim saw similarities with his own behaviour over the years and realised that instead of confronting his feelings, he had put out smokescreens. It was an image he thought made sense – the infantry that hid their movements on the battlefield by letting clouds of smoke grow against the sky.

He had become a pro at pretending that everything was fine. With his smokescreens he had misled not only himself but also Arash and Klas and all the others. Of course, they were annoyed every time he came up with excuses for not doing an interview or a photo shoot or a promo, every time he had stayed under the covers even though he knew that those waiting for him in the lobby would end up dealing with the shit.

He had become a good illusionist, really good. But this somewhat clumsy strategy, to push the problems out of way, had in turn created even more anxiety.

It had not really started with Avicii even, he now realised. In an email, he explained to his mother:

This behaviour goes back to when I started getting acne in my teens, how I started skipping school etc if I had a bad day. You just escape the problem, it's really the same thing as a medicine, you just deflect and deflect and it all turns into super anxiety in the end, not only for myself but for everyone else of course.

After a month in the clinic, everything felt so different. Tim had shaved off his hair. The crew cut symbolised his fresh start, so did the muscles from boxing. He longed to see how those at home would react when they saw his new style.

He had found a video on YouTube, a clip of a show he'd done three months earlier in the Moroccan city of Rabat. The camera, held up by a hand in the middle of the sea of people, filmed yellow and green laser beams dancing over the heads of the crowd. A bare-chested guy sat on his friend's shoulders, a little further up in the audience waved a Swedish flag.

Tens of thousands of people chanted in 'Wake Me Up', while images of beautiful desert landscapes illuminated Tim's silhouette from behind.

'ALL THIS TIME I WAS FINDING MYSELF AND I DIDN'T KNOOOW I WAS LOST!'

His songs really touched people, it was clear to see. He had been so far into the furious madness that he had not had time to take that in. He had bought the premise that Avicii would be nothing without marketing and interviews, without pyrotechnics and laser beams. But what it really came down to was something stemming from within himself. Something that people could relate to. What was in him also lived in others.

'It kinda made me feel proud for real for the first time in a while,' he wrote to Paul Tanner.

He seemed to have matured several years in just a few weeks and wished someone had taught him to think like this before. The negative emotions were not something you needed to be

264

afraid of or turn away from. The pain did not have to signal anything bad but, on the contrary, it could well be the first sign of health.

A warning flag.

'Gonna be taking charge now,' he wrote in a text message to Jesse Waits.

Listen to your other emotions and to what they are telling you about the world around you, what advices they are giving you. Got a bad feeling about something? If interpreted correctly, following that bad feeling will always provide you with the best possible outcome.

A FEW MONTHS LATER, Tim was sitting in a folding chair in the middle of the American desert, in front of Monument Valley's bright red rock formations which towered in the distance. They were iconic silhouettes, depicted in lots of old western movies from Hollywood's childhood. The wind swept over the deserted landscape, grabbing the microphone stand that stood in the gravel. Tim bounced in front of the computer as large speakers shouted a powerful drum break out in the wilderness.

It was one of Tim's bros who had suggested to get away for a while after his time in rehab, get inspiration from new surroundings.

Maybe they should go out and travel?

Said and done. They were a large company of Swedish musicians who had started from Malibu and set off east in three buses. The idea was that in just over a week they would travel across the country to Miami, where Tim was again booked on Ultra Music Festival's main stage in March 2016. On the way, they would stop in various national parks, unpack the equipment on stone and sand, and write songs in the cool spring sun.

Sebastian Furrer from Cazzette was with them, as were Sandro Cavazza and Dhani Lennevald, a couple of young singers who had assisted on two of the tracks on *Stories*. Another of the travellers was Carl Falk, a Swedish songwriter who on his CV had hits for such diverse artists as the boy band Westlife and hip-hop star Nicki Minaj, and who now stood by one of the synths and tried out a chord progression.

The journey took place in a new musical landscape. Recently, the tempo in house music had slowed down and the sonic explosions had faded. The leader of the style called tropical house was Kygo, a Norwegian two years younger than Tim who had grown up with Avicii as his greatest role model. Kygo dressed just like his idol, in check shirts and a back-facing cap, and in many ways his style built on Tim's most playful periods. Conga drums and meditative pan flutes met restrained dance-hall and Mediterranean pop. Martin Garrix now made songs with deep whistles and in Calvin Harris and Rihanna's latest collaboration, 'This Is What You Came For', the hard crescendo shone with its absence. Instead, the drop made the melody slowly swim, pulsating and restrained. Justin Bieber's world hit 'Sorry', produced by Skrillex among others, smelled of Puerto Rican reggaeton and evoked images of haze in the rainforest.

The new direction suited Tim's mood perfectly. The open expanses surrounding him made the productions feel rested and newly awakened, with feather-light parts and bouncing hits against steel pans.

Out in the desert landscape, the puppy that Tim just got could tumble around completely freely. Liam was a pit bull with black streaks in his white fur and a dark pirate patch over his left eye. Inside the bus, it was more difficult to travel with the dog, which slid back and forth across the floor and pooped impressive amounts in piles that no one bothered to pick up.

Filmmaker Levan Tsikurishvili was also on this trip, just as he had been on tour in Australia three years earlier. He had got to know Tim by now, practically become one of the gang, and collected material for another film about Avicii. On a specially built website, parts of the trip were broadcast live. The most loyal fans could therefore follow how the gang sat on the bus after a day in the Grand Canyon, worn out and quite giggly. A couple of months earlier, Salem Al Fakir and Vincent Pontare had sent a demo to Tim. The chorus was a mighty roar after liberation – the first association was a break-up from a relationship, but the lyrics of 'Without You' could be interpreted more broadly than that. To leave something, to make a divisive but necessary change in life.

The chorus in Salem and Vincent's sketch was as powerful as could be, but the verses were too slow and fuzzy. Someone had brought a cheap plastic synthesiser on the bus and Carl Falk this evening came up with a more efficient riff. It felt like Swedish folk music in a major key. Tim loved the new idea and Sandro Cavazza's singing made a mighty addition to the song. Tim looked forward to playing it before the crowd in Miami.

As the bus drove on to a mountain range in New Mexico, there was plenty of time to kill. Tim had found a personality test online. The questions were about how he handled different situations – when he felt anxious and when he was calm.

'You enjoy vibrant social events with lots of people.'

Tim tapped to the far edge of the seven-point scale to mark that the statement was incorrect.

'The time you spend by yourself often ends up being more interesting and satisfying than the time you spend with other people.'

Tim clicked on the other end of the screen – that's exactly how it was. When all the statements were answered, the computer thought for a moment before concluding that Tim was INTP, or in other words a logician. A long text stated that the logician was introverted, and to explain that concept, the script also talked about the man behind the ideas.

Carl Jung was one of the twentieth century's most influential psychologists and thinkers. One of the Swiss man's most significant theses was that of two basic human types. According to Jung, extroverted people were dependent on their surroundings and could skilfully adapt. To them, socialising was fun and valuable, through the eyes of others they gained their self-worth. Introverts, on the contrary, were self-sufficient and driven by their own emotion. They did not need many friends and could have difficulty with social situations. Even introverts could certainly become good at small talk, but rather out of necessity than desire. They came home tired from parties, exhausted.

Tim ploughed through the text, more and more amazed. It felt like he was reading about himself in a whole new language.

In addition to being introverted, Tim had been categorised as intuitive and thinking, which was apparently an unusual combination. These types, the logicians, could have a hard time relating to others. Professionally, they often ended up in science or technology, immersed themselves and became prominent in their field. They could have trouble with deadlines, difficulty understanding the signals of others, hard to find a partner to share their lives with. But what did it matter? They gave birth to new thoughts and expressions, they brought society forward. The text listed some examples: Albert Einstein and Isaac Newton. The philosopher Socrates. And then Carl Jung himself, this thinker that Tim now wanted to know all about.

'I had so much fucking fun today,' Tim told Cazzette member Sebastian Furrer when he came out to the sofas in the bus again. 'You know who Carl Jung is?'

'Yeah, I recognise the name,' Furrer said a little hesitantly.

'He was like an old psychologist, you know? He had a system with a lot of different personality types. It's so fucking cool!

I've been sitting all day reading. It kind of explains the psyche completely for me.'

Tim waved his hands. He described how he had now acquired concepts that described exactly the discomfort he had always felt making small talk backstage with different industry people.

'I have always felt that I have been judged for not being an extrovert. I finally understood why I should not care what others think. It's so nice. For me, it becomes a kind of path . . . to feeling better.'

Tim bit his nails, pleased.

'That sounds really nice. Carl Jung?'

'Carl Jung. A fucking king, man.'

A few weeks later, on 19 March 2016, Tim and Carl Falk sat in the back seat of a large black car, each with a computer in their lap.

They had finally arrived in Miami and it was terribly hectic. Tim wanted to open the gig at Ultra with 'Without You', the new song from the bus trip, but the blocks on the computer screen were not where they should be. Inspired by U2's magnificent arena gigs, Carl Falk had made a majestic intro that would set the mood for the entire performance, but they were still unsure of what should happen after the chorus.

While the car was driving towards Bayfront Park, Tim and Carl sent files between them, editing and fine-tuning. As they approached the festival area, the noise of the crowd increased. Tim had not been on a stage for more than six months and recognised the tingling that welled up in his body.

It was not a good feeling.

The driver steered into the tumult, among the tens of

thousands of people crowded in their neon wigs, butterfly wings and body paintings, longing for a party.

'Oh damn, it's Avicii!'

Someone had seen Tim in the back seat and now people ran towards the car, swarming around it like angry bees.

'AVICII! AVICII! AVICII!'

Tim stared at the screen. There was trouble with the USB stick where the songs would be. The roar was deafening. He needed to pee. When his bodyguard pulled open the car door, the phone cameras were immediately there and the flashes lit up the dark.

The performance was great and no one in the audience could have guessed how Tim felt. He premiered nine songs, found his rhythm, moved with vigorous control and authority up there. But afterwards it was possible to read in Tim's entire body language that something was wrong.

'Tim, shit. How's it going?' asked Carl Falk when they were back in the green room, surrounded by artists and roadies rushing around preparing for the next performance.

'I can't do this any more,' said Tim.

'What do you mean?'

'I just feel like I'm done with this shit. All these stares. I'm gonna call Ash and tell him. I can't even look people in the eye.'

Tim disappeared for yet another greeting with someone.

It had been his first gig in more than six months and he was put off by his own reaction in several ways. On the one hand, there was the pressure of facing so many people again, and the stress that some technical part of the stage production would fuck up. But even scarier was that somewhere deep down he felt how much he had missed this too. To be Avicii. To live through the ego.

After a late dinner, they ended up at the club Liv, in front of a packed dance floor. Tim called over visual producer Harry Bird.

'I just want to tell you before it's official. I've made up my mind.'

'What?'

They had to scream through the crowd.

'I'm cancelling all of my shows!'

'Fair enough. Shouldn't you just consider it overnight?'

'No, I felt it as soon as I got off the stage tonight. I don't want to do this any more.'

Harry was surprised by Tim's determination. If he cancelled gigs he had already signed, he would be forced to pay back advances and in addition it would surely upset a lot of people.

'Why don't you just see the last shows through? So that the fans can say goodbye and wave you off at least?'

'No, I'm gonna tell everybody now. I can't fucking do this any more.'

Just a week or so later, Tim, Fricko Boberg and the other friends from school were lying in the newly renovated glass house on Blue Jay Way in Hollywood.

After more than two years of construction and fixing, the house was finally habitable. Tim had picked up a blanket and lay down on the beige sofa right by the glass wall. Outside, Los Angeles glistened under a moon high in the sky.

'A special thank you to everyone who has been ... with ...'

Tim read the words aloud as he wrote, nervous about how the message he was trying to formulate would be received by his over three million followers on Instagram. But now that he had made up his mind, he wanted the audience to know as soon as possible.

Those who had not seen the other side of his life, how would they react when he told them he would stop touring? Many would surely be upset, thinking he was spoiled and lazy. Either way, this was the right thing to do.

All the hustle and bustle in Miami had become a confirmation that he had previously thought wrong. Take the pancreas, for example. The inflammation in his stomach had been interpreted as a threat, even by himself, something that slowed down his career. Now Tim reasoned they should all have interpreted the disease the other way around: like a throbbing plea from the body. A potential first step towards better health.

Tim wrote:

My path has been filled with success but it hasn't come without its bumps. I've become an adult while growing as an artist, I've come to know myself better and realize that there's so much I want to do with my life. I have strong interests in different areas but there's so little time to explore them.

I know I am blessed to be able to travel all around the world and perform, but I have too little left for the life of a real person behind the artist.

He stopped, bit his nails, trying to remember everyone he wanted to thank. Everyone who had made possible a career that would now drastically change. The music would never disappear, on the contrary: it was also to be able to fully focus on writing songs that he did this.

'There is a great risk that people will talk shit about you,' said one of his friends.

'It's fine,' Tim replied. 'I'd really like to send this out as soon as possible.'

'But are you in a hurry to post it?'

'Yeah, I am.'

'Why?'

'Because my body is telling me. That's the thing. What you said now is the same thing I have heard all along: "Calm down, there is no stress."'

Tim Bergling sat up on the sofa, arguing his case.

'It is so difficult for me to explain that stress is my life. That's what my body is telling me. And has been telling me for eight years.'

AS SOON AS THE letter was posted online, Tim felt himself lift off the couch. It was such a complete sense of happiness that he had never experienced anything like it. He lay there next to Fricko and his other childhood friends, bingeing documentaries and films, feeling like he was weightless. It was reminiscent of the game nights on Linnégatan a long time ago, but was even more wonderful.

For several days, Tim hovered in the air.

He followed the reactions closely. To his relief, he was met with understanding rather than protest. Many of the fans seemed to feel compassion for him, they too recognising the crazy pace of the times. Instagram and Facebook were filled with crying emojis and broken hearts.

Sometimes you just have to make yourself happy and not think about everyone else.

You deserve the life you want. Not because you're a superstar DJ but for the same reason we breathe. As a human.

Enjoy your youth and your freedom, travel the world and live all the experiences that you have always wanted to live.

Enjoy yourself babe. You are a free birdy now.

It turned out, however, that it was a little harder than that. Tim had about thirty gigs during the spring and summer of 2016 that had been planned for a long time and in principle were impossible to cancel. Reluctantly, he agreed to tour for a few more months. He went to the Arabian Peninsula, did Bahrain and the United Arab Emirates. To the great delight of his fans, Avicii finally returned to Asia – three years in a row he had cancelled performances in Shanghai, now they finally happened. He travelled between Osaka and Tokyo; he was in Bangkok and Seoul.

Ironically, the production on the farewell tour was more ambitious and beautiful than ever. Harry Bird had spent time in a forest outside London and with string lights, plywood and a sledge he'd created films depicting Màni, the god of the moon, who dragged the crescent after him. Harry himself had dressed in a bathrobe and masquerade mask, a friend had swung a toy sword, and with double exposures and tempo shifts, the images looked fateful and quite suggestive. They had found their ultimate visual language just when it was all over.

In addition to the decision to stop touring, Tim now made another radical decision – he would end his collaboration with Arash Pournouri and At Night. It was a feeling that had grown since the time in the rehab centre, and that felt more and more right. He would always love Arash, he was a brother. But they had been rubbing up against one another for so long now, and the quarrels had become more and more petty. Tim hired a man with background as general counsel of the furniture giant IKEA, to create an overview of the financial history and negotiate an end after eight years of collaboration between the artist and his manager.

Pournouri also communicated through a business lawyer, in a process that became divisive and complicated and where both felt that the other had betrayed trust. That was where they had ended up. Their different personalities, which had so often complemented each other, were now on a collision course.

The fundamentals of Tim's decision, however, had nothing to do with dull business law.

Tim wanted to be free from a lifestyle that was unsustainable.

Beyond the hectic touring life, he saw something completely different. Lying on the couch at home and playing computer games and cooking pizza in sweatpants. An existence that left time to have some beers and laugh with his siblings.

By the end of July, the tour had reached the Middle East. Between gigs in Tel Aviv and Beirut, Tim spent time watching lectures on YouTube. There was a whole world of gurus, life coaches and inspirational speakers that he got increasingly interested in after the months in the clinic.

In one particular clip, a well-dressed woman rose from the audience. She approached a microphone and introduced herself as Mary, saying that she worked in the human resources department of a big tech company. They had recently taken a course to learn how to support their colleagues, she said, and there was of course nothing wrong with helping others. But it was all the more difficult to be kind to oneself.

'You know, if I didn't accomplish anything I'm a failure to myself,' said this Mary. 'So, I was wondering if you have any advice for those of us who don't have as much compassion for ourselves.'

Tim watched the little man on the computer screen, the one who sat huddled in the armchair on stage. It was Eckhart Tolle, the self-help author that Tim has become so fond of in the last six months.

'When the enjoyment of what you're doing is lost, then you have to be careful,' Tolle said in a softly broken English that hinted at his German background. 'That's a dreadful thing to live with, living with a voice in your head that continually criticises you and tells you that you haven't done well enough. I mean, if you had to live with a person like that, you would leave.'

Big laughs from the audience, while the star smiled his gentle smile. It was the ego that spoke those negative words, according to Tolle. But there were ways to stop the mental chatter.

Tim had understood that these thoughts were inspired by Eastern philosophy and therefore sought further. On his tablet, alongside the comic book *Watchmen* and books by Carl Jung, Tim had also downloaded ten books by Thich Nhat Hanh, a Buddhist monk with an impressive life story. In the early 60s, as the civil war in the monk's native Vietnam intensified, Nhat Hanh and his allies had smuggled banned literature, rice and medicine to the civilians, prompting Martin Luther King to nominate him for the Nobel Peace Prize. From his monastery in France, the old man now continued to organise aid workers in his homeland, while teaching the basic ideas of Buddhism to Westerners.

Tim was attracted by the tangibility of the philosophy, that Buddhism was not only a religion but also a practical doctrine that required physical practice and application. There were no gods, no predetermined destiny. All people could change for the better, that was the conviction – that anyone could be enlightened.

The fundamental notion was that people were never satisfied. The longing for more was so deeply rooted in our nature that we always continued to chase in our hamster wheels. The endless cycle of birth and death was kept going by this human desire and could only be broken by self-knowledge and peace. That was what the pampered and spoiled Prince Siddhartha once realised under a tree at the foot of the Himalayas, when he reached Enlightenment and was transformed into the first Buddha of mankind.

Tim read *Peace Is Every Step: The Path of Mindfulness in Everyday Life*, in which Thich Nhat Hanh described mindfulness, a way of life that was part of Buddhism's eightfold path, the collection of actions that were considered to steer man away from suffering.

In essence, mindfulness was about developing one's ability to pay attention to what was happening in and around oneself. In silent meditation, the practitioner would observe the thoughts, feelings, fantasies, desires and sensations that flowed through the body. It was important to explore with an open and curious mind: no feeling was worse than another, the intention was not to value. By acknowledging one's anxiety or stress, one could eventually free oneself from its power. But the first step was to just register. Thich Nhat Hanh wrote:

> It is best not to say, 'Go away, Fear. I don't like you. You are not me.' It is much more effective to say, 'Hello, Fear. How are you today?'

It was now August 2016 and the road crew were on their last legs. Everyone was tired and nervous about Avicii's last appearance ever, which would take place in Ibiza. In a car outside the hotel, siblings Anton, David and Linda were waiting for Tim to come down from his room.

'Damn, it's the last one now,' David said as they set off for the beach and Ushuaïa.

'I know,' Tim said in a tone that revealed he was more on edge than usual.

He had prepared a set with an unusual number of obscure favourites from the past, such as an electro bootleg of rapper Dizzee Rascal's song 'Dirtee Cash', which he had done in the pad on Kammakargatan seven years earlier. 'Street Dancer', with its unexpected mix of pan flutes and breakdance drums, was also unearthed from that time, as well as 'New New New' and 'Tweet It'.

The three siblings stood at the VIP tables to the right of the stage and saw a magnificent end to an era.

'Hell, now we're doing it,' Anton shouted in David's ear.

They had started discussing the idea the day before, mostly jokingly: that they should give their brother a surprise. In the theatre world, it was a tradition during the last performance to play a prank on your fellow actors to get them off balance. In front of eleven thousand jumping people, it would take something very special even to be seen.

The brothers each sipped a confidence-boosting beer and pushed their way to the edge of the stage, where they were let through after some explanation and persuasion. Hidden behind the DJ booth, out of sight of both Tim and the audience, they began to take off their jeans and sweaters.

Just as Tim had turned up 'Silhouettes', Anton pulled his black underpants as high up his butt as possible. He tried to look calm as he slowly stepped on to the stage, followed by David in white boxer shorts.

They jumped and clapped their hands above their heads and Anton waved his butt a little extra, before concluding the dance number by turning to the high booth and bowing to their little brother.

Behind the yellow pillars of light, Tim laughed so much that the roll of tobacco slipped out from under his lip.

KLAS BERGLING HAD FOUND his favourite place out in the garden. Later in the day, the light would be too intense, but while the sun was still rising over the old fishing village in Skillinge, the air was saturated and pleasant.

Now that he was alone at the family's country house, Klas did not care about setting the table and stuff. He sat directly on the stone steps that led down to the lawn, eating his porridge.

He had taken the archaeological find out with him. The discovery was made the night before, when he cleaned out a cardboard box in the small office next to the kitchen.

The notebook with waxed covers must have been there for over twenty years. Among Klas's own reflections and drafts of jokes, the yellowed pages were full of things Tim had said when they had been here in previous years.

In the winter of 1993, when Tim was four years old and they attended the funeral of Anki's father:

'The skeleton is buried and the skin goes up in the sky.'

'Grandpa won't get any sand in his eyes, because the box is closed, right?'

Klas laughed as he read. An intelligent and sensitive boy, full of his own thoughts and formulations. 'Mother sick' meant longing for Anki, 'tune up a little' was a wish for Klas to raise the volume on the stereo.

'Sometimes the giants are very angry and today is sometimes.'

'What does nothing look like?'

Another note, this one from a six-year-old Tim:

'Dad, you see how I've changed? I help out, I do not leave the table right away. Soon I will probably start eating potatoes.'

Klas's youngest son had turned off his phone. Tim was bouncing among acacia trees and dry greenery, on the equator. They had already seen a herd of elephants, giraffes and a lioness wandering past the car, a jeep that had been rebuilt so that the sides were open.

Now their guide put a halt to their bumpy ride, and Tim and his friend each raised binoculars.

'Those are wildebeest,' said the guide, and pointed to a herd of black giants about forty metres away.

After the last show in August 2016, Tim had gone straight to south-western Kenya. Together with a childhood friend from high school, he was staying in a beautifully decorated tent right on the edge of the Maasai Mara, a game reserve known as one of the world's most abundant with animals. At this point of the year, The Great Migration was still underway, the period when over a million animals moved in from the dry fields of Tanzania in search of water and fresh grass.

Further away in the yellow landscape stood not only wildebeest but also some grazing zebras. They were waiting to cross the water, where the crocodiles were sunbathing on the riverbed. In a flash, the predators could catch a scent and mount an attack.

'Damn, I should have brought my real camera with me,' Tim laughed to the guide.

But not carrying any stuff, being completely surrounded by mile after mile of land that was never cultivated by humans, was overwhelming in a way that not even the most hysterical festival came close to. There were no film crews here, no demanding tour managers, and in just a few weeks the constant flow of requests and bickering in the mailbox had ebbed away. Apart from their safari guide, who cheerfully said that he loved 'Hey Brother', there were not many who recognised him on the Kenyan savannah.

Tim was, in short, free.

A few nights into the stay, he and his childhood friend sat reclining in beanbag chairs with the vastness of nature at their feet. Tim recognised the view, thinking that the environment was reminiscent of Barrens, the arid savannah landscape controlled by the Horde faction in World of Warcraft. The light was the same, as were the boundless expanses. The staff had lit a crackling fire in front of the crooked trees of the savannah, which slowly disappeared at dusk. While Tim sipped a drink made with honey, lime and a splash of gin, a group of men clad in red gathered in a circle in front of the hotel guests. They were Maasai warriors, belonging to the nomadic people who had lived off nature since time immemorial, before the armed colonisers arrived from Europe.

One of the men in red was apparently the leader of the choir. When he began the note of a first phrase, the others responded by throwing their heads back in synchronised movements. The warriors sang with humming sounds as their heads rose again. Tim watched in delight as the dancers alternately bent their upper bodies forward and backward, like a well-oiled zipper, while the wordless song increased in intensity and their bracelets rattled between the hand claps.

Then one of the men raised the spiral-shaped horn of an antelope and blew a forceful fanfare out over the wilderness.

Tim was struck by the drive, by the complexity of the rhythm.

'I have to work with these musicians,' he said afterwards to his guide. 'I'm coming back here, recording some songs. Then I will donate all the proceeds to you, to the Maasai.'

Then Tim went home to Stockholm for a longer visit. He had sold his apartment on Karlavägen and in the spring of 2017 instead rented a place on the same street where his parents lived, right by the rock cavity where he and his friends had had their secret parties in the past.

He had time to pick up his exercise routine again. Tim had received a training schedule from a new personal coach, this one also recommended by Vincent Pontare. Tim would alternate cycling and boxing at one-minute intervals for twenty minutes, followed by fifteen or eighteen reps with weights, depending on muscle group.

Tim also filled the kitchen cupboards with amino acids that would build protein and enzymes for better digestion. Vitamin D and probiotics were useful for the intestines and he would take a pill for optimal acid balance in the stomach.

'Look at my posture, Mum! I'm not walking crooked any more.'

Proudly, Tim strutted back and forth in the apartment, showing off for his mother. He had an attitude she had never seen before. He walked with his back straight and a steady gaze.

'Well, look at you my son!' Anki exclaimed. 'Damn, you're handsome!'

Tim felt that the insights came one after another. He sent a message to Paul Tanner, the head of treatment at Ibiza: 'This time after retiring is a good ego-handling bootcamp,' he wrote. 'I think my ego had found a lot of comfort in my "old" way of living and looking at the world – even tho it made me feel miserable!'

Feeling that his and Avicii's identities were no longer one and the same was unusual and a little painful. But at the same time, it felt just right. 'I don't have anxiety, nervousness or anything any more, not in the same way,' he wrote.

Tim thought the coping mechanisms he and therapist Paul Tanner had discussed were very interesting. He wondered why it had taken him so long to set boundaries – and not in that desperate way that had forced him to lay out smokescreens and hide in hotel rooms, but in a healthier way. Why had there been such resistance to addressing his feelings? It could very well be, as Paul said, that in all families there were dysfunctional behaviours that were passed on to a child. Unconsciously, generation after generation of parents taught their offspring to escape negative emotions rather than confront them.

But wasn't the question even bigger? The entire society applauded achievement and success, but seemed happy to look away as soon as things became more complicated.

Wasn't there a lot that society also kept quiet about? It had really started in school, Tim reasoned when he wrote down his thoughts in an email to Tanner.

My school experience in Stockholm, like most people's, was not very confidence building nor was it functional.

I was taught to suppress my emotions in a very unhealthy way from a very early age. It was promoted to talk about feelings, just not the bad ones, which in any human would cause a tremendous amount of confusion.

If there was home economics at school, where you had to learn how to cook a damn potato, why did the students not get to know more about how to handle all the hard feelings that came with adulthood? Why didn't they learn more about stress management? How to overcome sleeping difficulty and dark thoughts – that should be on the timetable.

Why should you be so strong and hard and quiet in the face of pain?

MANY OF THE IDEAS TIM got during this period were not primarily musical. He wanted to challenge himself in new areas, find artistic ways to comment on social issues. The video for 'For A Better Day' was a first step in this direction.

Many of Avicii's previous videos had been exuberant but trivial stories. Now Tim wanted to spark a debate about the children who, in the shadow of war, ended up in the clutches of cynical smugglers and were sexually exploited. Out of a container full of children, a cold-blooded trafficker chose his victims. The acclaimed actor Krister Henriksson, one of Tim's mother's closest friends, portrayed the heartless profiteer. Two of the children eventually retaliated by burning 'PEDOFILIA' on their tormentor's back and hanging him in front of a jubilant crowd.

It was a ruthless film, but nonetheless a dream of everyone's right to live out their full potential, free from the shackles of misery and poverty. To the audience, the story was an unexpected move from the otherwise so euphoric Avicii, and the video whetted Tim's appetite.

Now he wanted to do more similar things, and after his time in the clinic, it was spiritual development that was the closest to his heart.

He invited Per Sundin to his apartment to discuss how they should outline the next musical project. It would be a trilogy, three parts of five or six songs each. That way, they could present new music more often and keep the impatient music consumer in their grip. The music itself was not really much to talk about, Tim thought. In the computer he still had 'Without You' and lots of other sketches from the bus trip a year earlier. He had recorded 'What Would I Change It To' with guitarist Mike Einziger, and 'Friend Of Mine' had been added recently, another song written by Vincent Pontare and Salem Al Fakir with the help of Martin Garrix.

Tim was more interested in the framing of the tracks. He had a meticulous sketch of how the trilogy could be presented. The project would include sixteen songs, each inspired by the different levels of Buddhist hell. The idea was that each video would also represent part of Tim's journey towards insight and strength.

The main character would begin his journey in *arbuda*, a dark world surrounded by inhospitable mountains. He would walk alone as hail and ice hit his naked body. The pictures represented the self-doubting school days, when Tim tried to find his place in the hierarchies at Östra Real without really succeeding. Song number six would be inspired by *utpala*, a frozen environment where the character would turn blue when he got drunk before a gig. When he was prescribed painkillers in song eight, his body would instead become pleasantly warm and red.

The destructive spiral would then become increasingly apparent. The pancreas became infected: more pills. Gall bladder ruptured: more pills. The appendix burst: more pills. The same mistake would be repeated over and over again, and the main character would grow redder as he tried to buy himself out of his torments. But neither a new dog, expensive watches, a house nor more tattoos helped. They were just coping mechanisms.

In the end, this walk of hell would show that no one was

stuck in their circumstances, that it was possible to get a grip of one's emotions and life. To clarify the point, the first part of the suite would have the Buddhist spelling of the hell that Tim was named after – *Avīci (01)*. The tree on the cover represented hope.

'You can get out of the hole,' said Tim. 'When you turn your face up, you see the whole blue sky. The birds and the light.'

During the summer of 2017, Tim continued to travel. Despite having done so many laps around the world, he had seldom seen more than hotel suites, taxis, green rooms and the seats of private jets.

The Amazon River was something completely different. The brown and cloudy water stood almost still in the heat, while the freighter carried Tim further and further into the Peruvian rainforest. Bananas and livestock were transported on the ship's lower deck, Tim, Jesse Waits and some of the childhood bros were sitting on top.

It was Jesse's uncle, the old hippie who had lived in the jungles of Hawaii, who had given them the idea to go to Peru and drink *ayahuasca*. The brew was a concoction of hallucinogenic plants that had been used by South American natives for hundreds of years. After being a ritual that only appealed to the most daring tourists, the drink had in recent years begun to become hip in the US and Europe as well. The rite was said to help the practitioner get closer to the intuitive, the natural and the eternal.

Whatever the case, the brew certainly provoked physical reactions. There were many stories of people who had vomited in cascades at the same time as diarrhoea erupted from them in what the indigenous people called the purification. Then came the visions. What hallucinations the brew set off seemed to depend a bit on your own current state – if you were unlucky you could get the feeling of being nailed underground, suffer from malformed growths on your face or feel snakes crawling up your nostrils. But the intoxication could also lead you to magnificent valleys or uncover magical energy fields before the inner eye. A single ceremony, some said, was as significant as several years of therapy.

On the boat, Tim was excited about what was waiting further into the jungle. He sat on a rickety plastic chair with a computer in his lap and played his latest songs for Jesse Waits. Recently, he had been in Nashville for a couple of weeks, working with country music stars such as Kacey Musgraves, Keith Urban and Anderson East. His favourite song from the visit was 'You Be Love', which he had written together with, among others, Taylor Swift's producer Nathan Chapman.

Tim was proud of the lyrics, which he himself had been a driving force in formulating and which had become poetic and rich in images. The verses could be interpreted as a story of unconditional love, but also as something greater. Tim thought strange things had started to happen since he'd made the decision to stop touring. He had learned to play the piano magically fast, for example.

It was as if the universe, or perhaps even a spiritual energy, wanted him to be well. He was like clay in the hands of a great force that transformed him, cast him into who he wanted to be.

You can be the potter
I'll be the clay
You can be the blacksmith
and I'll be the blade

After more than a day's journey along the river paths, the travel companions went ashore deep in the Amazon. A medicine man greeted them by blowing some kind of tobacco mixture into their noses with a pipe, and showed them to a number of wooden huts built on piles above the muddy ground. Here, among bats and huge mosquitoes, they would live for almost a week.

In the evening, after dropping off their backpacks, the friends helped capturing frogs to get hold of the discharge that the giant leaf frog secreted when it became stressed. The shaman stabbed Tim with a burning stick, and when the top layer of skin had burned off, the medicine man stuck the frog secretion into the wound. The poison was said to stabilise blood pressure, strengthen the immune system and was the first part of the purification. As the poison spread in his bloodstream, Tim felt how difficult it was to breathe. The skin began to tighten around his mouth and his lips swelled up. The company looked at each other and laughed with tear-filled eyes. They all looked grotesquely wrinkled and distorted, as if they were three hundred years old.

The next day, the first ceremony would take place. Tim and the others had to go out into the jungle in search of the roots, vines and bark varieties that the brew consisted of. In a cauldron over a fire, the plants were boiled together and the friends took the worn mattresses from their shacks and placed them on the floor in a communal hut. Then the shaman blew tobacco smoke in their faces and began waving a leaf rattle as he whistled and sang hymns to nature and the holy spirits.

Tim and the others were served the green, viscous brew in small cups. Only with great effort could they keep the musty mud down, it tasted disgusting.

But Tim enjoyed every second. To lie down on a mattress in the middle of the rainforest and wait for a great cleansing, that was to experience life for real.

*

Neil Jacobson and the others at the record company in Los Angeles had no choice but to get used to an artist who had started to protect his free time passionately. *Avīci (01)*, the first part of the EP trilogy, was to be released in less than two weeks and Tim had still not approved the final mix of 'Lonely Together', the song he had done with singer Rita Ora. There would probably be no major issues, it was almost a formality. Tim only needed to listen to the song a couple of times so that they all agreed on how the drums would be in relation to the bass and if the sonics were clear enough. It used to take about half an hour.

Universal had worked out a marketing plan where the icing on the cake were ten black boxes to be sent to some particularly loyal fans. When a box was opened, the inside lit up at the same time as a speaker at the bottom started playing 'You Be Love'. The record company had calculated that the recipients would post videos of the box in their social media channels, and in this way they would get promotion that looked organic. There was a lot more that the record company was planning, but of course that presupposed that Tim was available.

But Tim's mobile was turned off, or perhaps lacked coverage – when Neil Jacobson called, he got nothing.

Just over a week later, at the end of July 2017, Jacobson prepared for an evening of some significance: he and his wife had invited an influential film agent to dinner with Neil's in-laws. Just as he was tying his tie, Universal's marketing manager called.

'You're not gonna believe this. Take a look at Avicii's Instagram!'

What Neil saw on his mobile screen was a llama, filmed from behind. A cool breeze seemed to make the fur dance, as the animal gazed across some valley in South America. Was it Machu Picchu?

Over the short film were tones that Neil recognised. It was the introduction to 'Friend Of Mine', the song by Salem Al Fakir and Vincent Pontare that would be the opening track on the EP.

Tim had written a short caption: 'New music is coming very (very) soon!'

'What the actual fuck is this?' mumbled Neil to himself. For months, they had been preparing the perfect way to launch Avicii's return, after a two-year silence. And then he posted a video of a llama?

Neil started scrolling through the comments on Instagram.

I CAN'T WAIT!!!!! THIS MUSIC IS JUST AMAZING!!!!!!!! WOW!!! <3

Gonna be craaaaaazy!!!!!

YES! OH MY GOD WE'VE BEEN WAITING FOR SO LONG!!! I LOVE YOU SO MUCH.

This song sounds so good @avicii <3 Your album is going to be a damn perfect masterpiece.

Everything about this post makes me happy.

For the next few hours, every online newspaper that Neil cared about picked up the news. Tim's new song began to be discussed wildly on Twitter – the evening with the film agent became a single long celebration.

When Tim finally called a few hours later, he seemed completely unaffected, barely aware that Neil had been chasing him for several days.

'Hey, dude. How's it going?'

'You fucking ... Tim. You lunatic. We've spent weeks strategising, putting all this money on elaborate plans. You post a picture of a fucking llama and everyone goes nuts. The internet is on fire, Tim. You're a genius!'

'Well, I don't know. I just felt like doing it. It felt right.'

TIM BERGLING BECAME increasingly comfortable talking openly about his emotional life. He had informed his team that he wanted to do bigger, more serious interviews about his health with journalists who could do his journey justice. Radio personality Howard Stern, for example, or music journalist Zane Lowe. Or the Canadian CBC cultural programme *Q*, where Deadmau5 had been portrayed in a respectful way. If Tim could just end up in the right context, he wanted to tell his story, and with some distance reflect on substance dependence, spirituality and mental health. He had told some of his friends that he eventually wanted to write a memoir – surely his story could help someone else in a similar situation.

In August 2017, he did a candid interview with *Rolling Stone*, where he explained why he had stopped performing.

'I needed to figure out my life,' he summed up for the reporter. 'The whole thing was about success for the sake of success. I wasn't getting any happiness any more.'

Avīci (01) had just been released, but fans had begun to get used to Tim Bergling suggesting self-help books rather than discussing melodic loops.

Tim had contacted the architect who had designed his glass house in Los Angeles and asked him to devise a certain kind of meeting place. Fashion designer Calvin Klein, who lived nearby, had an underground garage blasted into the rock below his house, and Tim envisioned a similar solution.

The idea was that talented creators, the foremost in their

respective fields, would meet up and collaborate. Game developers, film directors, inventors and philosophers would form a society that Tim wanted to call Aeterni – he thought the Latin word gave off the sense of tradition and education. They would reach the room via a shaft next to Tim's studio. In a lift, the meeting participants were to descend into the mountains of Hollywood, and just below the pool, Tim wanted to decorate seven underground bunker rooms. There, brilliant brains would sprout ideas that had real potential to change the world.

Among other things, Tim had sketched out a computer game, a further expansion of the game Spore. In the original, the player began as a primitive microorganism and the challenge was to develop into a carnivorous creature. Tim imagined a similar model, but with a completely different content. The game would be realistic, based on everything he had learned about personality types and coping mechanisms and the cycle of life and death. In the end, when the main character had beaten the game, it would have evolved into a human free from desire, someone who attained enlightenment like the Buddha under the tree. Spiritual fulfilment.

'None of us today can fucking handle our emotions,' Tim told *Rolling Stone*. 'That's why I had to stop touring, because I couldn't read my emotions the right way.'

Tim finally had time to live in the house in Hollywood that he had bought four years earlier. The decor had become just as relaxed and elegant as he had always wanted. The sturdy coffee table in bronze and high-lacquered stone, the chandelier whose chains fell to the floor like a soft lock of hair. The speckled marble tiles that dominated the bathroom, the black bed overlooking the entire city. Down in the movie theatre he had hung original posters of his favourite films such as *The Godfather* and *A Clockwork Orange*; in the bathrooms were the worn *Donald Duck* comic books from his childhood flea markets in Skillinge.

At the entrance stood the centrepiece of the home – a sparkling black grand piano by the manufacturer Steinway & Sons. It had cost nearly sixty thousand dollars, but it was worth it given the rich and clear sound that sang from the strings, made from Swedish steel. Tim, by this point, loved playing and had developed a technique that was quite peculiar. He did not use regular chords with both black and white keys; instead he played almost exclusively on the black ones. He often played only two notes with his right hand, a fifth or a quarter. It was at the other end of the keyboard that he made the big moves. When the incomplete chords on the right met the full bass tones on the left, unexpected and unconventional sounds filled the air.

However, Tim did not care about the theoretical side of things. He was just looking for what felt right in his gut.

The days in Los Angeles passed by at a comfortable pace. Tim would lie in bed watching *South Park*, which was still one of the funniest things he knew. The latest season of the series was about fake news on Facebook, microbreweries and Cartman, who had fallen in love with a virtual assistant.

In one of the episodes, the city's children's entertainers began to drop like flies. It turned out that Stan's grandfather was being blackmailed by an old lady who forced him to smuggle OxyContin out of the nursing home with the help of his unknowing grandson.

The granny farted loudly as she seized hold of the painkilling opioids, and Tim's boisterous laughter filled the bedroom. In the autumn of 2017, his new girlfriend often sat beside him. Tereza Kačerová had swept into Tim's life with intensity and spirit. They had started chatting with each other on the dating app Raya, and already on their first date Tereza had incited Tim to jump in a pool with his clothes on. On the second, she had shown him her favourite junk food: cheese puffs dipped in Nutella.

Since then, they had been inseparable; Tereza had practically moved in and they seldom got out of the bed. They ordered popcorn from ArcLight, the cinema, poured M&M chocolates into the cups and mixed it all together. They had become so lazy that Tim no longer walked to the kitchen but rode his Segway there. The two-wheeler's blue neon lights lit up the parquet floor on his journey towards more juice and ice cream.

Tereza was born and raised in the Czech Republic but had come to Los Angeles to become a model. She had worked for Diesel and been in a music video for the pop group Maroon 5. Now she was thinking about moving on from modelling. Putting on a jacket and laughing while ruffling her hair was too mindless. She wanted to write children's books and screenplays. Tim liked her creative side, the fact that her apartment was full of textbooks on psychology and that she knew very well who Carl Jung was.

Despite her spirited creativity, Tereza felt mature – perhaps because she already had a child, a nearly two-year-old son named Luka.

At first, Tim had been stiff and nervous in front of the boy. That passed once they had sat down in front of the grand piano and Tim showed Luka the basics of playing. Soon they created their very own worlds. When Tereza came to the bedroom with breakfast, she found Tim and Luka in a hut they had built with the duvet. They were sitting cross-legged – Luka in his nappy, Tim in underwear – and discussing something in gibberish. Tereza tried to crawl under the covers and was met by loud protests from her son.

'Mummy! Just boys!'

The newfound friends would lie out in the narrow pool for hours and toss Luka's stuffed fish back and forth, the ones that looked like Dory and Nemo from the animated films. Tim learned to change nappies and when Luka pooped in the pool, Tim helped find a strainer to fish up the mess. He was amazed at how much fun it was to take care of a child. In the evenings, he read bedtime stories about an affectionate truck that taught the other vehicles how to drive politely while Luka crawled up on the pillow next to him.

Tim thought about how he would fit as a father himself. It was probably time now; he had always wanted to be a young dad, unlike his own father.

He talked about it when he had dinner with Tiësto: pasta and a couple of glasses of wine at the Waldorf Astoria in Beverly Hills. He and Tijs Verwest had not seen each other in several years and Tim was bubbly and talkative. They reminisced about the nights in Ibiza a long time ago.

'I've actually been thinking a little about performing again,' Tim said.

Now that Tim was more comfortable at the piano, he and Carl Falk had discussed starting a band with Salem Al Fakir and Vincent Pontare. Tim envisioned that he would control the live music from his booth, distorting and manipulating it with filters and effects, and when the spirit fell upon him, he could sit at the piano himself or pull out a guitar. It would be a completely new experience for the audience, and he would not have to be alone on stage. The tours would not be as extensive as before, but maybe they could try their hand at a few gigs at the new club that Jesse Waits was about to open in the casino resort The Palms in Las Vegas. See how it was received, take it from there. He was thinking of the band name Avicii and the Animals.

Tim apologised to Tiësto for disappearing for those few years, becoming so elusive. They should start hanging out again, as before. Maybe go and see Swedish House Mafia, who would be reunited at Ultra Music Festival in March 2018?

It was a time of reconciliation, of calm.

Tim filled his villa with exciting technical equipment. He ordered drones, a set of binoculars with a wide-angle zoom and a state-of-the-art camera. He was most pleased with the three microscopes: heavy and sturdy instruments, intended for biological analysis in laboratories.

Tim had become interested in new research findings on mushrooms. He had read that a single fungus could have threads that spread for miles underground, a fine-mesh extension of the forest's root system that helped the trees absorb nutrients. Unfortunately, very few mushrooms grew in the mountains of Hollywood. Instead, Tim went out into the garden and looked for a leaf or a piece of bark, in the best case an insect, which he could put under the lens.

Tereza looked at him as he sat over the microscope. She thought his hands were so beautiful.

———————

I need to learn how to listen to music again. Uncondition myself from all these stressful thoughts connected to music that don't even make sense.

I need to find a calm or ambition that negates my worldly ambitions of success since that's not a wholesome mode to be in, causes more stress and 'need' than happiness.

———————

WHEN IT CAME TO PRODUCING tracks, Tim Bergling had stagnated.

It was easy to see that the house music bubble in a way had burst. The aged entrepreneur Robert Sillerman's grandiose plans for a conglomerate of EDM festivals and music sites had quickly vanished – a couple of years after he proudly posed with Afrojack when the company went public, his corporation had gone bankrupt.

A businessman with close ties to the sheikh who invested in the giant club Hakkasan in Las Vegas had been arrested by police, suspected of money laundering in a corruption scandal that was still growing.

That way, the party was over, the gold rush over.

But house music still continued to shape the sound of modern music. On the radio in Los Angeles in the autumn of 2017, lots of songs made by Tim's peers were played. The Chainsmokers, Zedd and Kygo now made music where the drop was basically gone. Instead, unassuming build-ups, like a radiator slowly warming a room. Maybe it was not so strange. The raw and uncompromising elements of a style always tended to soften after a while. That had been the case when rock music slid out into the California sun in the early 70s, or when the punk explosion turned into a smart new wave in the 80s. Puff Daddy had done the same in the 90s when he polished up the first wave of aggressive hip-hop.

Few talked about EDM any more, which in fact was a telltale

sign of the influence that house music had: the sounds that felt challenging ten years earlier were by 2017 incorporated into almost all contemporary pop music.

The Swedes were not insignificant in this development. In Los Angeles, a small colony of Swedish songwriters had emerged, which influenced how American radio sounded.

Max Martin, who had made hits for Britney Spears and the Backstreet Boys already in the 90s, had solidified his position as interpreter of American teenage life and recently built his own studio in Hollywood. In that house, which was previously owned by Frank Sinatra, sat in addition to Martin himself a bunch of Swedes who carved out world hits for Taylor Swift, Adele and Ariana Grande. Another of the Swedish collectives included Erik Hassle and the artist Zara Larsson, named by *Time* magazine as one of the most influential teenagers in the world. It was now well established that the Swedes arrived on time, were reliable and willing to work, not afraid to make shamelessly melodic pop that made people hum along.

Many of the songwriters were women. Jonnali Parmenius, who under the artist name Noonie Bao had her breakthrough when she sang on Avicii's 'I Could Be The One', had by this time done songs for Katy Perry, among others.

Parmenius would think of that first time she landed in Los Angeles a handful of years earlier. After struggling for a long time in a basement in Stockholm, she had saved up enough money to be able to work in Los Angeles for three weeks. On the way in from the airport, Parmenius had turned the radio on in the car and immediately heard her own voice over Tim Bergling's and Nicky Romero's elated beat, and understood that her life was about to change.

That was the type of thing that could happen in the city of dreams, a door stood ajar and you stepped inside. A small

Swedish miracle that Tim Bergling had been a crucial part of. But what did it help him now, as he sat in his studio downstairs, scrolling through his colleagues' Instagram posts and feeling that he did not really belong any more?

He felt creatively drained. The songs he wrote in Nashville at the beginning of the year had come to nothing; Tim wasn't fond of them any more. He dismissed his new song ideas without giving them any real chance. The worst thing was that he had stopped trusting his gut feeling. At the grand piano, the melodies still came to him, and it was fun to write the songs directly on the instrument rather than on a screen. It was in the colouring he had lost his touch.

'That's where I get stuck,' he wrote in a text message to a friend. 'I have song ideas for years but with the production/ sound design part I'm way out of the game.' Music had for so long been linked to tension and execution that he got stressed out as soon as he tried to work.

At Universal, they became increasingly frustrated. Tim pretended to be interested in their suggestions but never completed anything. He said he wanted to work with Chance the Rapper, a young and hot artist, but wouldn't get on a plane to Chicago. He had got the first option on the demo version of 'Sixteen', a song that instead ended up with Ellie Goulding. He was offered 'Back To You' before anyone else – when Selena Gomez eventually grabbed it, it became a hit on charts worldwide. Neil Jacobson and his colleagues had even arranged a meeting with Quincy Jones, the legend who had produced Michael Jackson's *Thriller*, in the composer's house.

'I'm super down!!' wrote Tim, then he cancelled.

Tim had started to miss Arash Pournouri, or at least someone who had the same function. There was no clear leader now, just a bunch of group emails between him, Neil Jacobson and

Per Sundin. Sure, he trusted them both, but they had plenty of other artists to take care of, other deadlines to deal with.

He needed someone who could put all his focus on who Avicii would be in 2017, and perhaps more importantly, in five years' time. Or ten.

'Without Ash whipping me, so to speak, and telling me what tracks to focus on/his excitement over what tracks to go with etc, I've really had a hard time being excited over making music the same way I did before,' Tim wrote to Neil Jacobson. 'The reason I don't finish the billion ideas I have is because no one is rly pushing me to, and if I don't finish them it's impossible to hear the real potential!'

Being completely free of obligations wasn't as easy as Tim had imagined. Now he had a lot of time left to ponder and he became almost obsessed with staying healthy.

In the spring, he had been examined by a doctor at an alternative medicine practice that Coldplay's Chris Martin had recommended. At the fashionable clinic in Agoura Hills, Tim had his lymphatic system drained, received blood transfusions and had cupping on his back, which would increase blood circulation.

Still, there were signals from his body that Tim did not really know how to interpret. 'Started feeling a bit nauseous in the mornings last week,' he wrote to a dietitian he was in touch with. 'Not sure why!!'

The discomfort would subside after a while, especially if Tim started the day off with kombucha, a fermented tea drink that had become popular in Los Angeles. But it was worrying not being able to tell why he felt ill and sometimes got stomach-aches. It was the same with the pain in his ears that appeared from time to time. It seemed to come out of nowhere.

He also had a liver spot on his back that looked unpleasant. It was oblong, and had it not changed colour a bit? Could it be cancer?

The more Tim thought about it, the more convinced he was that he had finally got the disease he had feared most of all since he was little.

He smoked quite a bit. In a drawer at the top right in the kitchen was the cannabis box and the rolling paper and ashtrays. When Tim woke up ahead of lunch, he would stroll out into the kitchen and roll some joints, which he'd take back to the bedroom. He felt the weed calmed his anxiety and opened new, creative doors in his mind.

Attitudes towards marijuana had shifted at a furious pace in the United States, not least in Los Angeles. Barely a year earlier, while California residents were choosing between presidential candidates Hillary Clinton and Donald Trump, they had also voted to legalise recreational use of cannabis in the state. At any moment, a regulated market was expected to open up, and entrepreneurs had already begun decorating stores and putting up signs along the highways boasting of UNRIVALED POTENCY and the BEST CANNABIS IN LA.

Opinions about psychedelic mushrooms were undergoing a similar change in the US. What was previously considered a destructive remnant of the hippie culture of the 60s had now become hard currency for hip tech companies in Silicon Valley. Several startups competed to be the first to develop a synthetic version of psilocybin, the hallucinogenic substance in fungi, in order to manufacture completely new types of antidepressant drugs.

Tim was fascinated with the effects of magic mushrooms. Some believed that they could restart the brain and relieve depression and anxiety for months. He had been enchanted by psilocybin during his expedition to Peru a year earlier, when the group of friends had received a bag of shrooms from their guide in the jungle. On the boat back to civilisation, they had all tripped, and in the gleaming sunset on the Amazon River, Tim had an experience that made him feel like he understood life better than ever before, that every single piece of the puzzle had fallen into place. On the terrace in Los Angeles as well, he would get warm, vibrating visions that he felt gave him new insights and perspectives.

Sometimes, however, the trips led to more unpleasant experiences.

'Kind of like I understand the universe but hard to not really grasp it,' he wrote to a friend about one ordeal. 'Feels a bit like going crazy.'

17 August 2017

Tim Bergling

My friend :D! Just thought of you
and I miss you!

Would love to catch up and talk for
a while when you have time <3

> **Paul Tanner**
>
> Wow. Sounds so corny but I also
> was about to text you.
>
> I am on Dubai time. Yesss
> let's speak :D

Tim Bergling

Haha that synchronicity
phenomenon is a real
head-scratcher to me,

it's been happening so much these
last 2 years!!

Ah its late there! Maybe we can
talk tomorrow?

They continued to stay in contact: the therapist Paul Tanner and his former client.

Tim never beat around the bush when he called. He would dutifully say something about his girlfriend or talk about the progress his pit bull was making, but most of all he wanted to dive right into philosophical and existential discussions. Avidly, he would describe documentaries about alchemy or levitating generators that produced electricity from nothing. He thought that the most meaningful and exciting things happened on the edge of science. He had read about a virologist who argued that electromagnetic signals could be stored in water and transferred to a new water source via email – if such a thing were possible, it would turn all accepted theories on their head!

Tim had big ideas about making a change. For example, he had got in contact with his favourite director Darren Aronofsky, whose film *Requiem for a Dream* had made such an impact on Tim when he was a teenager, and asked if the filmmaker wanted to collaborate. Maybe they could do a documentary that went behind the scenes of the party life in Ibiza – showcase how many people died from overdoses on the island every summer. Or a biographical story about the Buddha as a young man, perhaps?

To Paul Tanner, Tim's striving to help others was truly beautiful. But how was he actually feeling himself?

It was frustrating that Tim couldn't just pick a concept and stick with it. The same restless inventive joy that came across in his music-making was clear in his spiritual endeavours. It had been two years since Tim was in the clinic and Paul's impression was that he now should remember some of his most basic insights from that time. Tim seemed to be pretty alone in his quest, and it annoyed the therapist that they most often stayed up in the realm of ideas during their conversations.

What did Paul actually know about his former client's daily life? Tim had indeed mentioned the new dog, and had talked a little about Tereza and her son. Occasionally, a friend of his or Klas and Anki would come up in conversation – but they were still just fragments.

Tanner suggested that they should travel somewhere together. Perhaps a few weeks by the rice fields in Bali? Tanner, who himself was spiritually inclined, knew a guru there who Tim would love to meet. Or Paul could just take a flight to Stockholm sometime when Tim was there?

But none of these plans ever came about; Tim was hard to pin down.

Paul sensed that Tim was not feeling as well as he wanted everyone around him to believe.

Or as good as he himself wanted to believe.

Maybe Tim had started putting up smokescreens again?

John McKeown, the owner of the rehab centre in Ibiza, was worried too. If exercise and meditation gave Tim an inner peace, that was great, but the therapist felt that the basis for better well-being was much simpler than that.

It was about something as basic as staying sober.

Before Tim left the clinic, McKeown had tried to impress upon him that total sobriety was the only actually sustainable path to recovery. He realised that it sounded damn miserable for a twenty-six-year-old, but he was speaking from experience.

Just like Tim, the young McKeown had discovered a simple way to relax: a line, a pill, a few ounces of alcohol that soon became a bottle. He had taught his body to hotwire its emotional life, and it was a skill that could not be undone. For an addicted person, the button was always there, whether they wanted it or not. The escape route to relapse was well maintained. That's why John McKeown still went to self-help support groups, even though he had been sober for over thirty years. Meeting other addicts was a reminder of how easily everything could go to hell. That day when you were especially happy with yourself, when you felt like rewarding the system, when you relaxed and thought that you had developed into a person who would be able to numb yourself in moderation.

Rumours had reached McKeown that Tim was using mind-expanding mushrooms at his home in Los Angeles, and that he was apparently smoking a lot of pot.

Relative to opioids, marijuana could sound innocent, but in fact cannabis was a risk factor when it came to psychosis.

The ability to interpret reality would falter during a psychosis, or be completely knocked out of play. It was a condition difficult to assess, especially for those who had never encountered it before. The illness could creep in over several years or bloom in a few days. The line between normal and irrational thinking was seldom clear, and it became even more difficult to judge because those affected often felt happy and content themselves. They could experience a magical ability to see invisible connections, make original associations or have close contact with God or the universe.

The condition could occur in direct connection with drug intoxication, but also appear several days or weeks later. After a sometimes gentle start, the situation often became more and more anxiety-inducing and the unwell person would feel like he had lost contact with his surroundings and himself.

It was a feeling of unreality.

THEY WENT TO Big Bear, a ski resort east of Los Angeles; it was just after New Year's Eve 2018.

Tim and Tereza had started getting annoyed with each other in the car already. They had not arranged any accommodation, but instead of just quickly booking a cabin online, Tim wanted to get his travel agency involved – the people who had arranged hotel rooms and flights during his tours. Tereza thought that if he wanted to get away from the stress of being a superstar, he should at least be able to book a hotel room himself.

They rented skis and boots for three days, but Tereza got tired of the gentle slopes after only an hour. She was an experienced skier and needed some challenge and speed. She wanted the two hundred dollars that she had put down for the equipment back, and tried to persuade Tim to lie that they had collided with each other and therefore couldn't keep going. Tereza limped into the store, moaning and grimacing, but Tim revealed her plan to the rental staff. So silly to lie about such a thing, and for such a small amount, at that.

It had ignited a real quarrel and they might have even broken up – or at least Tim had left the ski slope without saying goodbye and returned to Los Angeles alone.

When Tereza came home to Tim a few days later, the atmosphere was one of irritation. Tim was lying tucked up in the bedroom; he had neither showered nor changed clothes since he got back.

'Are you still sad?' Tereza asked.

'No, it's not about that any more,' Tim responded. 'I'm just having like an existential crisis.'

It was the first time Tereza saw Tim depressed in this way, but he had been thinking intensely about life before as well. One time he had told her that his whole surroundings felt surreal.

'What if everyone around me is just a projection in my mind? What if nobody is really here, and I'm all alone in the world?'

Tereza hadn't known what to say in response. It was a fantasy without end, one that felt scary to fully consider.

'That's all right,' she had tried. 'I know how it is to be depressed; it happens to everyone sometimes.'

This time, Tim wanted to be at peace with his thoughts, so Tereza left him there in the darkened bedroom. A few days later, Tim was happy and wanted to hang out again, but there had been something disturbing about the whole situation that Tereza had a hard time letting go of.

Tim tried to reassure his girlfriend. There was nothing to worry about, he was fine again.

'Sometimes I just think about these things. About how nothing really matters.'

'What do you mean?' asked Tereza. 'That's such a sad thought!'

'No, it's not really. It means you can do whatever you feel like, whatever you want. It's freeing.'

In February 2018 Tim flew home to Stockholm. He and Tereza had got in a fight again and he needed a break.

He rented a large apartment far up on Upplandsgatan, in the north of the city, and immediately turned it into a game hall. Soon he was in the middle of a battle, where machine guns rattled, laser beams fluttered over the walls and artillery shells exploded over the opponents.

Tim had bought a curved screen which he placed on the dining-room table and he invited his childhood friends Fricko Boberg and Johannes Lönnå to a game night. They had bought crisps and soft drinks and launched Overwatch, a game by the same developer behind their old favourite World of Warcraft. The surroundings looked different here, the adventure took place in a dystopian metropolis, but Tim had still picked a hero that was indispensable for the team.

While Fricko was a buff pig and Johannes a chesty soldier, Tim's character was a monk hovering in a lotus position. He spoke words of wisdom as he healed the others.

'True self is without form,' said the creature with a metallic voice as he shot healing spheres from his rattling robot hands.

Fricko thought it was a perfect character for Tim, who had got so involved in spiritual development in recent years. It felt as if his childhood friend was moving in exactly the right direction, as if he now understood the value of rest and recovery in a different way from before. Wasn't this situation a good example of that? The apartment on Upplandsgatan turned into a pocket of air, a place where Tim's fingers slammed against the keyboard and time ran away just like in the old days. Even the crisps tasted the same as before.

It was nice that they could hang out like this again, just as friends, no longer as co-workers in the entertainment industry.

'The universe shall embrace you,' said the robot voice, creating a circle around him so that no one else on the team could be injured for a few seconds. The life force returned to Johannes's injured soldier, who again peppered the enemy with automatic gunfire.

In the breaks between battles, Fricko fried frozen meatballs and served them with macaroni and pesto. Tim told them he was done with Los Angeles. He was tired of being treated differently all the time, it felt as though everyone he met related more to Avicii than to Tim. It fed his ego in a way that wasn't helpful.

During the winter, Fricko had helped Tim look for houses in Stockholm. Among other properties, he had been on a tour of an estate on Norra Djurgården that had once been owned by King Gustaf VI Adolf. The villa was right on the beach and Tim had loved it, apart from one important detail – no evening sun reached the garden.

But there was no question that he wanted to move home to Stockholm. Down the line, he wanted to build greenhouses and plantations, perhaps even become self-sufficient.

'I'll get a kick-ass house so we can all just hang out there,' he said. 'It's gonna be fucking awesome!'

While Tim was in Stockholm, he also took the opportunity to meet Arash Pournouri.

Although he now received practical help from Mark Sudack, a manager with whom Neil Jacobson used to play golf, Tim had realised that he missed the ear of his former partner. And not just his ear, by the way: he missed Arash.

Sure, they had worn out the relationship, clashed on epic levels, seen each other at their worst. But they were also forever intertwined, connected by experiences no one else shared.

About six months earlier, Arash had sent an email and spoke his heart. He had embarked on new paths now – Strandvägen had never really become the creative superhub that Arash had imagined, and he was working less with music these days. Together with the well-known financier Mats Qviberg, he had launched a digital talent show, and with, among others, Per Sundin at Universal, he had become a partner in a company that rented out office space. Another project he had started with

Sebastian Ingrosso was to cultivate influencers on YouTube – a couple of twins from Västerås who dribbled and juggled with a football, for example. Brilliant Minds, the conference that Pournouri and Spotify founder Daniel Ek were behind, had by this time established itself in Stockholm's business world and attracted various big names, including Google's former CEO Eric Schmidt, to the city.

The tone of Arash's email had been conciliatory and calm; he had emphasised that he was neither angry nor bitter.

In his answer, Tim had written:

It's hard to say exactly where we went from being a super team with a passion for music and set on taking over the world to a complicated machinery without passion where nothing worked anymore.

For my own part, I can say in retrospect that I pushed myself way too much in something I thought was hard (doing gigs) year after year after year and after a while my lust for life disappeared. And it was scary to pause and stop the train because everything was going so well, but nor was it the end of the world, and I should have done it very much earlier, before crashing into and through the wall multiple times.

Tim did not want Arash to run his business any more. But as a creative sounding board, he had been invaluable. Musically, there was simply no one that Tim trusted as much as Arash. If they accepted each other's differences, created new roles for each other, they might be able to find a way back to those magical years in the beginning.

They finally met, for the first time in almost two years. They first had dinner at a luxury hotel in Lärkstan that Tim's big brother David worked for. Then they went to Berns, the club around the corner from Stureplan where Fricko Boberg had now got a job as a guest manager.

Fricko thought it was so nice to see that it seemed to have got better between Tim and his former manager. They were laughing together again. Fricko got them some drinks and invited the two to a separate part of the bar, where it was possible to talk without shouting in the crowd.

Tim and Arash sat and talked, as Friday night turned into Saturday morning and the sun started to rise over the bay outside. When they parted at five in the morning, they agreed on how much love they had for one another and that they would be in touch again soon.

BOXES OF HEALTHY FOOD arrived at the house in Hollywood, full of brown rice, fish and broccoli. One of the housekeepers prepared salads with pine nuts, peppers and rocket. As a snack, unsalted almonds, walnuts or pumpkin seeds were okay. If it was a training day, he could treat himself to a couple of lightly fried eggs with pink Himalayan salt. And apparently the fatty fish at the bottom of the food chain were extra nutritious, so it was important to eat sardines.

Salem Al Fakir was sitting in the kitchen upstairs and listening while Tim lectured Vincent Pontare on diet and nutrition. The scene made him happy. This Tim felt so far removed from the weary shadow they had been working with a few years earlier. Now Tim had muscles on his body and colour in his cheeks. He seemed to be feeling good again, was almost as happy and playful as when they'd got to know each other seven years earlier in the small basement studio in Östermalm.

That was, in any case, Salem Al Fakir's feeling.

Tim's new manager Mark Sudack had tried to break the creative deadlock by asking Tim to list which musicians he would like to work with. Not the ones he thought would achieve the most, but simply the ones he had the most fun with in the studio.

Salem Al Fakir and Vincent Pontare were obvious. In fact, there were only Swedes on the list: soon Carl Falk and Jocke Berg, singer in the rock group Kent, would also join. A few weeks later, Albin Nedler and Kristoffer Fogelmark, the pair of producers who had co-written the song 'Pure Grinding' a few years earlier were also invited.

Musically, however, the first two days with Salem and Vincent were slow. They recorded sketch after sketch in the studio downstairs and Tim was as receptive as usual; it wasn't that – he obviously still had his ear, sharp just like before. But then it stopped. Tim seemed uninterested in taking the drafts further; he was self-conscious in a way they had never seen before. As if he was just looking for that first nice feeling, a chord progression that gave him a flutter in his stomach. He didn't really care about the style and expression of the song.

'That was fucking great,' he'd say every time. 'We can figure out the rest of the production later, I don't want to get caught up in that now.'

'But we have to start getting something into the computer,' Vincent countered. 'So we can begin working out what we have.'

'Let's do one more idea,' said Tim. 'It seems like we have a good flow going!'

On the third day, the songwriters worked up the courage. When they came back up to the mountains, Vincent spoke his heart immediately.

'We have to do it differently now, Tim.'

They agreed to try and find an empty space, musically. What wasn't playing on the radio at the moment? That was where they would go.

The release came when they started talking about that strange period in the 90s when every metal band and rocker had made brave attempts to rap. For Tim, those songs were the sound of childhood. In parallel with favourites such as Kiss, Linkin Park and System of a Down, in Tim's youth there had been bands such as Crazy Town, a group that made blond and bare-chested soft metal. They listened to the group's song

'Butterfly', which had been a huge hit when Tim was still in primary school.

Vincent Pontare, who was significantly older than Tim, put on a sort of prototype for this strange hybrid. The song 'Loser' had been the singer Beck's big breakthrough in the 90s. It was a self-ironic slacker song, with a sloppy hip-hop beat and a lyricist who didn't even care about coherent verses.

Out of this energy came 'Excuse Me Mr Sir', the first song in a very long time that Tim wanted to complete. With a rapper's cockiness, Salem delivered an almost sarcastic nod to those who doubted that Avicii would make a grand comeback.

The three friends sat on the terrace and talked about the times they were living in. There was so much stress, such a manic buzz. The cell phone, this wonderful device that the three of them loved but also felt just a bit too attached to. They were always available, never turned off. The last thing they did in bed in the evening was scroll; the phone their first companion in the morning. And despite the fact that so many people were now connected through shared playlists, chat threads and Instagram comments, it was easy to feel isolated and alone. Overstimulated and bored.

They went down to the studio and wrote 'Peace Of Mind', a song about the never-ending noise of information and their own longing for silence and stillness.

In the mornings, Tim sat with his legs in the lotus position on a low stool he had carried out on to the balcony. From YouTube sounded the vibrations that arose when a wooden stick was gently rubbed against the edge of a metal bowl, a Tibetan tradition of unwinding. The soft sound filled the bedroom and travelled out into the morning light, where Tim sat with his hands on his lap and palms facing up.

Tim tried to get back to his mantra, but his thoughts kept racing. He got a tune in his head, he thought about what he wanted to eat for breakfast, felt a tension in his back. He had learned that it was the same for everyone, even those who had practised this form of meditation for a long time – the attention drifted elsewhere and you had to constantly remind yourself to return to the personal and secret sound. The mantra had no real meaning and would reset the focus without creating new thoughts. The sound was to be repeated over and over during the twenty minutes that the ritual lasted.

Tim's search for different ways to feel better continued. He had recently discovered transcendental meditation, a technique launched by an Indian guru in the late 1950s. Maharishi Mahesh Yogi had wanted to achieve what he called the Age of Enlightenment, and had received significant support from the stars of The Beatles, who had begun to take an interest in his teachings. Paul McCartney and John Lennon had written parts of the classics *White Album* and *Abbey Road* in the guru's meditation centre on the banks of the Ganges, even though the journey had ended in conflict. It was alleged that the guru had made sexual advances on the actress Mia Farrow, who had come to India with her sister Prudence after her break-up with Frank Sinatra. And after weeks of persistent spiritual search, Prudence had entered into a condition similar to a psychosis. For four days she had been sitting perfectly still in her bungalow. She had stopped eating, did not sleep and had become obsessed with being freed from all her insecurities in life.

An instructor from a meditation centre in Los Angeles had come up to Tim's house and taught the basics of this technique. Most modern instructors stressed that transcendental meditation was not something fuzzy; on the contrary, it was a simple technique to get rid of stress, but faithful to his habit,

323

Tim wanted to get to the original sources and therefore read *Science of Being and Art of Living*, Maharishi's book that the guru had dictated on tape at the beginning of the 60s. It had been a long time since Tim had been so blown away by a text. He was attracted by the transformative power. This form of meditation differed from those he had previously attempted. While mindfulness was about calmly observing one's inner self, transcendental meditation made it a bigger point to be able to reach new states of consciousness. Tim wrote:

Reading a book by transcendental meditation founder Maharishi about getting to the beginning of thought and how the world is double faceted with one part being the absolute never changing and the other being the ever-changing world of manifestation.

The basic idea was that, on the worldly level, there were things that were relative and unsteady, but with practice and many hours of meditation, all people could come into contact with a more subtle level of consciousness, the one that Maharishi called Being. It was the source of all aspects of life – all time, space and contexts. It was everything that had been, everything that was and would ever be. The all-encompassing beginning and end of existence, the absolute constituents of creation.

According to the guru, one who was dedicated enough could attain cosmic consciousness. Such a person became free from all sins and would not have to be born again in earthly form. In fact, this form of meditation was said to be an unusually rapid path towards liberation from worldly conditions, from the cycle of life and death and the suffering that was otherwise the lot of humanity.

A tourist bus swayed on the narrow streets up in the

mountains and the passengers saw Tim sitting cross-legged on the balcony. He waved happily to the tourists, well aware of how the scene must look from their perspective. Here was Avicii sitting outside his glass villa meditating: it could hardly get more Hollywood.

But Tim actually felt that the meditation helped him. He and Tereza were going through a rocky period, and Tim had started chatting a bit with other girls on the Raya app. To his great surprise, he now dared to be the one to start the conversations, something he had never done before. He thanked his secret mantra for it.

Tim now knew what true joy was, he told Albin Nedler when the twenty-seven-year-old songwriter visited him in the villa. Happiness was what Tim had felt when he had just published the message that he would stop touring. He could still get goosebumps when he thought of those first days of ease two years earlier.

'I've never felt so free,' he told Albin over a glass of red wine in the kitchen. 'Like, it's as if I was almost hovering.'

That was the feeling of liberation he wanted to achieve once more.

Musically, Tim had now been picking up steam. He wanted to experiment with Arabian rhythms and African sounds. His brother David had sent a clip with the Algerian folk musician Khaled, who in the 90s had made the traditional Bedouin music raï known to the general public. In the digital synthesiser Omnisphere, Tim found North African lutes and West African djembe drums. On 'Freak', he used the sound of a thumb piano from Zimbabwe; 'Bad Reputation' included the traditional Japanese string instrument koto.

Tim thought the songs were interesting, different. The traditional instruments gave the beats their own character.

He showed Albin Nedler yet another book he was reading. It was a real thick one, in which a controversial biologist argued that man, with the help of his subconscious, could change his DNA.

Albin did not really know what to think. It sounded highly unlikely. But it was hard to stay focused when Tim ran away in thought as he sometimes did; it was hard to take in all the theories about quantum computers, alchemy and water's ability to feel positive energy.

The smell of tobacco and marijuana filled the downstairs. Tim stuffed cannabis into cigars and blew out the sweet smoke. One evening when they had grilled vegan burgers and hung out on the terrace, one of his friends reacted.

'Damn, Tim, chill with the weed. How much do you actually smoke?'

'A little too much maybe. But it's fine. It really helps me too. It just makes things so much fucking easier.'

In the beginning of April, after a month's work, Tim had around twenty demos to choose between. 'It feels INSANE strong,' he reported to Mark Sudack. 'The hit potential is rly big.'

Tim emailed the hotel in the wilderness in southern Kenya where he had stayed when he had just stopped touring, and explained that soon he wanted to rent the entire facility: 'We would be 20 people coming then maybe and would have to build a studio somewhere,' he wrote. The plan was to fly in all the musicians and complete the second EP on the savannah, maybe even the third. The Maasai people he had seen dancing a year and a half earlier, with their rhythmic choirs and complex hand claps, could give the songs a whole new touch.

'Is there someone specific that is known in the different tribes to be the "best", to know most about Maasai music?' he wrote to the hotel.

He showed Albin Nedler photos of the place on his phone.

'We should be able to set up a studio in these tents,' he pointed out. Tim's eyes glowed when he talked about recording music among lions and gazelles.

On the evening of 7 April 2018, they all stood at the grand piano and looked out over Los Angeles. They composed 'Never Leave Me', a ballad about the healing power of love, Tim's fingers moving in their special way over the black keys.

Everything Tim had gone through – the impossible pace, the walls he had crashed through – perhaps it had all been necessary to find an artistic expression that felt as rich and precious as this?

A couple of days later, the housekeeper packed Tim's bags. He was going on a week-long trip to Oman. A group of friends that Jesse Waits knew had planned it all. Some of them had apparently been to the Arabian Peninsula during the autumn and fell in love with the area. Unlike its neighbours, Saudi Arabia and the United Arab Emirates, Oman lacked large oil reserves, which had made the country a quiet and somewhat forgotten enclave in an otherwise turbulent region. More and more tourists were now discovering the untouched and barren desert, which could be visited on comfortable adventure trips, designed for those with a large wallet and a taste for something new.

This holiday group consisted of about ten people, and they had hyped each other up a lot over email: they would paraglide in the desert, drink fine wines and get lessons in kitesurfing on the coast. At the last minute, Jesse got stuck in Las Vegas – he was busy planning the new nightclub at The Palms casino resort. It stressed Tim out a little, because even though he had met several of the other travel companions before, none of them were close friends. But anyway, he was still looking forward to the trip.

Albin Nedler and Kristoffer Fogelmark would stay in the house in Los Angeles, refining the new songs while their host was away.

Tim hugged them in the hallway before dragging his bag to the taxi.

9 April 2018
Tim Bergling

I've been reading and talking about
this stuff for years now but last
weeks have been insane, it has
changed my life

> **Jesse Waits**
>
> Please anyway you can persuade
> me to be a better person

Tim Bergling

The second u start clearing all the
nonsense out your mind – which u
only can do with meditation (not TM
specifically but any meditation!!!)
all the other parts fix themselves!
For instance I've been for 10 years
thinking I need to fix something in
order to be happy/confident but in
reality I know now I only need to
'exercise' my brain with meditation
and I will be happy and the rest
will follow

Aaaand I might fall back in 2 weeks
time and not uphold this new

'insight' so not saying I've figured
anything out yet – but I can feel the
fn difference

The last 3 weeks I've felt like
every insecurity I've had has been
lifted, I keep noticing how I'm no
longer anxious

And I'm a very, very anxious person!

As soon as Tim had checked in at The Chedi beach hotel in Oman's capital of Muscat, he went up to his room. There waited record label executive Per Sundin on the line; Neil Jacobson and Mark Sudack were on the phone in Los Angeles too.

They needed to discuss which singers would fit with which song. At this point, none of them got surprised by the unorthodox crew that Tim imagined. He wanted to ask Michael McDonald or Peter Gabriel. Maybe Shakira, if she reined it in a bit and sang, like, normal? On the song 'Freak', perhaps the rapper Post Malone would fit? 'SOS' needed someone with a full-bodied voice. 'Peace Of Mind' could do with somebody a little scarred by life, maybe Anthony Kiedis from Red Hot Chili Peppers? It would be cool to have an African singer on one of the songs, a voice with character and depth. Neil Jacobson suggested the veteran Angélique Kidjo.

'Sure, that's perfect!'

Tim wanted to get over to Kenya and finish twelve songs as soon as possible. Then they could release six of them this summer and the final part of the EP trilogy in the autumn of 2018.

The next day, Tim and the other tourists were picked up by a young and energetic guy who arranged tailor-made adventure trips in the Oman desert and coastal areas.

The white stone houses shimmered in the heat as the company's jeeps drove out towards the ravines on the coast – already in the morning it was nearly thirty degrees Celsius. As they turned off towards the mountains, the air got thinner. Here, black goats roamed the cliffs and the cars teetered on unstable roads: until very recently, the gravel trail they travelled uphill could only be traversed by donkey.

After a simple lunch by some ancient cemeteries, they reached the first camp of the journey later in the afternoon.

Food was served: slow-cooked meat, chicken and rice, a simple flatbread, juicy vegetables. Someone in the party had brought vintage wines from his cellar in England that ended up pairing really well with the traditional dishes.

As pleasant shadows stretched out, Tim and the others sat on pillows and listened to a troubadour playing quiet melodies on an oud, the kind of short-necked lute that was so common in Arabic music. The strings sat in pairs and gave off a softly swaying sound that slid out into the evening air. The musician, who was wearing a foot-length dishdasha, let his hand slide along the instrument's neck and Tim thought that of course he should also put a lute on his next record – why not?

After darkness had fallen, the sky remained open to their eyes. Between the pieces of music, the troubadour told of the constellations that lay strewn across the firmament up there. Taurus and Orion, of course, the Big Bear. Auriga was easy to recognise. Cassiopeia in the east, Sagittarius in the west. The Bedouins had always used the starry sky to navigate. The days were too hot to travel long distances, so at night the constellations and the moon became their map and compass.

The stories about space made Tim think of Hubble, the telescope that had fascinated him since he was little, when he sat in his room in Östermalm studying colourful images of gas clouds and supernovae. For almost thirty years, the Hubble Space Telescope had spun around in its orbit, day in and day out, helping researchers realise that the number of galaxies was many times greater than previously thought. In cosmic terms, the Milky Way was only an insignificant suburb.

The myriad stars they now saw in the sky were thus only the beginning of something, a first layer. Behind it was the incomprehensible unknown, what had not yet been mapped, what was really enticing.

KLAS BERGLING STOPPED to catch his breath. The narrow trail rose steeply up the valley.

The surroundings up here in the mountains were completely different to those down in the stone town of Las Palmas. On the plateaus the lush vegetation spread out, the air was damp and thick. Together with a couple of other Swedish retirees, Klas had left the city by bus in the morning and walked purposefully along the winding paths for hours. In the distance the goats' bells rattled and rang, which meant that they would soon arrive in a mountain village with white houses and could treat themselves to a well-deserved beer.

At the same time, Anki was lying down on the beach, devouring detective stories in the sun. This time of year, in the beginning of spring, the tourists had not yet invaded the city: the beach was far from full, only a few exercisers plodded on the boardwalk. Anki always read a lot when she was here, and when she finished her books she would walk to the Scandinavian tapas bar in the old market hall and pass them on to other Swedish tourists. Not much more happened. In other words, the days were as lazy as always when Tim Bergling's parents were in the Canary Islands.

Their youngest son had been hard to get hold of for a few weeks, but this time it felt only positive. Tim had been so proud when he sent them his latest songs. That seemed to be the way creativity worked, Klas thought as he sat with his beer up in the mountains: it came and went in ebbs and flows, just like the waves down in the Atlantic.

Now Tim was finally experiencing the flow again.

While Klas and Anki were there on the island, Levan Tsikurishvili's documentary about Tim had finally been broadcast on Swedish television, in early April 2018. The film was titled *Avicii: True Stories*, and his parents watched it on the sofa in their small apartment by the beach.

There were images of their son in a car in Australia four years earlier, newly discharged from hospital and already on the road to the next festival gig. The parents saw Tim's tired eyes when his agent Robb Harker suggested a new interview slot in order to show the fans that the star was feeling good again.

In the film, Tim talked about how alcohol had helped him to dampen his fears before performances and had also approved showing the pictures from Ibiza, where he, stressed and faded on pills, hadn't touched his food in hours.

Anki and Klas thought their son was impressively sincere.

'I was feeling like shit,' Tim explained in one of the interviews. 'And the only solution that I got was to take a medicine, or battle through it. Every time I went into the hospital it was like that: "Take this and you'll kind of feel better."'

Tim laughed as he talked. With just a little distance he realised how absurd the situation had been. He had relied on the doctors' advice – a generation of physicians that he now thought prescribed opioids way too easily. In the end, the medication had only given him more anxiety.

'The pain medicine made me feel shitty,' he continued. 'To me, it felt like I was constantly in, like, a haze.'

Anki Lidén walked out on to the balcony and lit a cigarette. She had a hard time watching those clips. But she couldn't be anything other than proud. It was brave of Tim to speak openly about how terrible he had felt. Just think that their son had still got through all of it, that he'd made it over to the other side.

The final scene in the documentary was filmed on the beach in Madagascar. Tim had just stopped touring and was sitting with his guitar in his lap, relaxed and special.

The group in Oman continued on their expedition. The sharp lines that the wind had drawn in the sand were blurred when the four-wheel-drive jeeps roared through the dunes, which at times stood more than a hundred metres high. The cars swayed and bounced, it was like being at sea; the dust that was whipped up formed a long tail attached to the motorised caravan. Then the terrain suddenly transformed into something that resembled glimmering snow. The cars drove on to a salt flat, traversing mile after mile of white ground, before the group finally reached the coast. Just at the water's edge, a modern camp was built, with spacious tents lined up along the beach. There each person would stay separately in their own bed. Beautiful mats were laid out at the entrance of each residence; in the shadow of a wind barrier a table was set.

Far out on the horizon, the tankers sailed with their oil from the Persian Gulf down towards India.

After a cool night, most of the guests woke up early. As the milky-white fog gradually dissipated, several of the group prepared for kitesurfing lessons, others waited for breakfast. Coffee, cereal and dates would soon be served on the table down by the water.

Yet no one had seen Tim Bergling. His tent was towards the end of the row by the shoreline and the breeze made the pale brown canvas flutter gently, but inside was quiet.

Eventually Tim came out, brimming with excitement, and explained that he had spent the morning hours meditating.

Focused on his breathing, he had swum deeper and deeper into his own mind. In the book about transcendental meditation he had just read, Maharishi Mahesh Yogi had articulated it with just such a metaphor: he wrote that the one who meditated regularly was a diver who took himself from the upper reaches of the water and further down. Eventually, this swimmer became more familiar with the deeper levels of the pond and he was able to move himself easily and freely, from the surface to far down towards the bottom. In the same way, it was possible to approach one's own inner self, until nothing was concealed any more – that was what the founder promised. According to the Indian guru, there were seven states of consciousness and the ones who reached all the way in would not have to be reborn into the world of suffering. On the contrary, the mind would gain such strength that it would never again have to endure the pressures of work, stress or illness. Beyond the limitations of the conscious mind, life's desires and meagre problems would then appear to be what they really were: insignificant. In other Eastern traditions, this enlightenment was spoken of as something almost unattainable, a state that took many lives to achieve. Maharishi, on the other hand, had wagered that those who followed his instructions would be able to reach what he called cosmic consciousness in five to eight years.

Tim thought it sounded incredibly hopeful, but he wanted to get there even faster. Therefore, he deviated from the instructions to sit for only twenty minutes at a time, instead meditating persistently for hours on end.

'It's amazing,' he said to anyone who would listen. 'I'm breaking through the layers of my consciousness really quickly. It's supposed to take years to get there, but I've reached deep already.'

Tim was proud of what he had accomplished. Sure, he was still an unrealised human, one who hadn't reached all the way to cosmic consciousness. But he was devoted, and had made progress.

He was about to elevate his mental capacity to the maximum, on his way to a life of completion. And the most amazing thing was that when he improved himself, society would also change – that was one of the basic ideas in Eastern philosophy. The causes of the suffering of existence were not so much in the material world but more in man himself. The anguish and pain of the whole world could thus be dissolved through meditative work.

He wanted the world to know this.

ON 16 APRIL 2018 Paul Tanner received a phone call. The therapist had left Ibiza and started working for a clinic in Switzerland. It was on their behalf that Tanner was now in Dubai helping a family whose son was in the middle of a rampant cocaine addiction.

When Tim called unexpectedly, Paul immediately heard that his old client was burdened with something.

'I don't feel too good,' Tim said. 'I'm really confused, Paul.'

The desert expedition was over, Tim's travel companions had returned home and Tim remained with a few guys from Oman that he had got to know. They had spent a couple of nights at Muscat Hills Resort, a trendy hotel in Al Jissah Bay. There they had swum, gone out on a boat trip and had a few drinks. At the hotel, several tourists recognised Tim and he had smiled into the camera for photos that were now up for public viewing on Instagram. There he was once again Avicii, the superstar rather than Tim, this mirror image that seemed to haunt him wherever he went in the world.

Tim longed to return to nature. He wanted to go to the desert again, try to catch a night with an even clearer sky than last time so that he could study the stars properly. Apparently, it was also possible to see both octopuses and orcas along the coast here, so maybe he would end his stay by going diving. In any case, Tim had decided to extend his trip by an extra week or so.

He didn't talk about these earthly practicalities with Paul Tanner. Instead, as usual, he wanted to quickly get up into the sphere of ideas. He was finding himself in a particularly turbulent period at the moment, he explained. It wasn't at all easy. He had been meditating and thinking so much for the past few weeks that thoughts were colliding in his head. In his phone he had made notes about it, to try to understand all the new insights. 'It feels like I am in a new default mode of being which is very new and a little bit scary,' he wrote. 'It felt like the fears the last couple of days caused havoc in me, but I remember the tip to focus on my breathing.'

'Well, the thing is that I want to have a normal life,' he told Paul. 'I want to have a girlfriend and a family. But I also feel like I have to reach enlightenment. I've got to help the world, I need to serve a purpose.'

It was a theme that Paul recognised: Tim who so sincerely wanted to help the world along. The king of euphoria, who created the soundtrack to so many wonderful experiences for others, but who at the same time put an impossibly heavy burden on his own shoulders. Tim longed for a tomorrow when everything had changed, when humanity was free from hopelessness and misery. Now he seemed to have gone so deep into his thoughts that everything ended up spinning. His voice cracked as he spoke, the feeling of being insufficient, of not achieving earth's recovery fast enough, seemed to hurt him.

'You could do both.' Paul tried to put him at ease. 'You can live your own life and still seek enlightenment for everybody else.'

Paul reminded Tim of Buddhism's focus on compassion and the shared experience. By transforming his own inner self, he would also transform his surroundings. Everything was connected, the truth lay within every being, and he who found peace himself treated his surroundings with greater understanding. The fear, envy and greed that lived within oneself could be dissolved also in the world, only it was named and made conscious. There was no contradiction whatsoever between developing oneself and striving for the healing of the earth; on the contrary.

As they continued to talk, Tim sounded calmer, relieved. In the middle of the conversation, he suddenly turned away from the phone.

'I'll have eggs and toast please,' he said.

Paul Tanner, who had assumed that Tim was in Los Angeles, only now understood that they were in the same time zone. Apparently Tim was just about to have breakfast.

'Hey, Tim, where in the world are you?'

'I'm in Oman.'

'What a coincidence! I'm in Dubai. Come and see me and we'll explore these ideas together. It sounds as if we really need to talk.'

What a happy fate, Paul thought, that they were only an hour's flight apart. Tim said he was happy to take a plane and come and visit Dubai, so they could talk more. Paul hung up and thought that it would finally happen, that he would at last see Tim again. It would be so interesting to get to the bottom of some of the discussions that had been postponed for far too long.

A few hours later, shortly after lunch, Tim sent a message: 'Hey brother! I just had an amazing meditative experience and wrote some stuff down so I would remember to tell you – let me know if anything resonates!!'

Paul relaxed: it was so nice that things seemed to have taken a turn.

'I am coming to Dubai in a couple days or weeks,' Tim went on. 'I'll call you when I know when exactly!!'

The same afternoon, record company manager Per Sundin also received a message. Tim had discovered Arlissa, a young

British singer, and asked Sundin to listen to her single 'Hearts Ain't Gonna Lie': "Yo brooo!! Check this chick out!!'

Tim also contacted Neil Jacobson with suggestions for even more collaborators on the new songs. He wanted to work with reggaeton artist Ozuna, underground rapper MF Doom and Egyptian singer Amr Diab. Tim saw 'Tough Love' as a duet between a man and a woman, who could play out the aching lyrics almost theatrically – why not Bruce Springsteen and his wife Patti Scialfa?

Neil Jacobson thought it was great to see that Tim was on his toes.

'And also, will stay in Oman for another 8 days!!'

In Las Palmas, the easy life continued for Tim's parents. Anki went for walks with her son's new songs in her headphones. She had been listening intensely lately and had become particularly fond of the oriental strings in 'Tough Love'. 'Maybe I'm harping on it . . .' she wrote in a message to Tim, 'but loooove several of your songs, they are so damn good!'

Tim responded a few hours later, on Monday 16 April 2018.

'Love you mum!!' he wrote. 'Oman is just incredible! Miss you and daddy!!'

Anki was delighted by the tone. Tim had recently sent a sweet message on her birthday saying that he was feeling better than he had in a long time. Self-confident, he claimed. In just over a week, he and his siblings would go on an adventure together. Linda was having a birthday and they were going to Iceland to swim in the hot springs. Apparently, it would be just nine degrees Celsius and rainy in Reykjavik, but Anki was still happy that all four siblings would be together, as it was rare for their schedules to match up.

Over the course of his stay in Oman, Tim had definitively

made up his mind, he wrote to his mother. He would sell the house in Los Angeles and move home. If he was going to start a family, he wanted to do it in Sweden. The search for the perfect accommodation continued: one of his friends had been on a tour of the ice hockey star Peter Forsberg's apartment on Birger Jarlsgatan and there were spots in both Saltsjöbaden and on the island of Värmdö that were also interesting.

In response, Anki filmed her husband, sitting at the small kitchen table in the apartment in Las Palmas. Klas was tanned, his shirt off, drumming on the edge of the table to the beat of 'Never Leave Me', one of the latest songs that Tim had sent to his parents.

'Oh, it's just so great!' Anki shouted into the camera.

On 19 April, a Thursday afternoon, Klas's cell phone rang. It was a number he didn't recognise.

The man on the other end introduced himself as Amer and explained that he had been with the group during the desert expedition in Oman. He and Tim had got to know each other in the tent camps, he continued. They had discussed music and wondered about the universe; Tim had loved staying out in the wasteland.

Since the Swede had wanted to stay longer in the country after the excursion, Amer had invited him to stay for a few nights on his family's estate, a property just west of Muscat. Tim had been accommodated in a guest house with a small terrace facing the garden and the pergola.

'They have had such a good time,' Klas scribbled down as he listened.

It turned out, however, that Amer was calling for another reason. In the last few days, he had begun to worry about his guest's well-being.

Tim had become passive and reclusive. The tour guide described the most concerning part: his guest had not eaten in a long time, and had become increasingly quiet.

'Not talking,' Klas wrote on his notepad, which was now filled with frustrated, hasty circles in blue ink.

Tim had spent the days meditating by the pool. He had been sitting there for hours on end, engrossed in his own thoughts. When Amer or someone else had tried to get him to at least move into the shade, Tim hadn't responded. Instead he had just jumped into the water and cooled off, then got back out and continued to ponder. Apparently, he had cried a lot too, but it was difficult for the host to understand what was getting him so upset. Tim didn't speak when they asked, but instead communicated through text.

'He writes things on paper,' Klas jotted down. 'Last days not talking.'

Amer said that now something even more disturbing had happened.

Tim had hurt himself. It was a superficial wound, not dangerous in itself, he had been to the hospital and got it bandaged up.

But the worry made Klas's stomach churn. His pen moved round and round, pressing down so hard that the tip almost tore the pad apart.

AT THE SAME TIME, Albin Nedler and Kristoffer Fogelmark were sitting downstairs in Tim's house in Los Angeles. Tim had invited them to stay and continue working on the songs while he was away. They had set up microphones and speakers in Tim's private cinema, making themselves at home in the soft armchairs. They were working on a tricky guitar lick in the song 'Freak'; Tim had been very specific about how he wanted the rhythm of it to feel. Into that song he had also thrown the whistled melody from 'Sukiyaki', a decades-old classic by the Japanese singer Kyu Sakamoto. It was a typical whim of the musical madcap Tim, Albin thought – to use a whistle from the early 60s to tie together verse and chorus.

The final days before Tim left for Oman had been special. Rather than staying in the studio, they had sat on the sofa upstairs, focusing entirely on the content of the lyrics. Albin had been impressed by how vigorous Tim was about the meaning of the songs. Albin and Kristoffer had helped change a word here and there, refine a phrase, but it was clear that Tim had a narrative vision. He sought after a rawness, had used swear words and clear images. No one should miss that the storyteller was frustrated.

> *I don't want to be seen in this shape I'm in*
> *I don't want you to see how depressed I've been*
> *You were never the high one, never wanted*
> *to die young*
> *I don't want you to see all the scars within*

It was only now that Albin really took in the meaning of the words. Why were the lyrics so gloomy? Tim had certainly always had dark motifs in his songs, but, before, the clouds had burst open, liberation was within reach. Songs like 'Freak' and 'Bad Reputation' were more hopeless.

Still, Albin was really happy about the songs. He perceived the lyrics as a constructive flashback, a reflection on a time that Tim had struggled his way through. It felt sincere and beautiful. Tim obviously had some experiences he wanted to share.

Albin Nedler too knew what it meant to feel like shit. Just over a year earlier, he had been in the middle of a painful break-up that had dragged him down to rock bottom. Albin had had a hard time acknowledging his feelings even to himself – he had always seen himself as a happy guy with energy and a lust for life. Ambitious and reliable, stable and determined. When his friends told him they were feeling down, he just shook his head. Life was ahead of them, what the hell was there to complain about?

After months of depression, the situation quickly worsened. The aching melancholy escalated and became something much more acute. The sedatives that Albin had been prescribed no longer had any effect and during a week without sleep, unfamiliar thoughts began to nestle in his head.

Albin looked at the bridge over the bay in Årsta and terrible ideas came over him. He walked along the platform at the Södra train station and became afraid of what he could do. He hated these new impulses, didn't want anything to do with them. Yet it felt like they commanded his every move.

In retrospect, Albin could see how quickly the darkness had enveloped him. He had learned that this was how suicidal thoughts worked – they attacked fast and could take over completely.

During this short period, he had been in a tunnel that was rapidly shrinking at both ends. As the light was disappearing, the air was becoming difficult to breathe and the future impossible to imagine. No physical pain he had ever endured could compare to what was going on in his head. It was as if his brain was rotting from the inside, as if he had no choice but one.

That thought was especially difficult to get rid of.

If he just got in the car, drove out to a distant country road and steered into a tree, he would finally be able to sleep.

THE SUN ROSE over the horizon in Las Palmas. The few tourists in town this Friday, 20 April 2018, began to leisurely make their way from their hotel breakfasts towards the beach. Over by the pier, early-morning retirees did their group gymnastics, their movements synchronised.

The night had been wide awake and endless. It had been impossible for Tim Bergling's parents to gather their thoughts, difficult to breathe deeply. Klas had paced back and forth through the apartment's few rooms, talking anxiously with the travel agency that used to book Tim's tour trips. The first connection between Las Palmas and Muscat was a cumbersome flight with a stopover in Frankfurt – the parents had bought tickets and were to arrive in Oman the next day, on Saturday.

It felt like an eternity, Anki thought as she sat glued to the sofa, disoriented and paralysed. What were they actually going to do while they waited for that plane? They tried to encourage each other, but the words that came out of their mouths just sounded hollow. Slowly they drifted through the thick and viscous hours. Never before had the distance to their son been so physically palpable.

Once again, Klas had spoken with the man in Oman, who the day before had sounded the alarm that Tim had injured himself. Amer had now cancelled his planned commitments so that he could watch over his Swedish guest and Tim's parents told themselves that they should try to stay calm despite everything. After all, Tim was in an upmarket suburb of

Muscat, an area where the country's upper class lived. A large property with manicured lawns, high walls and security staff. Their son would be safe until they got there.

The thought that Tim would hurt himself had never occurred to either of them. For a while they had feared an overdose. Or some kind of medical complication, given all the hassle with his stomach. But this? It chilled them, in spite of the morning sun warming up the rooms.

Below the balcony, waves crawled in towards the sand. During the night, the tide had exposed the dark ravine out in the bay; it would take a few more hours before it was filled and it was possible to swim properly. A restaurateur opened up an umbrella on the outdoor terrace, a woman spread a towel over a deckchair – Las Palmas quietly waking up down there felt surreal.

Thoughts swirled restlessly in Klas's head. Why was there no earlier flight? How could Oman be so far away? A vast continent, the entirety of Africa, separated the parents from their son.

Ahead of lunch, the phone rang again. Klas pressed the green button to answer. He stood silently, staring into the air, immediately realising from the tone on the other end what had happened. Everything was chillingly clear. Yet the voice repeated the same thing again, saying words that should not exist.

The white village far away in the mountains, where Klas had hiked a few days earlier, lay hidden in fog.

He listened and understood. It was too late.

Spread positivity through my music, in message. And enjoy success but not materialistic success.

Transfer emotion to the song, what emotion the song is written in will be transmitted.

Most important mantra you can have is 'I love you'.

IN STOCKHOLM, IT was the first truly warm day of spring. After patiently waiting for six months of darkness and cold, the city's residents hurried out of their offices early on Friday afternoon, bought cheese and wine and sat on blankets across the islands and islets on which the city was built.

The magnolias outside Östra Real were about to blossom with their white shimmer, the lawns were drying out and turning green, and on the slopes in the city parks the blue petals of the squills were standing tall again. There would be a summer this year as well.

Shortly after seven in the evening, tens of thousands of pockets buzzed. The daily newspaper *Dagens Nyheter* had sent out a news flash:

'Tim "Avicii" Bergling is dead – was 28 years old.'

The first news update was followed in a blaze by others. The Stockholmers stared, puzzled, at their cell phones. The topics of conversation changed from workplace gossip and weekend plans to what possibly could have happened.

Avicii? He who was so young? In Oman? What was he doing there?

Soon 'Levels' was thundering in the park at Söder Mälarstrand while 'Wake Me Up' was heard from Kungsholmen on the other side of the water. At the clubs at Stureplan, the dance floors fell silent to show respect, and while the news travelled around the world during the night, the sorrow spread on Twitter and Facebook.

Just read the news. I am absolutely sad and my heart just shattered into million pieces.

You have no idea how much your music saved me.

Nobody had the vibe you had brother!

I wish somewhere how you can read our comments ... how much we loved you ...

The next day, thousands of people gathered at Sergels torg, the square in the very centre of the capital. A couple of young guys had brought large speakers, camera crews from TV and newspapers had come to broadcast the tribute live. At four o'clock in the afternoon the murmurs ceased and thousands of people gathered together for a minute's silence. The only thing that broke the peace was sobs and cries. Slowly, the melody of 'Lonely Together' began to play, as those gathered hesitantly clapped their hands. Were you allowed to applaud and dance as you mourned?

One of the organisers took a microphone and stood on the steps that led up to the entrance of the City Theatre. He gave a speech about how Tim Bergling let his soul be heard in the music, which was why he spoke in a language that everyone in the world understood.

'Can we please get the whole of Sergels torg to put their hands up in the air and make a heart to honour Avicii? Do you want to dance? Do you want to rejoice? Do it!'

Then, when 'Levels' revved up, the crowd erupted. Cheers and applause and a girl who was hoisted up in the air by her friends, a square that rocked in the release of thousands of feet dancing together in grief.

Anki stood in front of the computer in the small living room in Las Palmas. She had received a text message from a friend who told her about the broadcast from Stockholm. Anki saw what was happening on the screen – people dancing and crying to her son's music – but the images just seemed far away. She had a hard time understanding that they were about her son. Instead, she pondered about things that in this context seemed banal. Who would have thought that receiving news of someone's death really was just like in the movies. She had always had her reservations and doubts about those scenes before, feeling as though they had been an overdone cliché that had no equivalent in real life. But when they received the call, she really had collapsed on the floor. The scream had come from a depth in her body that she did not even know existed.

Klas was now speaking to David and Anton via a shaky telephone connection. Because their parents were stuck in Las Palmas, Tim's brothers had flown to Oman as soon as they could. Now they were sitting in a police station in Muscat, trying to arrange for an autopsy report and a death certificate. Staff from Sweden's nearest embassy, located in Saudi Arabia, had arrived to assist the brothers.

There was no uncertainty over what had happened.

In a brief, unguarded moment, Tim had withdrawn to the guest house where he was staying. Neither the police nor his brothers had reason to suspect any crime. Tim had taken his own life.

For Anki and Klas, that information did not really change anything.

Tim was still dead.

In no way was the Stockholm they came home to the same city any more. Familiar environments had become foreign. Their home on Linnégatan was filled with bouquets and letters from fans lamenting their loss. But the apartment was another, now that Tim would never be there again and eat shrimp pasta and smoke on the balcony. Even simple tasks such as emptying the bins and vacuuming felt different, the pavements leading down to Oscar's Church appeared hazy and soft.

One day, Anki and Klas took the short walk to the sanctuary, which was a stone's throw from Tim's first recording studio on Styrmansgatan and the cliff where he had partied in his teens. They stood on the promenade across the street from the parish chapel, hoping no one would notice them behind the trees. At twelve o'clock the church bells began to play 'Wake Me Up', and when Tim's well-known melody sounded over Östermalm, it seemed almost sacred, resembling a psalm.

A few weeks later, Anki stood in Anton's garden on Kungsholmen and made an effort to put one leg in front of the other. She was just going to the kitchen, but her body refused to obey the demands of her brain. That the grief was also a physical pain was obvious. Tim existed in his mother's every moment, which was also why he was so painfully absent. Anki collapsed there by the rose bush.

That summer was the warmest in hundreds of years. On TV, happy and sweaty Swedes were interviewed on swimming jetties, while the newspaper placards shouted about extreme weather and climate change. Anki walked cautiously towards the therapy clinic on Artillerigatan – when she leaned on Klas, she was able to slowly get around in the sparse holiday traffic. Laboriously, she forced her feet up the steps and into a small secluded room with tasteful curtains and lit candles.

The therapist she saw was a sharp and experienced woman who had helped many people in shock, when they were at their most vulnerable and angry both at themselves and the one who had suddenly disappeared. The therapy sessions helped Anki process her thoughts and feelings. She was told that for almost all relatives, a suicide came unexpectedly, even in cases where signals had existed beforehand. Often there was a trigger, which in itself could seem trivial and therefore could be difficult for those who lived on to understand. One wasn't to fixate on it. Instead, it was the sum of the small strains that was decisive. The tunnel vision that a suicidal person often suffered from made their perspectives limited. Their problem-solving ability deteriorated; the ability to judge consequences faltered; the options became few. What was easy for someone else could be impossible for someone stuck in the tunnel.

The therapist also explained that feelings of guilt were common in a situation like this. Memory loss was completely normal, as was insomnia. All the things that Anki was going through were actually typical reactions to shock.

The most meaningful thing for Anki was to begin to look at what had happened from a different angle. Just as she felt sad, she could also feel appreciative – find gratitude for the time that she had actually spent with her son, joy over the twenty-eight years he had been in her life, delight about the hearts that he had touched.

In addition, the therapist was never coddling. It was so refreshing to be with someone who did not tilt and nod her head but instead fired off a sharp and liberating line.

Klas tried to handle the situation as firmly and practically as possible. In July 2018, he flew to Los Angeles, where the glass house in Hollywood was to be emptied and sold. He went up into the mountains and hardly dared to unlock Tim's door, stepping into a house that was painfully quiet and empty.

Klas had already gone through many duties that just had to be powered through, even though they felt insurmountable and were difficult even to comprehend. He had drawn up an estate inventory, signed a death certificate and met with the funeral director to prepare a final farewell. He had used words like inheritance and residue. The most difficult thing had been to sign the document that approved a cremation. All these routines and concepts that were so formal and sterile, words that could not possibly have to do with his beloved Tim.

With a feverish feeling in his body, Klas made his way into the large rooms in Los Angeles, forcing himself to go through all the drawers and cabinets. He collected the clothes in the large wardrobe, all the small items ended up on the tables in the gaming room behind the kitchen. He put some chairs and other furniture in the garage: they were to be donated. Like a machine he ploughed on, not wanting to dwell on anything, thinking it better to just get it done.

Later in the evening he was pulled towards Tim's bedroom. He opened the door and looked around the sparsely decorated corner room with panoramic windows. He carefully lay down on Tim's bed, wanting to sense his presence, feel his touch. There he lay, staring up at the ceiling, feeling an endless longing, almost frightened by its intensity.

The images flooded over him. Tim had been at home with his parents during his last visit to Stockholm in February. It was just a few months earlier, still an eternity ago. Anki had cooked, and afterwards she and Tim had sat out on the balcony smoking and agreeing that Gene Hackman was one of the most outstanding actors ever: always restrained, never an expression that felt overdone. It had been just an ordinary conversation.

Then father and son had hugged goodbye and Tim had run down the stairwell. He had glanced over his shoulder and their eyes had met before Tim disappeared around the corner behind the elevator, like so many times before.

That picture was crystal clear in Klas's head.

He was still wondering about so much. What was it that his son had gone through during those difficult hours? In Tim's phone there were notes written during the last days, when he was sitting in the lush garden in Oman and seemed to have had a conversation with himself. They were half-formulated thoughts, fragments. Many of the notes seemed upbeat:

'I'm in tune with my mind and starting to get in tune with energy,' Tim had written. 'And this is all easy to maintain when you are taking good care of yourself and surround yourself with positive energies – which are people!'

'My job is to help the people who have the least control over their experience up!'

'Everyone needs a pat on their back.'

Sometimes another tone shone through, one that felt darker, more desperate and confused. Gradually, Tim seemed to have lost his footing, slipped away from reality. He seemed to have longed for liberation, but did he understand that the consequences of what he was about to do were irreversible?

'The shedding of the soul is the last attachment, before it restarts!'

'We need to feel strong fear sometimes and strong suffering to grow!'

'Aaaaaaah but I'm still trying to figure everything out all the time, I need to be OK with sitting by myself!'

'I need to learn how to handle those emotions.'

'Relax.'

After a few days in Los Angeles, Neil Jacobson at Universal arranged for a couple of guys to come and help Klas disassemble Tim's studio equipment. A removal company carried away the colourful paintings and a storage space that Tim had used nearby was cleared out.

Klas sat out on the terrace staring at a neon sign down on Sunset Boulevard. The first letter had gone out, so now it was just UNSET in capital letters. It bothered Klas a bit that no one had put in new lights. It couldn't be such an exhausting job, could it?

He was in a grumpy mood, falling into dark thoughts, unable to stop them from gaining a foothold. He was so upset at himself, felt naive and mindless. He could well understand that it was pointless to go on blaming himself, but right now it felt like he hadn't understood anything at all. He had walked next to his son all those years, seen Tim feel bad, he had known about everything.

So why had he never realized the full extent of the problem? Why had he never imagined that it would come to this? How was it even possible that Tim was dead?

That it would end this way had never crossed Klas's mind, not even in his worst nightmares, least of all when their son had been in the middle of his most creative flow in many years. The only thing his parents had heard from Tim in the days before he died was how fantastic the songs were, how beautiful it was in the desert, how much he was looking forward to travelling to Iceland with his siblings.

Klas had also talked to the therapist in Stockholm. She had called suicide a serial crash of the mind. A few days of anguish and anxiety that had thrown Tim back to a place that those around him thought he had left behind.

Restless, Klas went in and sat down at his son's black piano. He looked out over sun-bleached Los Angeles and cried as he played the chords to 'Wee Wee Hours', Chuck Berry's blues about lost love.

SALEM AL FAKIR and Vincent Pontare were sitting in their studio in Södermalm, wondering how they would even begin.

Salem had talked on the phone with Per Sundin and barely recognised the record company manager at Universal. Sundin, who was usually so efficient and focused, had cried when he explained that he thought that the last songs that Tim worked on should be completed and released.

Salem and Vincent were actually of the same opinion. They could testify to how excited Tim had been that the creative fuse had finally gone off during those days in March, days that now felt so distant. It would feel wrong if the world never heard the songs that Tim was so proud of.

Still, it was difficult to plug in the hard drive and open the files that were catalogued under the name 'TIM WHOLE FOLDER 2018'. Here were drafts in different states: some project files did not consist of much more than a few drum loops and mumbles over guitar, while other songs were practically finished.

The tunes were charged with electricity, and took Salem and Vincent back to those intense days when Tim had seemed so happy. They envisioned him bouncing around the studio downstairs, shouting instructions, and him out in the sunshine talking about how several of these songs were among the best he had ever made.

The contrast between those mental images and the miserable atmosphere in the studio on Södermalm made it impossible for Salem and Vincent to start work.

How could someone who seemed so satisfied suddenly disappear? Who were they even to be tinkering with Tim's stuff anyway? How could they know how he wanted these tracks to be completed? And did they even have it in them right now to produce songs? The mere thought of music felt unfitting. A beloved friend had disappeared; that was the only thing that mattered.

They let time pass. Eventually, one morning in October 2018, Salem and Vincent opened up the projects and looked at their files with a slightly clearer gaze. They had just played at Tim's funeral at the Woodland Cemetery and his death had begun to feel more definitive and real. In addition, Klas Bergling had come by the studio and explained that it was also the family's wish that the songs were finished.

Salem and Vincent began working on 'Peace Of Mind' and two of the other productions that had been nearly finished when Tim went to Oman. In 'Excuse Me Mr Sir', the verse, bridge and chorus only needed to be assembled in the right order; for 'Tough Love' a couple of singers were missing.

Vincent went back to his notes from an afternoon when he and Tim had sat on the balcony in Los Angeles and discussed what needed to be done for them to be ready. He and Salem became increasingly confident that the music was actually a part of themselves as well. They intuitively knew where the songs should go, had a whole well of memories to draw from, endless hours of conversations with Tim about music and the times they were living in.

The short period that had passed since Tim Bergling's death had made his significance as a musician even clearer. What he had always worked for – to be taken seriously as a songwriter and composer – had by now been emphatically fulfilled. The newspaper columns were full of words of remembrance that recognised Avicii as a fearless visionary, as someone who, through his unexpected choices, had been involved in reshaping an entire genre.

The creative, adventurous spirit had been evident even in the last weeks in Los Angeles, when Tim had thought it was as natural to find inspiration in a cheesy ballad from the Disney movie *Pocahontas* as it was to study the handclaps in the film adaptation of *Jesus Christ Superstar* that he'd watched with his school gang on the bed on Linnégatan. It was that same playful instinct that made Tim dare to invite a musician with a banjo on stage as had made him not hesitate to use pan flutes in his childhood bedroom. That same trait made him want to colour the last album with a thumb piano from Zimbabwe and finish it all together with Maasai warriors.

Salem and Vincent put new guitars on 'Excuse Me Mr Sir' and felt a growing calm ahead of the posthumous project. This would work; Tim would have liked what they were doing.

Laidback Luke cried when he opened Tim's project file for the song 'SOS'.

He had been asked to do the official remix of the single, but seeing Tim's files reminded him of once upon a time, on the online forum, when they had discussed how to mix a bass drum or when the epic drop should come in.

Laidback Luke had given the nature of the music industry a lot of thought lately. Two of the young producers he had invited to a small basement club in Miami in 2009 had moved on and become huge stars. Tim Bergling did his thing, of course. But also Hardwell made it to the top, making hits like 'Spaceman' and 'Apollo' and ending up at the top of *DJ Mag*'s list of the world's best DJs two years in a row.

Barely six months after Tim's death, Hardwell also decided to stop travelling. The touring had become an endless roller coaster, he wrote on Instagram. He needed to clear his calendar of interviews, deadlines and other musts; he needed to be Robbert van de Corput again.

There were other cracks in the proud façade of fame, signs of greater honesty. Musician Billie Eilish spoke in interviews about how her early breakthrough had made her feel like she was disjointed from society and how she had got impulses to hurt herself before she even turned seventeen. Actress Catherine Zeta-Jones talked about the relief of being diagnosed with bipolar disorder – finally she had a name for what she had felt for a long time. Sports stars such as Andre Agassi and Michael Phelps described how the constant demand for peak performance had led to addiction and depression, and when gymnast Simone Biles decided not to compete in the Olympics due to unreasonable pressure, she was hailed as a pioneer. Even a thick-skinned rapper like Lil Wayne now opened up about his mental health issues and the suicidal thoughts that had plagued him as a young man.

Laidback Luke began to live with a new code of conduct.

One day a week he was not allowed to do anything at all. He would lay in his bed, staring at Netflix, telling himself he was suffering from terrible flu. When the impulse came to check an email or scroll the feed, he ignored it; at most he slowly trudged to the toilet.

The practical change made a difference to his physical condition, but the biggest shift was mental. The same person who at the beginning of his career had been isolated and silent now wanted to talk openly about his panic attacks and his addiction.

Those who emailed Laidback Luke on one of his free days were met by an auto-reply: 'DJs need weekends, too.'

*

For many others who had crossed his path, Tim's death set things in motion.

For Filip Åkesson, it took a couple of months before he decided – the summer of 2018 would be Philgood's last months on opioids.

For a few confused and grieving weeks, Filip spent almost $5,000 on a final farewell to the pills he had loved and hated for so long. Then he flew home to Stockholm, went to a psychiatric clinic in Mörby and sought help.

Even in Sweden, abuse of prescription medications had by this time become a major social issue. While oxycodone was the substance that had started an epidemic in the United States, the Swedish equivalent was called tramadol. The opioid had increasingly been prescribed for sports injuries in the late 2000s and the rumour had spread among young people about a medicine that made one feel great – at first many people seemed to have thought that it was a simple headache pill. Just over a decade later, tramadol was the second most common illicit drug in Sweden after cannabis. In fact, Sweden now had the fourth highest numbers per capita in the world in terms of deaths due to opioids.

The withdrawal was tough for Filip. As his head cleared, the remorse came knocking. He regretted every shitty thing he had said to Tim in the fog of drunkenness, every accusation in the perceived clarity of intoxication.

Why had they laughed off their addictions, joked about the medication instead of talking seriously? Why had they not dared to sit down and talk for real? If Filip had been more honest about his own addiction, perhaps he and Tim would have been able to tackle their problems together? If Filip had not dealt with his defeats by fleeing to Los Angeles, perhaps Tim would have been put off by his friend's experiences and found it easier to resist?

Maybe everything could have ended differently?

Tim Bergling had nevertheless saved Filip Åkesson, that's how he saw it. Quitting the drugs was the least he could do to honour his friend. It was just so damn shitty that it took Tim dying for Filip to understand that he needed help to change his own life.

As Filip wiped away his tears, he saw the tattoo. In dark ink on his wrist sat a memory from a green sofa in Östermalm when he and Tim were still teenagers.

It was the title of the very first song they did together.

'A New Hope'.

And love is the feeling we love, the perfect compass to keep the system in balance and to remember our purpose even when we don't know it.

So the purpose of this system we call life has to be to, as cheesy as it sounds, to follow love.

Not because it's a sweet idea, but simply because the logic is sound.

AND SO THE DAYS passed, and strangely even months and years.

Anki Lidén sat at the kitchen table in Skillinge and ate two pieces of pickled salmon and a potato but she could manage no more. She who had always been so fond of food had not been hungry in three years now.

Tim had taken her appetite with him.

Her ability to concentrate had also suffered. Anki, who had previously loved to read, could no longer manage it. She couldn't get into the books, wasn't able to apply herself to the blocks of text. Her friends asked her and Klas if it hadn't got better with time. In all good faith, they wondered if the grief wasn't easier to bear now. In fact, it was the opposite. In the beginning, everything had been unreal, their surroundings covered by a veil of silk. Tim was still alive, it was impossible that he was actually gone.

Three years later it was different. The realisation grew with each passing day and the warm sensation of fever that had characterised the months after Tim's death was long gone. The grief now had sharp edges.

Anki watched every TV series she came across, everything except space adventures and vampires. It was her way of handling the days. She lived in the make-believe stories, stayed there for a while. In order to fall asleep she needed to be in another world.

Klas Bergling found relief in educating himself. He read

reports and studies, took notes to understand the mechanisms behind destructive thoughts and the times in which Tim had lived. Although the information was often disappointing, the knowledge softened the inner voices, those that lectured and blamed and wondered how it had ended up like this.

Klas learned that mental health issues had increased by almost seventy per cent among young adults in Sweden in the last ten years. With rising frustration, he read that seven times more people died by suicide than in traffic accidents across the country. Yet society invested far more in preventive road construction than in approaching the human psyche. There always seemed to be money to erect guard rails or rebuild intersections, but the level of instruction on how to deal with people in crisis was often low, even in healthcare settings.

As Klas read, the anger that lived within him became more outward-looking. He was angry at himself, but also increasingly at society. In the fury was also energy: if he and Anki felt so caught off guard by a suicide, there must be other people around them who were also unprepared for the worst.

The couple had long discussions at the kitchen table. Twisting and turning their thoughts, they agreed that they should try to generate something constructive out of all the despair. Together with the rest of the family, they decided to establish the Tim Bergling Foundation, a charity that would support organisations that worked towards preventing suicide and for a more open conversation about mental health issues.

Of course, it was partly to alleviate their own grief, but Tim's parents also saw it as a way to fulfil their son's wish – to encourage and help people reflect on the human condition.

Nervousness, anxiety, disquiet and loneliness could affect everyone, yet such feelings were often approached in an apprehensive manner. A physical ailment was something that afflicted someone: you broke your arm, you were in a bicycle accident. No one was characterised by their flu – but they were defined by their thoughts. Mental disorders were viewed as suggesting something about human dignity and strength. Unfortunately, to say that you had suffered from depression or a psychosis still meant to speak out, to confess something.

It was getting better, they noticed that. There were a lot of young people who, like Tim, genuinely talked about how they felt. But the stigma was not gone, there was much left to do. Anki and Klas asked themselves the same question that their son had when he was in the rehab centre in Ibiza, when he had learned to interpret his body's signals that something was wrong:

Why weren't these issues talked about more in schools?

Teachers should not just teach physics, chemistry and maths – the inner life was surely just as important. Students needed to learn early on how to relate to the shadows of life without feeling ashamed. Relationship problems, parents who divorced, achievement anxiety. Scheduled discussions about the darker corners of the psyche could help young people reach self-awareness and also become better at paying attention to the signs that someone else was not doing well.

At the same time, the discussion continued in public about the artist Avicii, he who had been snatched away far too soon and was well on his way to becoming both a martyr and a myth. News articles and social media posts looked for simple answers to the question of why the star had died. The grief and frustration turned into blood lust, people online hunted for people to accuse, someone to answer for what had happened.

Anki and Klas thought that kind of speculation was useless. In their eyes looking for scapegoats was not only destructive – it was also impossible. It simply couldn't be done; their son's journey had been too complex for that.

Klas Bergling changed gear, let the clutch meet the accelerator and felt how the low sports car hugged the curve. He was driving a shiny Ford Thunderbird, 1965, silver lacquered, with blue-upholstered seats.

It was the first car that Tim's friend Jesse Waits had bought when he came to Las Vegas a long time ago, back when European house music was still a marginal subculture on American soil. When Tim Bergling turned twenty-two, Jesse had given him the car as a birthday present and now it had ended up here, on a rain-soaked country road between rapeseed fields and winter-dry apple trees in Skillinge.

Jesse was one of Tim's friends with whom Klas kept in touch. The former nightclub king had recently made drastic changes in his life. The lavish house in Las Vegas was sold; he had abandoned his plans to be part of a new nightclub in the casino city. Instead, Jesse Waits had moved to Bali, where he now lived in a peaceful area in the southern parts of the Indonesian island. He apparently slept better at night nowadays, had quit drinking, took care of his soul in a way he had never been able to before – Tim's death had made him completely re-evaluate his life.

These kind of ripple effects continued among those closest to Tim.

Fricko Boberg, his friend since his childhood, had started going to a psychologist who gave him solid tools for how to act when unpleasant feelings came over him.

Songwriter Albin Nedler, who for a time had been tormented by the impulse to take his own life, was now doing much better. Suicidal thoughts were often just this fickle and short-lived: as soon as they appeared they could vanish. Nothing lasted for ever, not even hopelessness. And any day now, Albin would become a father.

These positive changes pleased Klas Bergling as he sat in front of the steering wheel of a sports car that vibrated with life. In the boot were six sturdy speakers currently blasting Tim's song 'I Could Be The One' out over the fields. Klas used to go for a ride when his thoughts were overflowing. Feeling the music pounding in his chest as the engine roared was also therapy.

Musically, his son's imprint continued to grow. Now Tim Bergling was considered one of the greatest songwriters in Swedish music history, someone who had been at the forefront during the years when dance music beat rock festivals and took over the world. At the same time, Avicii's name was respected by traditional musicians as well – those who had initially been suspicious of anything called electronic music. Tim Bergling had been one of those shifting the boundaries of dance music – the artists who came after him no longer had to face prejudices that a DJ was no real musician, but were seen as composers in their own right. Electronic music had become a fully integrated part of modern pop.

And Avicii's songs continued to be played – at festivals and celebrations and in the headphones of people who drew energy from the blissful melodies and hopeful lyrics. The letters to his family had continued to pile up, written by young people who described the importance that Tim's music had in their lives, the strength that his songs gave them: the courage to do a job interview, the hype before a workout session, the energy to get through a tough day at school. His beats brightened up weddings and funerals, were played at parties and in mourning. So many that had gone through similar problems to Tim's, or were in the middle of them, and pressed play to fight on.

That utopian and hopeful tone in Tim's music – the hole in

the clouds, the sunshine that peeped through, the warm light – now stood out so clearly to Klas Bergling. Everything would be fine in the end, that was what the music promised. That his son could continue to support other people was a consolation in itself.

The music made Tim live on a moment longer.

> When you need a way to beat the pressure down
> When you need to find a way to breathe
> I could be the one to make you feel that way
> I could be the one to set you free

The other day, Klas was standing in the kitchen, preparing a sandwich by the sink.

Then suddenly Tim was there beside him.

His hair was the same as before, short and blond, but he had grown taller than his old man.

A warm glance, something astute and secretive in the eyes.

'Hey, Daddy.'

That was all Tim said, his crooked smile beaming. Then they just stood there, keeping each other company while Klas slowly ate his cheese sandwich.

SOURCES

This book exists thanks to all of those who wanted to share their experiences. The vast majority of the story is built from interviews that took place over the span of more than two years, from spring 2019 to autumn 2021. Most of those interviewed chose to be named, others decided to speak on condition that they remain anonymous. They all have contributed valuable details and knowledge.

Most were generous not only with their memories, but also with material that allowed the story to stand on solid ground. In the background are text messages, chat conversations, personal notes, emails, receipts and tour schedules. I have gone through thousands of private photos, seen pictures from when Tim Bergling was a newborn baby to when he was spending his final weeks in Oman.

Through the generosity of the Bergling family, I've had access to Tim's own books, notes and emails, and I know which YouTube videos he saw at which point in time. As sources, I've also used Avicii's official accounts on Facebook, Twitter and Instagram, from which I occasionally cite comments.

The text's descriptions of the various locations build primarily on my own physical visits to apartments and grocery shops and nightclubs – and to the roof on Kammarkargatan where a young Tim slept in the mornings after having stayed up all night making beats.

Arash Pournouri was offered the opportunity to participate in interviews, but eventually decided against doing so.

The person in Oman that I have named Amer is actually called something else.

This book is an authorised biography. All the net proceeds of the Avicii AB corporation will go to the Tim Bergling Foundation, in order to support the prevention of mental illness and suicide.

CITED WORKS

Ludovic Rambaud, 'Avicii – La Relève Suédoise' (*Only For DJs*, April 2009), p. 70

Dancing Astronaut, 'The Top 10 Tracks of Las Vegas Memorial Day Weekend' (*Dancing Astronaut*, 9 June 2011), p. 96

Levan Tsikurishvili & Anders Boström, *Avicii på turné* (Stureplansgruppen Media Group, 2013), pp. 162-3

Kerri Mason, 'Robert F.X. Sillerman's Empire State of Mind' (*Billboard Magazine*, 17 September 2012), p. 173

Jon Caramanica, 'Global Pop, Now Infused With Country' (*New York Times*, 18 September 2013), p. 183

Anders Nunstedt, 'Imponerande debut av Avicii' (*Expressen*, 13 September 2013), p. 184

Per Magnusson, 'Aviciis nya är ett långfinger åt de gamla konventionerna' (*Aftonbladet*, 13 September 2013), p. 184

Eckhart Tolle, *The Power of Now: A Guide to Spiritual Enlightenment* (New World Library, 1999), p. 259

Michaelangelo Matos, 'Avicii expands his musical reach on "Stories": Album review' (*Billboard Magazine*, 2 October 2015), p. 262

Will Hermes, 'Stories' (*Rolling Stone*, 2 October 2015), p. 262

NERIS Analytics Limited, *16 Personalities Free Personality Test*, www.16personalities.com, p. 270

Levan Tsikurishvili, *Avicii: True Stories* (Opa People, 2017), p. 106, 271, 275, 334

Thich Nhat Hanh, *Peace Is Every Step: The Path of Mindfulness in Everyday Life* (Bantam, 1992), p. 281

Simon Vozick-Levinson, 'Avicii Talks Quitting Touring, Disappointing Madonna, New Music' (*Rolling Stone*, 5 September 2017), p. 296

OTHER SOURCES

Pages 5–7

Socialstyrelsen, *Utvecklingen av psykisk ohälsa bland barn och unga vuxna. Till och med 2016* (Socialstyrelsen, 2017)

World Health Organization, *Injuries and Violence: The Facts* (WHO, 2014)

World Health Organization, *Suicide worldwide in 2019: global health estimates* (WHO, 2021)

Pages 10–15

Bengt Jonsson, 'Hubble 10 år – hotande fiasko vändes i succé' (*Svenska Dagbladet*, 7 May 2000)

Sören Winge, 'Fantastiska bilder från universum' (*Upsala Nya Tidning*, 25 February 2002)

Pages 18–22

South Park, 'Make Love, Not Warcraft' (Comedy Central, 4 October 2006)

Stefan Lundell (et al.), *Stureplan: det vackra folket och de dolda makthavarna* (Lind & Co, 2006)

Calle Dernulf, *Swedish DJs – intervjuer: Axwell* (Telegram Förlag, 2013)

Pages 24–29

Michaelangelo Matos, *The Underground Is Massive: How Electronic Dance Music Conquered America* (Dey Street Books, 2015)

Pages 30–33

Flashback Forum, *Tankspridd/oro utan grund* (Accessed 19 November 2019)

Flashback Forum, *Första gången jag rökte* (Accessed 19 November 2019)

Flashback Forum, *Kan ej tänka!* (Accessed 19 November 2019)

Flashback Forum, *Känns overkligt?* (Accessed 19 November 2019)

Pages 34–43

Basshunter, *FL Studio Tutorial* (YouTube, 6 June 2006)

Christopher Friman, 'Ett bedårande barn av sin tid' (*Magasinet Filter*, 10 October 2009)

Matthew Collin, *Altered States: The Story of Ecstasy and Acid House* (Serpent's Tail, 1997)

Blogspot.com, Isabel Adrian, 'Mitt liv som det är!' (Accessed 23 November 2020)

Studio, mötesplatsen för musikskapare, *Feedback sökes* (Accessed 3 November 2019)

Studio, mötesplatsen för musikskapare, *Skulle behöva lite hjälp* (Accessed 3 November 2019)

Pages 44–50

Richard Flink, 'Den revanschlystne rugbykillen som blev musikmogul' (*Resemagasinet Buss*, No. 8, 2016)

Ebba Hallin, Nils von Heijne, *Fuckups och businessblunders: felsteg som framgångsrecept* (Lava förlag, 2016)

Niklas Natt och Dag, 'Andra sidan Avicii' (*King Magazine*, No. 6, 2013)

Sommar i P1 – Arash 'Ash' Pournouri (Sveriges Radio P1, 9 July 2015)

Stephen Edwards, 'Meet Ash Pournouri: The Man Behind Dance Music's Latest Phenomenon' (*Elite Daily*, 26 August 2013)

David Morris, 'The Guy Behind the Guy' (*Vegas Seven*, 16 August 2012)

Jane Alexander, *The Body, Mind, Spirit Miscellany: The Ultimate Collection of Fascinations, Facts, Truths, and Insights* (Duncan Baird, 2009)

Laidback Luke Forum (Accessed 16 November 2019)

Mark van Bergen, *Dutch Dance, 1988–2018: How The Netherlands Took the Lead in Electronic Music* (Mary Go Wild, 2018)

Pages 52–65

Kerri Mason, 'Blood On the Dancefloor: Winter Music Conference vs. Ultra Music Festival' (*Billboard Magazine*, 7 February 2011)

Geoffrey Hunt, Molly Moloney, Kristin Evans, *Youth, Drugs, and Nightlife* (Taylor & Francis, 2010)

Pages 66–86

John Dingwall, 'Radio 1's Big Weekend: Dance star Tiësto reveals how he lost out on love because of his music career' (*Daily Record*, 23 May 2014)

Door Wilma Nanninga, 'Tiësto draaide niet op bruiloft ex Stacey Blokzijl' (*De Telegraaf*, 17 September 2013)

Calle Dernulf, *Den svenska klubbhistorien* (Storytel Dox, 2017)

John Seabrook, *The Song Machine: Inside the Hit Factory* (W.W. Norton & Company, 2015)

Stephen Armstrong, *The White Island: Two Thousand Years of Pleasure in Ibiza* (Black Swan, 2005)

Neil Strauss, *The Dirt: Confessions of The World's Most Notorious Rock Band* (Dey Street Books, 2002)

Pages 87–91

Ingrid Carlberg, 'En dag med Salem Al Fakir' (*Dagens Nyheter*, 4 January 2007)

Patrik Andersson, 'Salem vill erövra världen' (*Göteborgs-Posten*, 19 February 2007)

Christoffer Nilsson, 'Här är artisterna som spelar i Slottskyrkan' (*Aftonbladet*, 11 June 2015)

Avicii, *Avicii in Scandinavia – Part III* (YouTube, 20 November 2010)

Pages 92–100

Philip Sherburne, 'The New Rave Generation' (*Spin*, October 2011)

Bryan Bass, 'Twin Engines: The Waits Brothers and Wynn's Innovative Tryst' (*Nightclub & Bar*, February 2007)

Martin Stein, 'Nothing Succeeds Like XS' (*What's On Las Vegas*, January 2009)

Sarah Feldberg, 'On a Night of Excess, the First Night of XS' (*Las Vegas Weekly*, 31 December 2008)

Pages 101–107

Tore S. Börjesson, 'Jag passar inte in i USA. Jag är för tråkig' (*Dagens Arbete*, 20 January 2012)

Levan Tsikurishvili, *Avicii: True Stories* (Opa People, 2017)

Kungl. IngenjörsVetenskapsAkademien, *Frukost IVA 20150310 Avicii manager Ash Pournouri* (YouTube, 18 March 2015)

Magnus Broni, *Det svenska popundret: 5. Ett paradis för pirater* (Sveriges Television, 2019)

Johan Åkesson, 'Stjärna i sitt eget universum' (*Dagens Nyheter*, 18 March 2012)

Pages 108–112

Barry Meier, *Pain Killer: An Empire of Deceit and the Origin of America's Opioid Epidemic* (Random House, 2018)

Jonas Cullberg, *En amerikansk epidemi* (Bokförlaget Atlas, 2019)

Christopher Glazek, 'The Secretive Family Making Billions From the Opioid Crisis' (*Esquire*, 16 October 2017)

Patrick Radden Keefe, 'The Family That Built an Empire of Pain'
(*New Yorker*, 23 October 2017)

Pages 113–120

Sean Hotchkiss, 'First Look: Avicii for Ralph Lauren Denim &
Supply Fall 2012' (*GQ*, 9 July 2012)

Denim & Supply Ralph Lauren House for Hunger Playbutton,
(Macy's, 2013)

Pages 121–123

John E. Hall, *Guyton and Hall Textbook of Medical Physiology*
(Elsevier, 2015)

Pages 140–152

Jon Häggqvist, 'Vincent gick sin egen väg' (*Allehanda*, 10
November 2007)

'SiriusXM's Town Hall Series with Avicii' (*SiriusXM*, 19
September 2013)

Pages 153–157

Helen Ahlbom, 'Vestberg på scen med Avicii' (*Ny Teknik*, 22
February 2013)

Lars-Anders Karlberg, 'Avicii och Vestberg på samma scen'
(*Elektroniktidningen*, 27 February 2013)

Pages 164–170

Zack O'Malley Greenburg, 'The World's Highest-Paid DJs 2012'
(*Forbes*, 2 August 2012)

Pages 171–182

David Ciancio, 'Nightclub & Bar Announces the 2013 Top 100'
(*Nightclub & Bar*, 14 February 2013)

Lee Moran, 'Instagram tycoons toast Facebook deal by partying at Las Vegas superclub … and post a (pretty fuzzy) picture using their app' (*Daily Mail*, 17 April 2012)

Leonie Cooper, 'Prince Harry to become reggae DJ after meeting Marley's widow in Jamaica?' (*New Musical Express*, 7 May 2012)

Brian Viner, 'Sheikh Mansour: The richest man in football' (*Independent*, 22 October 2011)

'Sheikh Mansour convinced of potential of "sleeping giant" Manchester City' (*Guardian*, 1 July 2009)

Josh Eells, 'Night Club Royale' (*New Yorker*, 23 September 2013)

Pages 183–189

Jan Gradvall, 'Avicii: True' (*DI Weekend*, 6 September 2013)

Zane Lowe, *In Conversation with Chris Martin* … (BBC Radio 1, 28 April 2014)

Mike Fleeman, 'Gwyneth Paltrow and Chris Martin Separate' (*People*, 25 March 2014)

Patrick Doyle, 'Avicii's Rave New World' (*Rolling Stone*, 16 August 2013)

Pages 192–200

Per Magnusson, 'Episkt och älskvärt av Avicii' (*Aftonbladet*, 1 March 2014)

Johan Åkesson, 'Så bygger han Sveriges hetaste varumärke' (*Veckans Affärer*, 17 April 2014)

Pages 201–204

Sean Pajot, 'Avicii Hotel Returning to South Beach, Charging $800 Per Night for WMC and MMW 2014' (*Miami New Times*, 11 February 2014)

Michelle Lhooq, 'The Avicii Hotel in Miami Is Completely Insane' (*Vice*, 30 March 2014)

Pages 206–214

Ryan Kristobak, '"SNL" Mocks EDM Culture With "When Will The Bass Drop?"' (*Huffington Post*, 18 May 2014)

Pages 215–220

David Armstrong, 'Purdue Says Kentucky Suit Over OxyContin Could Be Painful' (*Bloomberg*, 20 October 2014)

Laura Ungar, 'Lawsuit seeks to make drugmaker pay for OxyContin abuse' (*USA Today*, 29 December 2014)

BBC News, *US life expectancy declines for first time in 20 years* (BBC News, 8 December 2016)

Jessica Glenza, 'Life expectancy in US down for second year in a row as opioid crisis deepens' (*Guardian*, 21 December 2017)

Pages 237–248

Rasmus Blom, 'Här är bråket steg för steg: Avicii mot brittisk press och Madonna' (*King Magazine*, 8 June 2015)

Carol Martin, Elaine Player, *Drug Treatment in Prison: An Evaluation of the RAPt Treatment Programme* (Waterside Press, 2000)

Pages 257–259

Sissela Nutley, Siri Helle, *Mår unga sämre i en digital värld?* (Mind, 2020)

Jean M. Twenge, *iGen: Why Today's Super-Connected Kids Are Growing Up Less Rebellious, More Tolerant, Less Happy – And Completely Unprepared For Adulthood* (Atria Books, 2017)

Matt Haig, *Notes on a Nervous Planet* (Canongate Books, 2018)

Pages 262–265

Sara Martinsson, 'Avicii: "Stories"' (*Dagens Nyheter*, 30 September 2015)

Onesimus D. Zeon, *Avicii 'Wake Me Up' Morocco Live Concert (June 1, 2015)* (YouTube, 8 July 2015)

Pages 268–276

Avicii, *Avicii Live @ Monument Valley #thecrowningofprinceliam* (YouTube, 13 March 2016)

Stim, *Hitstoria: Så skrev vi musiken – Without you @ Stim Music Room* (YouTube, 14 December 2017)

Merve Emre, *What's Your Type?: The Strange History of Myers-Briggs and the Birth of Personality Testing* (William Collins, 2018)

Jon Blistein, 'Avicii Retires From Touring via Open Letter to Fans' (*Rolling Stone*, 29 March 2016)

Pages 277–282

Talks at Google – Living with Meaning, Purpose and Wisdom in the Digital Age with Eckhart Tolle and Bradley Horowitz (YouTube, 24 February 2012)

Kristin Olson, *Makt och medkänsla: Reportage om engagerad buddhism* (Cinta förlag, 2019)

Kulananda, *Principles of Buddhism* (Thorsons, 1996)

Pages 283–288

Pete Tong, *Avicii Chats To Pete* (BBC Radio 1, 12 August 2017)

Pages 289–295

Ted Mann, 'Magnificent Visions' (*Vanity Fair*, 11 November 2011)

Christopher Friman, 'I en annan del av Sverige' (*Magasinet Filter*, 11 October 2012)

Lee Roden, 'Avicii teases new album through mysterious "magic" music boxes' (*The Local*, 2 August 2017)

Pages 296–301

South Park, 'Hummels & Heroin' (Comedy Central, 18 October 2017)

Jeff Barnard, 'Oregon's monster mushroom is world's biggest living thing' (*Independent*, 17 September 2011)

Pages 304–309

Ryan Mac, 'The Fall Of SFX: From Billion-Dollar Company To Bankruptcy' (*Forbes*, 24 August 2015)

Robert Levine, 'Former SFX CEO Robert Sillerman Speaks Out for the First Time About His Company's Implosion: "I Don't Begrudge the Employees' Anger"' (*Billboard Magazine*, 9 June 2016)

Bradley Hope, 'Key Figure in 1MDB Probe Is Arrested in Abu Dhabi' (*Wall Street Journal*, 18 August 2016)

Fredrik Eliasson, *Musikplats LA – en svensk framgångssaga* (Sveriges Radio P4, 29 May 2017)

Rachael Revesz, 'Marijuana legalisation is the biggest winner of the 2016 presidential election' (*Independent*, 9 November 2016)

Michael Pollan, 'The Trip Treatment' (*New Yorker*, 9 February 2015)

Erin Brodwin, 'Peter Thiel Is Betting on Magic Mushrooms to Treat Depression – and He's Not the Only One' (*Business Insider*, 12 December 2017)

Pages 310–313

Johan Cullberg, Maria Skott, Pontus Strålin, *Att insjukna i psykos: förlopp, behandling, återhämtning* (Natur & Kultur Akademisk, 2020)

Marta Di Forti et al, 'The contribution of cannabis use to variation in the incidence of psychotic disorder across Europe (EUGEI): a multicentre case control study' (*The Lancet Psychiatry*, 19 March 2019)

Pages 320–328

Prudence Farrow Bruns, *Dear Prudence: The Story Behind the Song* (CreateSpace, 2015)

Maharishi Mahesh Yogi, *Vetenskapen om Varandet och livets konst* (SRM International Publication, 1973)

Diana Darke, Tony Walsh, *Oman* (Bradt Travel Guides, 2017)

Pages 329–332

Charlotte Kjaer, 'Hubble-teleskopet är jordens öga i rymden' (*Illustrerad Vetenskap*, 20 July 2021)

Pages 333–337

Susan Shumsky, *Maharishi & Me: Seeking Enlightenment with the Beatles' Guru* (Skyhorse Publishing, 2018)

Matt Landing, *My Enlightenment Delusion: Experiences and Musings of a Former Transcendental Meditation Teacher* (2017)

Pages 350–357

Monica Holmgren, Clas Svahn, 'Tim "Avicii" Bergling är död – blev 28 år gammal' (*Dagens Nyheter*, 20 April 2018)

August Håkansson, 'Fansen i tårar på Sergels torg: "Avicii har förändrat mitt liv"' (*Aftonbladet*, 21 April 2018)

Rickard Holmberg, *Till minne av Tim Bergling/Avicii på Sergels torg* (YouTube, 13 February 2021)

Pages 358–363

Jake Gable, 'Breaking: Hardwell announces retirement from live shows' (*We Rave You*, 7 September 2018)

Emmanuel Acho, *Mental Health Doesn't Discriminate feat. Lil Wayne* (YouTube, 16 August 2021)

Steve Keating, 'Many "twisties" and turns, but Simone Biles exits Games a champion' (*Reuters*, 4 August 2021)

Gayle King, *The Gayle King Grammy Special* (CBS News, 23 January 2020)

Co-Op Think, *Michael Phelps Shares His Experiences and Struggles Achieving Excellence* (YouTube, 19 June 2018)

Andre Agassi, *Open: An Autobiography* (Harper Collins, 2009)

Nancy Hass, 'No Time For Secrets' (*InStyle*, December 2012)

Maria Ejd, 'Gammalt läkemedel blir ny drog' (*Vårdfokus*, 7 October 2015)

Matilda Aprea Malmqvist, 'Tramadolmissbruk ökar kraftigt bland ungdomar' (*Svenska Dagbladet*, 24 December 2018)

OECD, *Addressing Problematic Opioid Use in OECD Countries* (OECD Publishing, 2019)

FURTHER READING

Bill Brewster, Frank Broughton, *Last Night a DJ Saved My Life: The History of the Disc Jockey* (Grove Press, 2014)

Matthew Collin, *Rave On: Global Adventures in Electronic Dance Music* (The University of Chicago Press, 2018)

Calle Dernulf, *Swedish DJs – Intervjuer: Eric Prydz* (Telegram Förlag, 2013)

Matt Haig, *Reasons to Stay Alive* (Canongate Books, 2015)

Tommy Hellsten, *Flodhästen på arbetsplatsen* (Verbum AB, 2001)

Ullakarin Nyberg, *Konsten att rädda liv: om att förebygga självmord* (Natur & Kultur Läromedel, 2013)

Dom Phillips, *Superstar DJs Here We Go!* (Ebury Press, 2009)

Simon Reynolds, *Energy Flash: A Journey Through Rave Music and Dance Culture* (Faber & Faber, 2013)

Alfred Skogberg, *När någon tar sitt liv: Tragedierna vi kan förhindra* (Ordfront, 2012)

Gert van Veen, *Release/Celebrate Life: The Story of ID&T* (Mary Go Wild, 2017)

Tobias Brandel, 'Kungarna av Ibiza' (*Svenska Dagbladet*, 28 August 2009)

Jan Gradvall, 'Swedish House Mafia: den sista intervjun' (*Café*, December 2012)

Jonas Grönlund, 'Veni, vidi, Avicii' (*Sydsvenskan*, 12 May 2012)

Kerri Mason, 'Avicii's Wake-Up Call' (*Billboard Magazine*, 21 September 2013)

Michaelangelo Matos, 'The Mainstreaming of EDM and The Precipitous Drop That Followed' (*NPR*, 13 November 2019)

Emil Persson, 'Avicii till Café: "Problemet är att varenda dag var en fest"' (*Café*, October 2013)

Jessica Pressler, 'Avicii, the King of Oontz Oontz Oontz' (*GQ*, 29 March 2013)

Fredrik Strage, 'Sommaren med Avicii' (*Icon*, 2012)

Future Music Magazine, *Avicii in the studio – The Making of Dancing in My Head* (YouTube, 3 September 2012)

FILMS

Dan Cutforth, Jane Lipsitz, *EDC 2013: Under The Electric Sky* (Haven Entertainment, Insomniac Events, 2014)

Carin Goeijers, *God Is My DJ: The Story of Sensation* (Pieter van Huystee Film, 2006)

Kevin Kerslake, *Electric Daisy Carnival Experience* (Manifest, 2011)

Christian Larson, Henrik Hanson, *Take One: A Documentary Film About Swedish House Mafia* (EMI Films Ltd, 2010)

Bert Marcus, Cyrus Saidi, *What We Started* (Bert Marcus Productions, 2017)

IMAGE SOURCES

Plate 1

Pages 1–6
Private collection

Page 7
Top Image: Filip Åkesson
Bottom Image: Emily Goldberg

Page 8
Top Image: Felix Alfonso
Bottom Image: Emily Goldberg

Page 9
Top Image: Felix Alfonso
Bottom Image: Racquel Bettencourt

Page 10
Felix Alfonso

Page 11
Top Image: Emily Goldberg
Bottom Image: Private collection

Pages 12–13
Levan Tsikurishvili

Pages 14–15
Top Image: Levan Tsikurishvili
Bottom Image: Mike Einziger

Page 16
Andy Kropa/Invision/AP/TT

Plate 2

Page 1
Top Image: Racquel Bettencourt
Bottom Image: Charlie Alves

Pages 2–3
Levan Tsikurishvili

Pages 4–5
Top Image: Levan Tsikurishvili
Bottom Image: Private collection
Illustration: Tim Bergling

Page 6
Top Image: Tim Bergling
Bottom Image: Levan Tsikurishvili

Page 7
Levan Tsikurishvili

Pages 8–9
Top Image: Private collection
Bottom Image: Jesse Waits

Page 10
Tereza Kačerová

Page 11
Josh Goldstein

Page 12
Albin Nedler

Page 13
Tim Bergling

Page 14
Levan Tsikurishvili

Page 15
Jesse Waits

Page 16
Top Image: Tim Bergling
Bottom Image: Private collection

CITED SONGS

SILHOUETTES
Lyrics & music: Ash Pournouri / Salem Al Fakir / Tim Bergling
© Ash Pournouri Publishing / Pompadore Publishing AB / EMI Music
Publishing Scandinavia AB
Printed by permission of Sony Music Publishing Scandinavia / Notfabriken
Music Publishing AB
© Universal Music Publishing AB. Printed by permission of Gehrmans
Musikförlag AB.

WAKE ME UP
Lyrics & music: Tim Bergling / Aloe Blacc / Mike Einziger
© EMI Music Publishing Scandinavia AB.
Printed by permission of Sony Music Publishing Scandinavia / Notfabriken
Music Publishing AB.
© Elementary Particle Music / Universal Music Corporation. For the
Nordic & Baltic countries: MCA Music Publishing AB. Printed by
permission of Gehrmans Musikförlag AB.
© 2011, 2013 Aloe Blacc Publishing Inc.
All rights for Aloe Blacc Publishing, Inc. administered worldwide by Kobalt
Songs Music Publishing.
Printed by permission of Hal Leonard Europe Ltd.

HEY BROTHER
Lyrics & music: Ash Pournouri / Salem Al Fakir / Tim Bergling / Veronica
Maggio / Vincent Pontare
© Ash Pournouri Publishing / Pompadore Publishing AB / EMI Music
Publishing Scandinavia AB.
Printed by permission of Sony Music Publishing Scandinavia / Notfabriken
Music Publishing AB.
© Universal Music Publishing AB. Printed by permission of Gehrmans
Musikförlag AB.

SOMETHING'S GOT A HOLD ON ME
Lyrics & music: Etta James / Leroy Kirkland / Pearl Woods
© EMI Longitude Music
Printed by permission of Sony Music Publishing Scandinavia AB /
Notfabriken Music Publishing AB.

YOU BE LOVE

Lyrics & music: Tim Bergling / Billy Raffoul / Hillary
Lindsey / Nathan Chapman
© EMI Music Publishing Scandinavia AB.
Printed by permission of Sony Music Publishing Scandinavia / Notfabriken
Music Publishing AB.
© Eighty Nine 89 Music / WC Music Corp / Warner-Tamerlane Publishing Co.
Printed by permission of Warner Chappell Music Scandinavia
AB / Notfabriken Music Publishing AB.
© 2017 Concord Sounds c/o Concord Music Publishing LLC
Printed by permission of Hal Leonard Europe Ltd.

FREAK

Lyrics & music: Hachidai Nakamura / Jeff Lynne / Rokusuke Ei / Sam Smith /
Tim Bergling / Albin Nedler / James Napier / Justin Vernon / Kristoffer
Fogelmark / Tom Petty / William Phillips
© Sony Music Publishing (Japan) Inc. / EMI April Music Inc. / Stellar
Songs Limited / EMI Music Publishing Scandinavia AB.
Printed by permission of Sony Music Publishing Scandinavia / Notfabriken
Music Publishing AB.
© Gone Gator Music / Wixen Music Publishing / Edition Björlund AB.
© Method Paperwork Ltd. For the Nordic & Baltic countries: Universal
Music Publishing AB. Printed by permission of Gehrmans Musikförlag AB.
© 2019 Salli Isaak Songs Ltd. / April Base Publishing / Albion Productions
AB / Birdground Productions AB
Salli Isaak Songs Ltd administered by Downtown Music Publishing LLC.
April Base Publishing / Albion Productions AB / Birdground Productions
AB administered by Kobalt Music Group Ltd.
Printed by permission of Hal Leonard Europe Ltd.

I COULD BE THE ONE

Lyrics & music: Ash Pournouri / Tim Bergling / Linus Wiklund / Måns
Wredenberg / Jonnali Parmenius / Nick Rotteveel
© Ash Pournouri Publishing / EMI Music Publishing Scandinavia AB.
Printed by permission of Sony Music Publishing Scandinavia / Notfabriken
Music Publishing AB.
© 2012 Lurpi Songs AB, Hipgnosis SFH I Ltd and Nicky Romero Music.
Lurpi Songs AB / Hipgnosis SFH I Ltd administered by Kobalt Music
Group Ltd.
Nicky Romero Music administered by BMG Talpa.
Printed by permission of Hal Leonard Europe Ltd.

ACKNOWLEDGEMENTS

There are so many people to thank. Over the past two years I have had hundreds of heartening and pleasurable conversations, but the process has of course also been hard for many of those who were willing to share their time and memories.

Therefore, many thanks to Fredrik Boberg, Johannes Lönnå, Jakob Lilliemarck, Filip Åkesson, Jesse Waits, Salem Al Fakir, Vincent Pontare, Tijs Verwest, Lucas van Scheppingen, Filip Holm, Marcus Lindgren, Per Sundin, Neil Jacobson, Emily Goldberg, Harry Bird, Robb Harker, Charlie Alves, Felix Alfonso, Malik Adunni, Mike Einziger, Nile Rodgers, David Guetta, Chris Martin, Audra Mae, Carl Falk, Alex Ebert, Racquel Bettencourt, Magnus Lygdbäck, Paul Tanner, John McKeown, Tereza Kačerová, Mark Sudack, Albin Nedler and Kristoffer Fogelmark.

Rest in peace, Mac Davis, a fantastic songwriter who passed away a short time after we met.

There are also people who in other ways have helped me to understand Tim Bergling's world. They are musicians, class-mates and friends, they work at record labels and promote events. Some of them were close to Tim, others helped me in completely different ways – take for example Max Rice, a young man in the real estate industry, who for several days took me all around Ibiza, so that I could see with my own eyes the houses that Tim stayed in during his time on the island.

Among other equally important people are Nick Groff, Joakim Johansson, David Brady, Josh Goldstein, Johnny Tennander, Joe

Gazzola, Austin Leeds, Anders Boström, Lynda Murray, Paul McClean, Jared Garcia, Cy Waits, Wilson Naitoi, David Komar, Amanda Wilson, Jonas Altberg, Carl Dreyer, Tom Harrison, Wayne Sargeant, Andrew McKeough, Lilian Orellana, Nathan Chapman, Mattias Bylund and Simon Aldred. I have talked to professionals who have taught me about the pancreas, addictive diseases and panic disorder. Those who have chosen to share information anonymously have also contributed important perspectives and details.

My editor Elisabeth Watson Straarup has on several occasions tightened up the text, made me re-evaluate and clarify. Then corrected and read again. Publisher Kerstin Almegård and agent Niclas Salomonsson have with patience and expertise helped to guide the book to publication. Matilda E Hanson and Matilda Voss Gustavsson, my clever colleagues at *Dagens Nyheter*, have come up with invaluable views on the text, as has journalist Robert Barkman. Ebba Lindqvist deserves special thanks for believing in me as a writer early in the process and for resolving many practical problems along the way. My family has been a constant support: Mum and Dad and Jonas and Fabbe. Olivia Liu has carefully transcribed large parts of the interview material and designer Miroslav Sokcic has made the beautiful cover and image sheets.

Above all I want to thank Klas and Anki and the rest of Tim Bergling's closest family, who have so generously shared their joyous, proud and painful experiences. You have been through so much. This book would not have been possible without you.
    My deepest gratitude.

Måns Mosesson, September 2021